DATE DUE

IL9799597 SENT 950711			

The *TCN* Guide
to Professional Practice
in Clinical Neuropsychology

edited by

Kenneth M. Adams and Byron P. Rourke

SWETS & ZEITLINGER B.V. AMSTERDAM / LISSE   PUBLISHERS

SWETS & ZEITLINGER INC. BERWYN, P.A

Library of Congress Cataloging-in-Publication Data

[applied for]

Cip-gegevens Koninklijke Bibliotheek, Den Haag

TCN

The TCN guide to professional practice in clinical neuropsychology / ed.
by Kenneth M. Adams and Byron P. Rourke. - Amsterdam [etc.] Swets en
Zeitlinger.
ISBN 90-265-1242-2 geb.
ISBN 90-265-1243-0 pbk.
NUGI 742
Trefw.: klinische neuropsychologie.

Cover design: Rob Molthoff
Cover printed in the Netherlands by Casparie, IJsselstein
Printed in the Netherlands by Offsetdrukkerij Kanters B.V.,
Alblasserdam

ISBN 90 265 1242 2 geb.
ISBN 90 265 1243 0 pbk.
NUGI 742

TABLE OF CONTENTS

Preface

The present volume is intended to provide a convenient single-source reference for some important documents relating to clinical neuropsychology. When the editors began publishing *The Clinical Neuropsychologist (TCN)*, it was with the view that:

> ...there is much need for the airing of models, concepts, and positions with respect to educational, clinical, and professional issues. TCN is designed to provide a forum for such presentations and discussions."

Editorial Policy 1
Volume 1, Number 1

It is clear that this book falls under this rubric. Through the cooperation of the Division of Clinical Neuropsychology (40) of the American Psychological Association, the American Board of Clinical Neuropsychology/American Board of Professional Psychology (ABCN/ABPP), and many individual authors, we are pleased to be able to publish what is perhaps the most comprehensive array of documents defining a speciality area of clinical psychology.

The cooperation between *TCN* and Division 40 and ABCN/ABPP has allowed *TCN* to serve as a viable professional news outlet in clinical neuropsychology. Recently, these relationships have been reaffirmed enthusiastically by Division 40 and ABCN/ABPP. This will allow *TCN* to continue to fill this need in the years ahead.

The definitions, guidelines, lists, and master lectures contained herein represent many hours of devoted labor by neuropsychologists of every theoretical and practical persuasion. These various documents have been in great demand by a surprising large number of people in the field of neuropsychology and its cognate areas.

Furthermore, there has been equally lively interest in these papers by those outside the neuropsychological profession. Institutions and individuals have requested and received reprints on one – and, more often, several – of the titles contained herein to the point that some of what we thought were healthy reprint stocks have been long exhausted. A number of colleagues have encouraged us to publish this book as well, if only to save wear and tear on their personal issues of *TCN* from being so frequently used.

Another consumer group – students of neuropsychology – is most important to us. The key reflection of the relative health of a scientific profession is its student talent pool. Students want to be informed about issues that impact directly on their professional development. For example, students obtain their training in a variety of settings, and our goal in publishing items such as the Training Program Listings has been to assist them in every way possible.

In asking each of the contributors for his/her permission to produce this book, we extended our thanks for the efforts that have made it possible to assemble this impressive volume. Once again, we affirm this gratitude and extend our thanks as well to all those whose efforts have facilitated the various committees whose work products we publish with pride. These have included the Division 40 Professional Affairs Committee, Division 40 Task Force in Education and Training, Division 40 *Ad hoc* Committee on Computer Usage, and the ABCN/ABPP Executive Committee. To all those who have also supported *TCN* in its development, we extend our thanks as well. Finally, we would like to offer special thanks to Klaus Plasterk of Swets Publishing Service for his assistance in the development of so many aspects of *TCN*.

The Editors

The Clinical Neuropsychologist
1987, Vol. 1, nr. 1, pp. 5-8

Evolution of a Clinical Specialty

Arthur Benton

Last year, when I was notified that I was to receive the Award for Distinguished Service to the Profession of Psychology of the American Board of Professional Psychology, I said that I regarded it not only as a great personal honor but also as an important symbol of the coming of age of clinical neuropsychology as a field of professional practice.

The status of clinical neuropsychology as a recognized specialty represents a remarkable development - all the more remarkable when one considers that the discipline of human neuropsychology, which forms the scientific basis of the professional specialty, has such a short history.

Even the term, neuropsychology, is of recent origin. Used occasionally in the 1930s and 1940s in one or another context, "Neuropsychology" was the title of a presentation by Hans-Lukas Teuber in a symposium on diagnostic psychological testing at the convention of the American Psychological Association in Boston in 1948. Teuber, who was primarily a researcher and a theorist and not a clinician, described the diverse procedures which he and the neurologist, Morris Bender, had been using to investigate different aspects of brain-behavior relationships in war veterans with penetrating brain wounds. Among these procedures were double simultaneous stimulation, mixed figures tests, the Wisconsin Card Sorting Test, the Visual Retention Test, tests of finger recognition, the "field of search" test to elicit evidence of lateral neglect, and flicker perimetry (this last procedure also having been used by Heinz Werner and Ward Halstead in their studies of brain-diseased patients).

Teuber argued that these specialized test methods were likely to be much more informative for diagnostic purposes than the tests which were then generally employed to detect the presence of brain dysfunction and he urged

Presented at the Annual Convocation of the American Board of Professional Psychology, Washington, D.C., 24 August 1986.

that they be adapted for clinical use, particularly for the purpose of lesional localization.

In retrospect it is clear that Teuber's paper was in the nature of a prophecy. In the 1950s and 1960s both the test procedures which he had described and many others which he had not mentioned were employed with steadily increasing frequency in clinical research and diagnostic evaluation as well as in normative neuropsychological studies. These tests thus provided the necessary tools for behavioral analysis in the emerging discipline of human neuropsychology. Concurrently, the formulation of fruitful guiding concepts (such as that of the pluralistic nature of hemispheric cerebral dominance) and a number of landmark discoveries (such as the demonstration by Scoville and Milner of the role of the mesial temporal lobes in the mediation of memory functions) coalesced to create a body of knowledge that formed the content of the discipline.

Over the course of about 15 years (roughly between 1950 and 1965) the discipline of human neuropsychology was established. Its status as a discipline was first signalized by the appearance of two international neuropsychological journals - *Neuropsychologia* founded by Henry Hécaen in 1963 and *Cortex* founded by Ennio De Renzi in 1964. The establishment of the International Neuropsychological Society followed in the late 1960s. Initially, the International Neuropsychology Society (INS) was a small organization. In 1970 its membership numbered about 175, and it could not really be counted as international in character since only about 10 members were not from the United States or Canada. I had the responsibility of organizing and presiding over the 1971 and 1972 meetings of INS which were held in conjunction with the American Psychological Association conventions of those years. Despite what I thought were excellent scientific programs, each meeting was attended by only 70-75 persons.

But this proved to be the calm before the storm. There was an explosive growth in the membership of INS during the next decade. No doubt the time was ripe for this to happen because by then human neuropsychology was firmly established as an important field of scientific study. However, the expansion of INS into a major organization was also due in very large part to the energetic and effective recruiting efforts of Stephen Goldstein, Paul Satz, and Aaron Smith in the early 1970s. Today the membership of INS stands at about 2000, including about 600 members from countries outside of the United States or Canada. INS holds two meetings each year, one in North America and one in Europe.

Psychologists made up the largest part of the membership of INS and this is still true today. However, neurologists with a special interest in brain-behavior relationships were also among the earliest members, as were some speech pathologists and linguists. Three clinical neurologists - Norman Geschwind, Marcel Kinsbourne, and Kenneth Heilman - have served as presidents of the Society. A distinctive source of strength for INS was that its meetings provided a forum where psychologists, neurologists, speech pathologists, linguists, and neuroscientists became aware of each others' work and characteristic approaches and also had the opportunity to interact with and mutually influence one another. These contributions from different fields of study to the discipline are surely one reason why human neuropsychology has been such a vigorous, exciting, and fast-moving field of study.

Two developments in the late 1970s signalized the emergence of clinical neuropsychology as a distinctive professional specialty that applied the knowledge, insights, and skills derived from both the discipline of human neuropsychology and the broader field of clinical psychology to the task of understanding adults and children whose behavioral, cognitive, or emotional difficulties were, or might be, determined by cerebral dysfunction. One was the founding by Louis Costa and Byron Rourke of the *Journal of Clinical Neuropsychology*, the specific purpose of which was to record advances in clinical, as well as investigative, neuropsychology. The second development, for which Louis Costa was largely responsible, was the formation of the Division of Clinical Neuropsychology (i.e., Division 40) in the American Psychological Association. The specific concern of Division 40, which now has about 1800 members, is with clinical neuropsychology as a scientific enterprise *and* a professional specialty.

Of course, this remarkable expansion did not take place in a vacuum. It was essentially a response to a social need (or, more accurately, a series of social needs), for example: the need to determine whether or not organic factors were playing a role in an older person's behavioral difficulties; the need to devise ways to help a patient who had sustained a stroke to recover his/her lost functions; the need to fathom why a school child of adequate general intelligence was failing academically or engaging in self-defeating behavior; the need to understand seemingly inexplicable disturbances in mood in persons of all ages. Many psychologists (and also many nonpsychologists) who felt that they were equipped to undertake these tasks, but who in fact were not qualified because of deficiencies in basic training and experience, made themselves available to meet these needs. The professional services provided by the majority of them were less than adequate and indeed sometimes actually deleterious to the welfare of their patients or clients.

It was in this context of extreme variability in the quality of neuropsychological services which were being provided in hospitals, clinics, schools, and private practice that the necessity for establishing standards of competence for the practice of clinical neuropsychology arose. Beginning in 1979, task forces under the able and inspiring direction of Manfred Meier undertook to specify the nature of the general and specialized training and the knowledge and skills that the professional neuropsychologist needs to have in order to qualify him/her for independent practice. By "independent practice" I mean not only private practice but also neuropsychological practice in hospitals, clinics, and schools because in reality the quality of neuropsychological services in these settings cannot be critically evaluated by the physicians or educators who make the referrals for neuropsychological evaluation.

The task forces worked long and hard on what proved to be a rather intricate problem - intricate because some degree of mastery of basic neuroscience, clinical neurology, and psychopathology is a necessary component of the competence of the clinical neuropsychologist in addition to the mastery of different fields of psychology. The truly arduous labors of Dr. Meier and the task forces have borne fruit. They are now reflected in part in the establishment of the American Board of Clinical Neuropsychology (ABCN), which is a component of the American Board of Professional Psychology. ABCN has defined in a realistic and practical manner the background of training and the knowledge and skills required for the competent practice of clinical neuropsychology. Needless to say, the present specifications of ABCN hold only for the *current* practice of clinical neuropsychology.

Clinical neuropsychology is in some respects a more complex specialty than the other professional specialties operating under the aegis of ABPP. Its very name - "neuro" and "psycho" - is a hybrid. When one surveys the practice of what is called clinical neuropsychology throughout the country, one becomes acutely aware that in too many settings vague terms such as "organicity," "brain damage," and "cerebral dysfunction," coupled with a concept of cerebral localization on the level of Gall and Spurzheim, still represent the sum total of the psychologist's knowledge of the structure and function of the central nervous system, how it operates to mediate behavior, and how injury or disease may modify behavior. The unfortunate consequences of this combination of ignorance with delusion are numerous, including the inappropriate application of tests to probe for evidence of cerebral abnormality, the uncritical interpretation of test findings and, most important from the standpoint of the patient or client, the drawing of unwarranted conclusions about the state of his whole brain or some geographically labelled part of it.

To my mind, one of the most important accomplishments of the American Board of Clinical Neuropsychology (but certainly not its only accomplishment) has been its insistence on and definition of the neuroscientific and neuroclinical knowledge and understanding that form an indispensable part of the basic equipment of the clinical neuropsychologist. The two fields with which clinical neuropsychology is most intimately concerned are human neuropsychology and human cognitive psychology. Both of these fields are currently in a very rapid stage of development. It is absolutely imperative that the American Board of Clinical Neuropsychology keep abreast of advances in these fields as they affect the practice of neuropsychology and that it review and be prepared to revise its own criteria and operations in the light of these advances.

Personally, I am very proud to have made a contribution to the development of the discipline of human neuropsychology and to have played a part in the establishment of clinical neuropsychology, the professional specialty which is based on that discipline. Coupled with my pride is my gratitude to my friends and colleagues for their longtime support and generous recognition of my efforts.

The Clinical Neuropsychologist
1989, Vol. 3, No. 1, pp. 22

Definition of a Clinical Neuropsychologist

THE FOLLOWING STATEMENT WAS ADOPTED BY
THE EXECUTIVE COMMITTEE OF DIVISION 40
AT THE APA MEETING ON AUGUST 12, 1988

A Clinical Neuropsychologist is a professional psychologist who applies principles of assessment and intervention based upon the scientific study of human behavior as it relates to normal and abnormal functioning of the central nervous system. The Clinical Neuropsychologist is a doctoral-level psychology provider of diagnostic and intervention services who has demonstrated competence in the application of such principles for human welfare following:

A. Successful completion of systematic didactic and experiential training in neuropsychology and neuroscience at a regionally accredited university;
B. Two or more years of appropriate supervised training applying neuropsychological services in a clinical setting;
C. Licensing and certification to provide psychological services to the public by the laws of the state or province in which he or she practices:
D. Review by one's peers as a test of these competencies.

Attainment of the ABCN/ABPP Diploma in Clinical Neuropsychology is the clearest evidence of competence as a Clinical Neuropsychologist, assuring that all of these criteria have been met.

This statement reflects the official position of the Division of Clinical Neuropsychology and should not be construed as either contrary to or supraordinate to the policies of the APA at large.

The Clinical Neuropsychologist
1987, Vol. 1, nr. 1, pp. 29-34

Reports of the INS - Division 40 Task Force on Education, Accreditation, and Credentialing

GUIDELINES FOR DOCTORAL TRAINING PROGRAMS IN CLINICAL NEUROPSYCHOLOGY

Doctoral training in Clinical Neuropsychology should ordinarily result in the awarding of a Ph.D. degree from a regionally accredited university. It may be accomplished through a Ph.D. programme in Clinical Neuropsychology offered by a Psychology Department or Medical Faculty or through the completion of a Ph.D. programme in a related specialty area (e.g., Clinical Psychology) which offers sufficient specialization in Clinical Neuropsychology.

Training programmes in Clinical Neuropsychology prepare students for health service delivery, basic clinical research, teaching, and consultation. As such they must contain (a) a generic psychology core, (b) a generic clinical core, (c) specialized training in the neurosciences and basic human and animal neuropsychology, (d) specific training in clinical neuropsychology. This should include an 1800 - hour internship which should be preceded by appropriate practicum experience.

(A) Generic Psychology Core
1. Statistics and Methodology
2. Learning, Cognition, and Perception
3. Social Psychology and Personality
4. Physiological Psychology
5. Life-Span Developmental
6. History

(B) Generic Clinical Core
1. Psychopathology
2. Psychometric Theory
3. Interview and Assessment Techniques
    i. Interviewing
    ii. Intelligence Assessment
    iii. Personality Assessment
4. Intervention Techniques
    i. Counselling and Psychotherapy
    ii. Behavior Therapy/Modification
    iii. Consultation
5. Professional Ethics

(C) Neurosciences and Basic Human and Animal Neuropsychology
    i. Basic Neurosciences
    ii. Advanced Physiological Psychology and Pharmacology
    iii. Neuropsychology of Perceptual, Cognitive, and Executive Processes
    iv. Research Design and Research Practicum in Neuropsychology

(D) Specific Clinical Neuropsychological Training
    i. Clinical Neurology and Neuropathology
    ii. Specialized neuropsychological assessment techniques
    iii. Specialized neuropsychological intervention techniques
    iv. Assessment practicum (children and/or adults) in University-supervised assessment facility
    v. Intervention practicum in University supervised intervention facility
    vi. Clinical Neuropsychological Internship of 1800 hours preferably in noncaptive facility. (As per INS - Div. 40 Task Force guidelines). Ordinarily this internship will be completed in a single year, but in exceptional circumstance may be completed in a 2-year period.

(E) Doctoral Dissertation

It is recognized that the completion of a Ph.D. in Clinical Neuropsychology prepares the person to begin work as a clinical neuropsychologist. In most jurisdictions, an additional year of supervised clinical practice will be required in order to qualify for licensure. Furthermore, training at the postdoctoral level to increase both general and subspecialty competencies is viewed as desirable.

GUIDELINES FOR NEUROPSYCHOLOGY INTERNSHIPS IN CLINICAL NEUROPSYCHOLOGY

The following report summarizes the recommendations of the subcommittee on internships of the INS/Division 40 Task Force. The report was prepared by Linus Bieliauskas and Thomas Boll.

At the outset, it is recognized that the Internship Program is designed primarily for students with degrees in clinical psychology. Such internship programs are those accredited by the American Psychological Association and or those listed in the Directory of the Association of Psychology Internship Centers.

Entry into a psychology internship program is a minimum qualification in a Neuropsychology Internship. Such entry must be based on completion of at least 2 years in a recognized Psychology Ph.D. Graduate Training Program in an area of Health Services Delivery (e.g., Clinical, Clinical Neuropsychology, Counseling, or School Psychology). Alternately, entry into a psychology internship program must be based on completion of a "retreading" Program designed to meet equivalent criteria as a Health Services Delivery Program per se. Within the training programs described above, the student must also have completed a designated track, specialization, or concentration in neuropsychology.

There are generally two models for psychology internship training: (1) Generic Clinical Psychology, and (2) specialty in Clinical Neuropsychology. The former does not concern us here since such training is not geared toward producing specialized experience or qualification. The latter type of internship program, when designed to provide specialized training in Neuropsychology, is what constitutes a Clinical Neuropsychology Internship.

A Clinical Neuropsychology Internship must devote at least 50% of a 1-year full-time training experience to neuropsychology. In addition, at least 20% of the training experience must be devoted to General Clinical Training to assure a competent background in Clinical Psychology. Such an internship should be associated with a hospital setting which has Neurological and/or Neurosurgical services to offer to the training background. Such an internship should not be associated only with a strictly psychiatric setting.

Experiences to be Provided
The experiences to be provided to the intern in clinical neuropsychology should conform to the descriptions of professional activities in the Report of the Task Force on Education, Accreditation, and Credentialing of the International Neuropsychological Society and the American Psychological Associaton (1981). Necessary training should be provided in both a didactic and experiential format. Supervisors in such an internship should be board-certified clinical neuropsychologists.

Didactic Training
A. Training in neurological diagnosis.
B. Training in consultation to neurological and neurosurgical services.
C. Training in direct consultation to psychiatric, pediatric, or general medical services.
D. Exposure to methods and practices of neurological and neurosurgical consultation (grand rounds, bed rounds, seminars, etc).
E. Training in neuropsychological techniques, examination, interpretation of test results, report writing.
F. Training in consultation to patients and referral sources.
G. Training in methods of intervention specific to clinical neuropsychology.

Experiential Training
A. Neuropsychological examination and evaluation of patients with actual and suspected neurological diseases and disorders.
B. Neuropsychological examination and evaluation of patients with psychiatric disorders and/or pediatric or general medical patients with neurobehavioral disorders.

C. Participation in clinical activities with neurologists and neurosurgeons (bed rounds, grand rounds, etc.).
D. Direct consultation to patients involving neuropsychological issues.
E. Consultation to referral and treating professions.

Exit Criteria
At the end of the internship year, the intern in clinical neuropsychology should be able to undertake consultation to patients and professionals on an independent basis and meet minimal qualifications for competent practice of clinical neuropsychology as defined in Section B, Neuropsychological roles and functions of the Report of the Task Force (1981).

GUIDELINES FOR POSTDOCTORAL TRAINING IN CLINICAL NEUROPSYCHOLOGY

Postdoctoral training, as described herein, is designed to provide clinical training to produce an advanced level of competence in the specialty of clinical neuropsychology. It is recognized that clinical neuropsychology is a scientifically based and evolving discipline and that such training should also provide a significant research component. Thus, this report is concerned with postdoctoral training in clinical neuropsychology which is specifically geared toward producing independent practioner level competence which includes both necessary clinical and research skills. This report does not address training in neuropsychology which is focused solely on research.

Entry Criteria
Entry into a clinical neuropsychology postdoctoral training program ordinarily should be based on completion of a regionally accredited Ph.D. graduate training program in one of the health service delivery areas of psychology or a Ph.D. in psychology with additional completion of a "respecialization" program designed to meet equivalent criteria as a health services delivery program in psychology. In all cases, candidacy for postdoctoral training in clinical neuropsychology must be based on demonstration of training and research methodology designed to meet equivalent criteria as a health services delivery professional in the scientist-practitioner model. Ordinarily, a clinical internship, listed by the Association of Psychology Internship Centers, must also have been completed.

General Considerations
A postdoctoral training program in clinical neuropsychology should be directed by a board-certified clinical neuropsychologist. In most cases, the program should extend over at least a 2-year period. The only exception would be for individuals who have completed a specific clinical neuropsychology spe-

cialization in their graduate programs and/or a clinical neuropsychology internship (Subcommittee Report of the Task Force, 1984) provided the exit criteria are met (see below). As a general guideline, the postdoctoral training program should provide at least 50% time in clinical service and at least 25% time in clinical research. Variance within these guidelines should be tailored to the needs of the individual. Specific training in neuropsychology must be provided, including any areas where the individual is deemed to be deficient (testing, consultation, intervention, neurosciences, neurology, etc.).

Specific Considerations
Such a postdoctoral training program should be associated with hospital settings which have neurological and/or neurosurgical services to offer to the training background. Necessary training should be provided in both a didactic and experiential format and should include the following:

Didactic Training
A. Training in neurological and psychiatric diagnosis.
B. Training in consultation to neurological and neurosurgical services.
C. Training in direct consultation to psychiatric, pediatric, or general medical services.
D. Exposure to methods and practices of neurological and neurosurgical consultation (Grand Rounds, Bed Rounds, Seminars, etc.).
E. Observation of neurosurgical procedures and biomedical tests (Revascularization procedures, cerebral blood flow, Wada testing, etc.).
F. Participation in seminars offered to neurology and neurosurgery residents (Neuropharmacology, EEG, brain cutting, etc.).
G. Training in neuropsychological techniques, examination, interpretation of test results, report writing.
H. Training in consultation to patients and referral sources.
I. Training in methods of intervention specific to clinical neuropsychology.
J. Seminars, readings, etc., in neuropsychology (case conferences, journal discussion, topic-specific seminars).
K. Didactic training in neuroanatomy, neuropathology, & related neurosciences.

Experiential Training
A. Neuropsychological examination and evaluation of patients with actual and suspected neurological diseases and disorders.
B. Neuropsychological examination and evaluation of patients with psychiatric disorders and/or pediatric or general medical patients with neurobehavioral disorders.
C. Participation in clinical activities with neurologists and neurosurgeons (bed rounds, grand rounds, etc.).
D. Experience at a specialty clinic, such as a dementia clinic or epilepsy clinic, which emphasizes multidisciplinary approaches to diagnosis and treatment.

E. Direct consultation to patients involving neuropsychological assessment.
F. Direct intervention with patients, specific to neuropsychological issues, and to include psychotherapy and/or family therapy where indicated.
G. Research in neuropsychology, i.e., collaboration on a research project or other scholarly academic activity, initiation of an independent research project or other scholarly academic activity, and presentation or publication of research data where appropriate.

Exit Criteria

At the conclusion of the postdoctoral training program, the individual should be able to undertake consultation to patients and professionals on an independent basis. Accomplishment in research should also be demonstrated. The program is designed to produce a competent practitioner in the areas designated in Section B of the Task Force Report (1981) and to provide eligibility for external credentialing and licensure as designated in section D of the Task Force Report (1981). The latter also includes training eligibility for certification in Clinical Neuropsychology by the American Board of Professional Psychology.

REFERENCES

Meier, M.J. (1981). Report of the Task Force on Education, Accreditation and Credentialing of the International Neuropsychological Society. *The INS Bulletin*, September, pp. 5-10.

Report of the Task Force on Education, Accreditation, and Credentialing. *The INS Bulletin*, 1981, pp. 5-10. *Newsletter 40*, 1984, *2*, 3-8.

Report of the Subcommittee on Psychology Internships. *Newsletter 40*, 1984, *2*, 7. *The INS Bulletin*, 1984, p. 33. *APIC Newsletter*, 1983, *9*, 27-28.

The Clinical Neuropsychologist
1988, Vol. 2, No. 3, pp. 213-220

Entry into Clinical Neuropsychology: Graduate, Undergraduate, and Beyond

Robert A. Bornstein
The Ohio State University

ABSTRACT

Psychologists at all levels of training have become interested in entering the field of clinical neuropsychology. The issues and obstacles pertaining to entry at various professional levels are discussed. Training and credentialing issues surrounding the question of minimal levels of competence have direct bearing on the protection of the discipline of neuropsychology and the population who receive neuropsychological services.

Clinical Neuropsychology continues to be an area of increasing interest to students and practitioners in Psychology. The recent decision by the American Board of Professional Psychology to award its Diploma in Clinical Neuropsychology (Bieliauskas & Matthews, 1987) serves to underscore the vitality of the field as a distinct area of practice. The interest in clinical neuropsychology is expressed at all levels of training and practice in psychology with students as well as established practitioners seeking to enter the field and engage in various neuropsychological activites. This interest has led to increased demand for training in the area, and the demand has resulted in opportunities for training at all levels of education in psychology. Thus, greater numbers of academic training programs offer courses which offer some exposure, and many internship settings offer rotations in neuropsychology (Cripe, 1988). Perusal of the APA monitor

A previous version of this manuscript was presented at a conversation hour at the American Psychological Association meeting in New York, 1987.

reveals an increasing number of postdoctoral fellowships, and a cornucopia of continuing education experiences.

The demand for training in neuropsychology, and the desire to engage in such professional activities, has raised for many of us (both inside and outside the field) the question of what is it that makes a neuropsychologist, and in the present context, how one goes about entering the field of neuropsychology. For several years, Division 40 of APA in a joint effort with the International Neuropsychological Society has generated a series of documents that provide proposed guidelines which describe basic requirements for academic training, internship, postdoctoral training (INS-Division 40 Task Force, 1987) and, most recently, continuing education in neuropsychology (Division 40-INS Task Force, 1988). These documents appear to represent basic information about the various levels of training in neuropsychology. A discussion of some of the issues regarding graduate and postgraduate training issues is neuropsychology may also be found in Meier (1981) and Costa, Matarazzo, and Bornstein (1986).

Obviously, these recommended guidelines represent an ideal situation, but current reality approximates these ideals to differing degrees in various settings across the country. The material that follows is a description of some of the vehicles for entry into the field of clinical neuropsychology that presently exist, some that may exist in the future, and to express my view of some of the contemporary issues and problems.

UNDERGRADUATE ENTRY AND ACTIVITIES

In some academic institutions, undergraduate students may have the opportunity to become involved in clinical neuropsychology through the various field experience courses offered by many psychology programs. The goal of such courses is typically to provide a first experience in research or patient contact. Where a bona fide clinical neuropsychology laboratory exists (and where the neuropsychologist involved has an appointment in the academic Psychology department), it may be possible for undergraduate students to obtain a glimpse into the world of clinical neuropsychology. Such a situation usually obtains where a neuropsychologist in an affiliated medical school or hospital has an appointment in the Psychology Department. Many aspiring clinical (neuro)psychologists obtain their first direct experience with neurological or psychiatric populations while working as aides or attendants in state institutions.

The increasing presence of neuropsychologists in major medical centers has resulted in another important avenue for undergraduate entry into clinical neuropsychology. The frequent use of psychometrists or technicians in North American style neuropsychology has generated a small cottage industry for baccalaureate graduates to obtain employment in Psychology. The increasing use of neuropsychological assessment in clinical activity and research suggests that this may be an increasingly common vehicle for undergraduates to enter the field.

While not all individuals will go on to postgraduate study, such experiences may be particularly valuable for those students wishing to delay entry into graduate school. Employment as a psychometrist provides first-hand experience in the nuts and bolts of neuropsychology, and also provides a wealth of assessment skills as well as exposure to wide varieties of patient populations. Most undergraduates, however, will not have any exposure to clinical neuropsychology, and for most the first such exposure will probably occur in graduate school.

GRADUATE ENTRY INTO CLINICAL NEUROPSYCHOLOGY

It is most likely that the majority of students entering graduate training programs will have had no previous exposure to clinical neuropsychology. In an attempt to remain in step with current developments in the field of psychology, many clinical training programs have perceived the need to offer some formal exposure to the burgeoning areas such as health psychology and clinical neuropsychology. This is done with varying degrees of effectiveness, largely related to the faculty members available to provide such coursework. Although the field of clinical neuropsychology has been extant for nearly three decades, there are still very few programs which offer formally defined areas of concentration in it. There are some exceptions, such as the University of Victoria and University of Windsor in Canada, and the Harvard/Boston V.A. group and the University of Oklahoma in the USA. At the University of Houston, a clinical neuropsychology program has evolved from biopsychology and has become a separate administrative area, much like clinical or developmental psychology. In recent years other institutions have emerged in which groups of widely recognized clinical neuropsychologists have come together. Notable examples of such groups include the University of California at San Diego, University of Michigan, and the University of Arizona. The concentration of such neuropsychological power at these institutions is an incalculable benefit to students pursuing training in clinical neuropsychology at these institutions. In most settings, however, the clinical neuropsychology expertise revolves around one or sometimes two individuals.

Because of the scarcity of formal training programs, the advice that I was given 15 years ago is still largely true today. That is, perhaps the best vehicle for a student seeking doctoral level specialization in clinical neuropsychology is to seek admission to programs which have, as part of their faculty, a person actively involved and specialized in clinical neuropsychology. That faculty member then serves as the student's advisor and mentor and prescribes the course of academic and clinical experiences to prepare the student for a career as a clinical neuropsychologist.

In view of the lack of a formal accreditation process for training programs in clinical neuropsychology, it should not be surprising that there is great variability in the coursework provided in various programs. This variability pertains both to the material being presented, and to the clinical neuropsychological expertise of those teaching the courses. In some institutions, the course materials represent what in the days prior to the popularization of the term, clinical neuropsychology, would have been called physiological psychology. In more clinically oriented courses, the material may deal with theoretical and/or practical issues related to neuropsychological assessment. Some of these clinically oriented courses include practicum or "hands on" experiences where students are required to administer and interpret some number of neuropsychological examinations. This often leads to a mistaken sense that having completed the basic or "advanced" neuropsychology courses in graduate school represents adequate training to establish competence. The degree to which such misconceptions are allowed to exist is to a large degree related to the neuropsychological expertise and training of the person teaching the course.

In some programs, the course is taught by a medical-center-based neuropsychologist whose principal position is in running a clinical-service-oriented neuropsychology laboratory. This, in my view, is the desirable situation in which students are taught clinical neuropsychology by an individual committed to that particular area of practice. More commonly, however, the coursework is offered by a clinical psychologist who is not involved for the majority of time in active clinical practice of neuropsychology. This is supported by a recent survey by McCaffery and Issac (1984) which reported a dearth of adequate neuropsychological background among instructors of neuropsychology courses in APA-approved graduate programs. Underscoring the importance of having clinical neuropsychology taught by an individual actively involved in clinical practice, the modal number of assessments among those respondents in the 12-month period preceding the survey was zero. In a subsequent survey of neuropsychologists in APA-approved internship programs (McCaffery, 1985), the modal number of assessments was 50, although the respondents had very similar educational backgrounds. In the specific context of doctoral level training in clinical neuropsychology, this reinforces the importance for students to work directly with individuals who are actively engaged in clinical practice of neuropsychology.

INTERNSHIP EXPERIENCES IN CLINICAL NEUROPSYCHOLOGY

A significant number of internship settings offer rotations in clinical neuropsychology (McCaffery, Malloy, & Brief, 1985), and some centers actually allow formal concentrations in the area. While this is very often in association with well qualified and productive clinical neuropsychologists, such an internship experience can at best serve as a rudimentary introduction to the field. Individuals who have taken a rotation in clinical neuropsychology should not labor under the delusion that they are competent in it. One bit of evidence that individuals do have these ideas is seen in the fact that a substantial number of applicants for a clinical neuropsychology position in a major midwest medical center presented their credentials on the basis of an internship rotation. In fact, many clinical neuropsychologists I know working in such internship settings actively attempt to prevent or correct such misconceptions. Four, six, or eight months of experience, with or without requisite academic experience, is simply inadequate for establishment of basic competence as a provider. Individuals who become interested in clinical neuropsychology via their internship experiences should follow this with postdoctoral work in which they may develop their specific clinical neuropsychological competencies.

POSTDOCTORAL EXPERIENCES

Apart from those students completing their doctoral level training in direct conjunction with a competently trained clinical neuropsychologist, the most common and effective route for entering clinical neuropsychology is with a postdoctoral training program. There are a rapidly expanding number of these opportunities (Cripe, 1988). The duration of postdoctoral programs may vary as a function of training needs for a given individual, programmatic requirements, or financial considerations.

May programs prefer to accept individuals with Ph.D. degrees from APA-approved clinical psychology programs, but this is neither uniform nor, in my opinion, absolutely necessary. Preference for clinically trained candidates is related to the fact that basic clinical skills are an inherent aspect of clinical neuropsychological practice. It should be clear from the above remarks that, while these general clinical skills are *necessary*, they are not *sufficient* to provide competence in clinical neuropsychology. Individuals without such clinical experiences in their doctoral programs (e.g., physiological or experimental psychology) are obligated to pursue such training in the postdoctoral years. Similar to the situation with training only in clinical psychology, simply knowing the brain is insufficient for competent work in clinical neuropsychology.

CONTINUING EDUCATION

The above comments make it clear that there are numerous avenues for entry into clinical neuropsychology. This will probably increase as a function of continued interest in the field and increased numbers of competently trained practitioners who are available as supervisors and mentors. Nevertheless, it is the case that some individuals get the neuropsychology bug after completion of their graduate training. Some individuals enter postdoctoral training or complete respecialization after some number of years of psychology practice. However, an apparently substantial number of psychologists gain their introduction through various continuing education activities. The role of continuing education in expansion and elaboration of established competence is well recognized, and in fact required by some state licensing laws. On the other hand, these continuing education experiences are not meant to provide, nor are they capable of providing, the training necessary for establishment of competence in any area.

In clinical neuropsychology, there appears to be an ever increasing number of basic or "advanced" workshops that, in my opinion, foster the belief that attendance at these workshops and purchase of certain books representing the distilled wisdom of the workshop presenters does indeed represent adequate preparation for entry level practice. Many of these workshops include preliminary caveats about the need for additional training, but this is buried in a mass of information that leads those attending the workshop to very different opinions about their level of competence. In fact, the message garnered by more than one graduate of such workshops is that they are in fact encouraged to believe that completion of the workshop provides the basic level of skill necessary to begin practice of clinical neuropsychology. This is dangerous for the patients subjected to these levels of clinical neuropsychological expertise, and therefore dangerous for the field of clinical neuropsychology. The threats to clinical neuropsychology and society as a whole engendered by these "weekend wonders" has been discussed elsewhere and need not be reiterated here (Boll, 1978; Matthews, 1976, 1981; Reed, 1976, Rourke, 1976).

In my opinion these workshops promote a naive and simplistic view of clinical neuropsychology by suggesting that basic or even advanced skills can be obtained after one week (however intensive that week may be). This contributes to the misconception that the field of clinical neuropsychology is simply just another group of tests and a few miscellaneous facts about brain function. It should be abundantly clear to anyone willing to sit and cogitate for a moment that the magic is not in the tests. In fact, it should be patently obvious that no valid field of endeavor is likely to be so simple that it can be mastered in one or even several intense weeks of training. By analogy, if an operant oriented behaviorist decided to switch his focus to dynamically oriented psychotherapy, most of us would agree that a one or several week intensive workshop would not be an acceptable vehicle. Similarly, competence in basic clinical psychological skills are necessary but not sufficient for mastering clinical neuropsychology. What is manifestly clear, as expressed by the Guidelines for Continuing Education produced by the Division 40/INS Joint Task Force (1988), is that continuing education workshops are inadequate for establishment of basic competence in clinical neuropsychology.

DIRECTIONS FOR THE FUTURE

At the present time there is little to be recommended for the established practitioner who wishes to enter clinical neuropsychology. The principal available route is completion of a postdoctoral program providing the necessary training and experience. It is unrealistic in many, if not most, cases for individuals with families or other financial responsibilities to abandon a successful practice to return to postdoctoral training. Some individuals have entered into supervisory arrangements with local clinical neuropsychologists who provide directed readings, academic experiences, and clinical supervision over a period of one or several years with the ultimate goal of establishing a basic level of clinical neuropsychological competence. In one situation of which I am aware, the result of such a one-year experience was that the individual realized that he had learned enough to know that he did not know enough to practice competently in clinical neuropsychology.

There has also been some discussion of the possible use of the assessment center concept. In this model, a series of competence-based modules would be developed and made available for study. Individuals could independently study and review these modules and then periodically come to a central location to demonstrate mastery of specific modules. A prescribed set of modules in addition to supervised clinical experiences could then be identified as prerequisites for recognition of basic competence. This model would allow for continuation of existing professional activities with simultaneous development of new competencies. Obviously, this model is theoretical at this point, but may in the future represent a vehicle for entry into clinical neuropsychology in the postgraduate or mid-career years.

SUMMARY

There are a number of effective avenues for entry into the field of clinical neuropsychology. There is an increasing number of well-trained neuropsychologists who can serve as mentors and supervisors for students in doctoral training programs. There are also expanding opportunities for postdoctoral training. Various self-directed or continuing education experiences may provide that initial fascinating glimpse of the promised land of clinical neuropsychology, but they do not represent adequate training for competent clinical neuropsychological practice. The popularity of the field will continue to create a demand for competently trained practitioners. Those individuals seeking an easy entry to the field through workshops or self-proclaimed expertise do a disservice to their patients and the field. New methods for providing adequate training will be developed in the future to meet the demand for training by individuals already engaged in other aspects of psychological practice.

REFERENCES

Bieliauskas, L.A., & Matthews, C.G. (1987). American Board of Clinical Neuropsychology: Policies and Procedures. *The Clinical Neuropsychologist. 1*, 21-28.
Boll, T.J. (1978). Diagnosing brain impairment. In B.B. Wolman (Ed.), *Diagnosis of mental disorders: A handbook* (pp. 601-675). New York: Plenum Press.
Costa, L.D. Matarazzo, J.D., & Bornstein, R.A. (1986). Issues in graduate and postgraduate

20

training in clinical neuropsychology. In S.B. Filskov & T.J. Boll (Eds.), *Handbook of clinical neuropsychology* (Vol. 2, pp. 652-668). New York: John Wiley and Sons.

Cripe, L. (1988). Listing of training programs in clinical neuropsychology-1987. *The Clinical Neuropsychologist, 2*, 13-24.

Division 40-International Neuropsychological Society (INS) Task Force (1988). Report of the INS-Division 40 Task Force on Education, Accreditation and Credentialing: Subcommittee on Continuing Education. *The Clinical Neuropsychologist, 2*, 25-29.

International Neuropsychological Society (INS)-Division 40 Task Force (1987). Reports of the INS-Division 40 Task Force on education, accreditation and credentialing. *The Clinical Neuropsychologist, 1*, 22-29.

Matthews, C.G. (1976). Problems in training of neuropsychologists. *Clinical Psychologist, 29*, 11-13.

Matthews, C.G. (1981). Neuropsychology practice in a hospital setting. In S.B. Filskov & T.J. Boll (Eds.), *Handbook of clinical neuropsychology* (pp. 645-685). New York: John Wiley and Sons.

McCaffery, R.J. (1985). Educational backgrounds of clinical neuropsychologists in APA-approved internship sites. *Professional Psychology: Research and Practice, 16*, 773-780.

McCaffery, R.J., Malloy, P.F. & Brief, D. (1985). Internship opportunities in clinical neuropsychology emphasizing recent INS training guidelines. *Professional Psychology: Research and Practice, 16*, 236-252.

McCaffery, R.J., & Issac, W. (1984). Survey of the educational backgrounds and specialty training of instructors of clinical neuropsychology in APA-approved graduate training programs. *Professional Psychology: Research and Practice, 15*, 26-33.

Meier, M.J. (1981). Education for competency assurance in human neuropsychology: Antecedents, models and directions. In S.B. Filskov & T.J. Boll (Eds.), *Handbook of clinical neuropsychology* (pp. 754-781). New York: John Wiley and Sons.

Meier, M.J. (1987). Continuing Education: An Alternative to Respecialization in Clinical Neuropsychology. *The Clinical Neuropsychologist, 1*, 9-20.

Reed, H.B.C. (1976). Pediatric neuropsychology. *Journal of Pediatric Psychology, 1*, 5-7.

Rourke, B.P. (1976). Issues in the neuropsychological assessment of children with learning disabilities. *Canadian Psychological Review, 17*, 89-102.

The Clinical Neuropsychologist
1991, Vol. 5, No. 3, pp. 226-237

Listing of Training Programs in Clinical Neuropsychology - 1991

Lloyd I. Cripe
Private Practice, Seattle, WA

This is the third publication of the list of training programs in clinical neuro-psychology. The previous published list (Cripe, 1989) had 101 listings (36 Internships; 24 Doctoral; and 41 Postdoctoral). The current list has 120 listings (40 Internships; 29 Doctoral; and 51 Postdoctoral). The reasons for this growth of listing are not known, but may represent an increased awareness of the list, the importance of being listed and an increase in available programs. Regardless, students now have more options from which to make their choices when searching and applying for training in clinical neuropsychology.

All of the directors of programs listed have indicated that they believe their programs are in compliance with the guidelines for training in neuropsychology published by Division 40 (TCN, Vol. 1, No. 1, 29-34).

Listing of a program does not represent any type of warranty by the author, TCN, Division 40, or the International Neuropsychological Society. Currently, there is no system of accreditation or credentialing for training programs in neuropsychology. Students pursuing training are encouraged to check for themselves to see if the programs are following the guidelines and meet their training objectives.

If you have comments, suggestions, corrections, additions, or deletions regarding this listing please send them to: Lloyd I. Cripe, Ph.D., Listings Coordinator, P.O. Box 2257, Sequim, WA 98382.

Reprint requests should be sent to: Kenneth M. Adams, Ph.D., Secretary, Division 40, Psychology Service (116B), VA Medical Center, Ann Arbor, MI 48105, USA.

REFERENCES

Cripe, L.I. (1989). Listing of training programs in clinical neuropsychology - 1989. *The Clinical Neuropsychologist, 3*, 116-128.
Reports of the INS-Division 40 Task Force on Education, Accreditation, and Credentialing (1987). Guidelines for doctoral training programs in clinical neuropsychology. *The Clinical Neuropsychologist, 1*, 29-34.

INTERNSHIP PROGRAMS IN NEUROPSYCHOLOGY

CANADA

Program	Contact	Address
Chedoke-McMaster Hospitals Psychology	Larry P. Tuff, Ph.D. (416) 521-2100	Box 2000, Station A Hamilton, Ontario Canada L8N 3Z5
University Hospital Department of Psychology Services	Jeffrey S. Martzke, Ph.D. (519) 663-3000	P. O. Box 5239 Postal Station "A" London, Ontario Canada N6A 5A5
Mississauga Hospital Department of Psychology	Lawrence Freedman, Ph.D. (416) 848-7387	100 Queensway West Mississauga, Ontario Canada L5B 1B8
Sunnybrook Health Science Ctr. Department of Psychology	W. Gary Snow, Ph.D. (416) 480-4438	2075 Bayview Avenue Toronto, Ontario Canada M4N 3M5

U.S.A. (Alphabetic by State)

Program	Contact	Address
University of Alabama at Birmingham Medical Ctr. Department of Psychology	Louis Fleece, Ph.D.	VA Hospital Birmingham, AL 35294
John L. McClellan Memorial Veterans Medical Center	Gary T. Souheaver, Ph.D. (501) 660-2071	Neuropsychology Services 4300 West 7th Street Little Rock, AR 72205
Camarillo State Hospital & Development Center Dept. of Development Services	I. H. Hart, Ph.D. (805) 484-3661	Box A Camarillo, CA 93011-1350
University of California at San Diego Department of Psychiatry	Dean Delis, Ph.D. (619) 552-8585 ext. 3916	Psychology Service (116B) San Diego VA Medical Center LaJolla, CA 92161
Veterans Affairs Medical Ctr. Psychology Service (116B)	Jeffrey Webster, Ph.D. Reda Scott, Ph.D. (213) 494-5604	5901 East Seventh Street Long Beach, CA 90822

Program	Contact	Address
VA Medical Center - UCLA	Wilfred Van Gorp, Ph.D. (213) 824-3166	Wadsworth & Brentwood Div. Wilshire & Sawtelle Blvds. Los Angeles, CA 90073
VA Medical Center Psychology Service (116B)	Amy M. Wisniewski, Ph.D. (415) 750-2004	4150 Clement Street San Francisco, CA 94121
The Institute of Living Dept. of Clinical Psychology	Geraldine Cassens, Ph.D. (203) 241-6932	400 Washington Street Hartford, CT 06106
VA Medical Center Psychology Service	Richard C. Delaney, Ph.D. (203) 932-5711 ext. 493	West Spring Street West Haven, CT 06516
University of Florida Department of Clinical and Health Psychology	Russell M. Bauer, Ph.D. (904) 392-4551	Director of Intern Training Box J-165, JHMHC Gainesville, FL 32610
University of Miami/ Jackson Medical Center Department of Psychology and Behavioral Medicine	Jay Weinstein, Ph.D. (305) 549-6919	Rehabilitation Center 1611 N.W. 12th Avenue Miami, FL 33136
Rush-Presbyterian-St. Lukes Medical Center Department of Psychology & Social Sciences	Martita A. Lopez, Ph.D. (312) 942-5932	1653 West Congress Parkway Chicago, IL 60612
West Side VA Medical Center Psychology Service	Linda Wetzel, Ph.D. (312) 633-2132	820 South Damen Avenue Chicago, IL 60612
VA Medical Center Psychology Service	Howard B. Marcum, Ph.D. (217) 442-8000 ext. 275	1900 East Main Street Danville, IL 61832
Lexington VA Medical Center Neuropsychology Section	John D. Ranseen, Ph.D. (606) 233-4511 ext. 4705	116A-CDD Lexington, KY 40511
VA Medical Center Psychology Service (116B)	John E .Mendoza, Ph.D. (504) 589-5235	1601 Perdido Street New Orleans, LA 70146
Boston VA Medical Center Psychology Service	Steve Lancy, Ph.D. Roberta F. White, Ph.D. (617) 232-9500	150 S. Huntington Avenue Boston, MA 02130
Children's Hospital Department of Psychology	Natalie D. Sollee, Ph.D. (617) 735-6398	300 Longwood Avenue Boston, MA 02115
North Shore Children's Hospital	Bob Lichtenstein, Ph.D. (617) 745-2100	57 Highland Avenue Salem, MA 01970

Program	Contact	Address
Allen Park VA Medical Center Psychology Service (116B)	Bradley Axelrod, Ph.D. (313) 562-6000 ext. 3623	Outer Drive & Southfield Allen Park, MI 48101
Ann Arbor VA Medical Center Psychology Service (116B)	Robert S. Goldman, Ph.D. (313) 761-7935	2215 Fuller Street Ann Arbor, MI 48105
Henry Ford Hospital Department of Psychiatry -CFP3	Phillip J. Lanzisera, Ph.D. (313) 876-3545	2799 West Grand Boulevard Detroit, MI 48202
VA Medical Center Geriatric Research, Education & Clinical Center	Kathy J. Christensen, Ph.D. (612) 725-6767 ext. 6507	(11G) One Veteran's Drive Minneapolis, MN 55417
University of Minnesota Medical School Neurosurgery (Neuropsychology Lab)	Manfred J. Meier, Ph.D. (612) 624-1412	Box 390 Mayo Minneapolis, MN 55455
VA Medical Center Psychology Service (116B-1)	Gustave F. P. Sison, Ph.D. (601) 865-1021	Biloxi, MS 39531
Long Island Jewish Medical Ctr. Clinical Neuropsychology Internship Program	Robert M. Bilder, Ph.D. (718) 470-8173 (718) 343-7018	Hillside Hospital - Research P. O. Box 38 Glen Oaks, NY 11004
Columbia-Presbyterian Medical Center Department of Psychiatry	Wilma G. Rosen, Ph.D. (212) 305-2214 (212) 305-1935	710 West 168th Street New York, NY 10032
International Center for the Disabled Behavioral Medicine Dept.	Robert J. Paluck, Ph.D. Marvin Z. Deluty, Ph.D. (212) 679-0100	340 East 24th Street New York, NY 10010
New York University Medical Center Department of Psychology	Rosemary S. Haraguchi, Ph.D. (212) 340-6168	Rusk Institute of Rehab. Med. 400 East 34th Street New York, NY 10016
Cleveland VA Medical Center Psychology Service (116B)	Robert W. Goldberg, Ph.D. (216) 791-4972, cxt. 4972	10701 East Blvd. Cleveland, OH 44106
University of Oklahoma Health Sciences Center Department of Psychiatry and Behavioral Sciences	Russell L. Adams, Ph.D. (405) 271-5639	P. O. Box 26901 Oklahoma City, OK 73190

Program	Contact	Address
VA Medical Center Psychology Service (116B)	Diane Howieson, Ph.D. Laurence Binder, Ph.D. (503) 273-5187	P. O. Box 1034 Portland, OR 97207
Hahnemann University Department of Mental Health Sciences	Sandra Koffler, Ph.D. (215) 448-4956	Neuropsychology Division 230 North Broad Street Philadelphia, PA 19102
Brown University Psychology Consortium	Paul Malloy, Ph.D. (401) 455-6355	Butler Hospital 345 Blackstone Blvd. Providence, RI 02906
VA Medical Center Psychology Service (116B)	Robert Lee Pusakulich, Ph.D. (901) 523-8990 ext. 5251	1030 Jefferson Avenue Memphis, TN 38104
Baylor College of Medicine Department of Psychiatry and Behavioral Sciences	Michael D. Cox, Ph.D. (713) 798-4840	One Baylor Plaza Houston, TX 77030
West Virginia University Department of Behavioral Medicine and Psychiatry	Paul D. Blanton, Ph.D. John C. Linton, Ph.D. (304) 341-1500	WVU Medical Center P. O. Box 1547 Charleston, WV 25326
West Virginia University Department of Behavioral Medicine and Psychiatry	Michael D. Franzen, Ph.D. (304) 293-2411	WVU Medical Center Morgantown, WV 26506-6302

DOCTORAL TRAINING PROGRAMS IN NEUROPSYCHOLOGY

CANADA

Program	Contact	Address
University of Victoria Department of Psychology	Esther Strauss, Ph.D. (604) 721-7534 (604) 721-7540 (Admin.)	P. O. Box 3050 Victoria, British Columbia Canada V8W 3P5
University of Windsor Department of Psychology	Byron P. Rourke, Ph.D. (519) 253-4332 ext. 2221	Windsor, Ontario, Canada N9B 3P4

U.S.A. (Alphabetic by State)

University of Arizona Department of Psychology	Alfred W. Kaszniak, Ph.D. (602) 621-5149	Tucson, AZ 85721
University of California, San Diego (UCSD) Department of Psychiatry & San Diego State University (SDSU), Department of Psychology Joint Program	Robert K. Heaton, Ph.D. (619) 497-6644 D. Saccusso, Ph.D. G. Rosenbaum, Ph.D.	LaJolla, CA 92093
University of Florida Department of Clinical and Health Psychology	Eileen B. Fennell, Ph.D. (904) 394-4551	Box J-165, HSB Gainesville, FL 32610
Emory University Department of Psychology	Marshall P. Duke, Ph.D. (404) 727-7456	Director, Graduate Education in Clinical Psychology Atlanta, GA 30322
Northwestern University Department of Psychology	Kenneth Howard, Ph.D. (312) 491-5190 Jerry Sweet, Ph.D. (312) 570-2000	Swift Hall, Room 102 2029 Sheridan Road Evanston, IL 60208
University Health Sciences Chicago Medical School Department of Psychology	Joseph Hatcher, Ph.D. (312) 578-3311	Director of Clinical Training 3333 Greenbay Road North Chicago, IL 66064
Ball State University Department of Psychology	Raymond S. Dean, Ph.D. (317) 285-8510	Neuropsychology Laboratory TC 517 Muncie, IN 43706
University of Kentucky Department of Psychology	David T. R. Berry, Ph.D. (606) 257-6844	Lexington, KY 40506

Program	Contact	Address
Wayne State University Department of Psychology	R. Douglas Whitman, Ph.D. (313) 577-2821	71 West Warren Detroit, MI 48202
Forest Institute of Professional Psychology Department of Psychology	Richard H. Cox, Ph.D. (417) 831-7902	1322 South Campbell Springfield, MO 65807
Washington University Department of Psychology	Suzanne Craft, Ph.D. (314) 889-6520 ext. 6511	Campus Box 1125 One Brookings Drive St. Louis, MO 63130
University of Nebraska Department of Psychology	James K. Cole, Ph.D. (402) 472-3229	209 Burnett Hall Lincoln, NE 68588-0308
State University of New York at Binghamtom Department of Psychology	Peter J. Donovick, Ph.D. (607) 777-2852	Box 6000 Binghamton, NY 13902-6000
Queens College, City University of New York Department of Psychology	Doreen Berman, Ph.D. (718) 997-3631	65-30 Kissena Blvd. Flushing, NY 11367-0904
City College, City University of New York Department of Psychology	John Antrobus, Ph.D. (212) 650-5721	138th Street & Convent Ave. New York, NY 10031
University of Cincinnati Department of Psychology	Bruce K. Schefft, Ph.D. (513) 556-5562	Dyer Hall, ML376 Cincinnati, OH 45221-0376
University of Oregon Department of Psychology	Jeri S. Janowsky, Ph.D. (503) 346-4966	College of Arts & Sciences Straub Hall Eugene, OR 97403-1227
University of Pennsylvania Brain Behavior Laboratory Department of Psychology	Andrew J. Saykin, Psy. D. Ruben C. Gur, Ph.D.	205 Piersol Building Philadelphia, PA 19104-4283
Pennsylvania State Univesity College of Medicine Neurobehavior Diagnostic and Research Laboratory	Paul J. Eslinger, Ph.D. (717) 531-8692	Division of Neurology, C-526 The Milton S. Hershey Medical Center 500 University Drive Hershey, PA 17033
Hahnemann University Department of Mental Health	Sandra Koffler, Ph.D. (215) 448-4956	Neuropsychology Division M.S. 341 230 North Broad Street Philadelphia, PA 19102

Program	Contact	Address
Drexel University College of Arts and Sciences Psychology, Sociology and Anthropology	Eric A. Zillmer, Psy.D. (215) 590-8672	Neuropsychology Philadelphia, PA 19104
Memphis State University Psychology Department	Charles J. Long, Ph.D. (901) 678-2821 (901) 523-9276	Memphis, TN 38152
University of Texas at Austin Department of Psychology Biopsychology Section	Michael Domjan, Ph.D. (512) 471-3627 Arnold Buss, Ph.D. (512) 471-3393	330 Meze Hall Austin, TX 78765
University of Houston Department of Psychology	H. Julia Hannay, Ph.D. (713) 749-2921	Houston, TX 77204-5341
University of Vermont Department of Psychology	James Rosen, Ph.D. (802) 656-2680	Burlington, VT 05405
University of Wisconsin Department of Psychology	Thomas Stampfl, Ph.D. David C. Osmon, PH.D. (414) 229-4747 ext. 6751	P. O. Box 413 Milwaukee, WI 53201
West Virginia University Department of Psychology	Michael Franzen, Ph.D. (304) 293-2360	Oglebay Hall Morgantown, WV 26506

POSTDOCTORAL PROGRAMS IN NEUROPSYCHOLOGY

CANADA

Program	Contact	Address
Sunnybrook Health Science Ctr. Department of Psychology	W. Gary Snow, Ph.D. (416) 480-4438	2075 Bayview Avenue Toronto, Ontario Canada M4N 3N5

U.S.A. (Alphabetic by State)

Program	Contact	Address
University of Alabama at Birmingham Med. Ctr. Neuropsychology Laboratory	Thomas J. Boll, Ph.D. (205) 934-8723	P. O. Box 109 Birmingham, AL 35294
Hill Crest Hospital Dept. of Neuropsychology	Douglas F. Robbins, Ph.D. (205) 833-9000	6869 Fifth Avenue South Birmingham, AL 35212
Barrow Neurological Institute Department of Neuropsychology	George P. Prigatano, Ph.D. (602) 285-3000	St. Joseph's Hospital and Medical Center 350 West Thomas Road Phoenix, AZ 85013-4496
Memorial Medical Center of Long Beach Dept. of Medical Psychology and Neuropsychology	John Knippa, Ph.D. (213) 595-3024	2801 Atlantic Long Beach, CA 90801
VA Medical Center Psychology Service (116B)	Jeffrey Webster, Ph.D. (213) 494-5605	5901 East Seventh Street Long Beach, CA 90822
University of California - Los Angeles (UCLA) Neuropsychology	Paul Satz, Ph.D. Wilfred Van Gorp, Ph.D. (213) 825-5360	760 Westwood Plaza (C8-747/NPI) Los Angeles, CA 90024
VA Medical Center Psychology Service (116B)	Amy M. Wisniewski, Ph.D. (415) 750-2004	4150 Clement Street San Francisco, CA 94121
San Francisco General Hospital Dept. of Psychiatry, 7G 16	Alicia Boccellari, Ph.D. (415) 821-5070	1001 Potrero Avenue San Francisco, CA 94110
The Institute of Living Department of Psychology	Geraldine Cassens, Ph.D. Leslie Lothstein, Ph.D. (203) 241-6932	400 Washington Street Hartford, CT 06106
National Rehab. Hospital Psychology Service	Joseph Bleiberg, Ph.D. Anne C. Newman, Ph.D. (202) 877-1695	102 Irvine Street, N.W. Washington, D.C. 20010

Program	Contact	Address
University of Florida Department of Clinical and Health Psychology	Eileen B. Fennell, Ph.D. (904) 392-4551	Box J-165, MSB Gainesville, FL 32610
University of Florida Ctr. for Neuropsychological Studies	Kenneth M. Heilman, M.D. (904) 392-3491	Box J-236, JHMHC Gainesville, FL 32610

University of Miami/
  Jackson Medical Center
Department of Psychology
  and Behavioral Medicine
	Jay Weinstein, Ph.D.
	(305) 549-6919
		Rehabilitation Center
		1611 N.W. 12th Avenue
		Miami, FL 33136

University of Iowa College of Medicine Department of Neurology	Daniel Tranel, Ph.D. (319) 356-2671	Iowa City, IA 52242
Rehabilitation Institute of Chicago Department of Psychology	Steven Rothke, Ph.D. (312) 908-6221	345 East Superior Street Chicago, IL 60611
Forest Institute of Professional Psychology	Mark Stone, Ed.D. (312) 635-4175	1717 Rand Road Des Plaines, IL 60016
Tulane University Med. Ctr. Department of Psychiatry and Neurology	F. William Black, Ph.D. (504) 588-5405	1415 Tulane Avenue New Orleans, LA 70112
VA Medical Center Psychology Service (116B)	Patricia R. Sutker, Ph.D. (504) 589-5235	1601 Perdido Street New Orleans, LA 70146
Children's Hospital Department of Psychology	Jane Holmes Bornstein, Ph.D. (617) 735-6398	300 Longwood Avenue Boston, MA 02115
Boston VA Medical Center Psychology Service	Roberta F. White, Ph.D. (617) 232-9500 ext. 3630	150 S. Huntington Avenue Boston, MA 02130

New England Medical
  Center Hospital
Neuropsychology
	Homer B. C. Reed, Jr.,
	  Ph.D.
	(617) 956-5725
		75 Kneeland Street
		Eleventh Floor
		Boston, MA 02111

Boston University School of Medicine Division of Psychiatry	M. Jay, Ed.D. S. Magocsi, D.Sc. C. Chase, Ph.D. (617) 534-5082	Boston City Hospital Neuropsychology Service 818 Harrison Avenue Boston, MA 02118
Braintree Hospital Neuropsychology	Richard S. Fischer, Ph.D. (617) 848-5353 ext. 2258	250 Pond Street Braintree, MA 02184

Program	Contact	Address
Johns Hopkins University School of Medicine Department of Psychiatry and Behavioral Sciences	Jason Brandt, Ph.D. (301) 955-2619	Meyer 218 600 North Wolfe Street Baltimore, MD 21205
University of Michigan Department of Psychiatry	Stanley Berent, Ph.D. (313) 763-9259	1500 E. Medical Center Drive Ann Arbor, MI 48109-0840
Henry Ford Hospital Div. of Neuropsychology (K-11)	John L. Fisk, Ph.D. (313) 876-2526	2799 West Grand Blvd. Detroit, MI 48202
University of Minnesota Medical School Neurosurgery (Neuropsychology Lab)	Manfred J. Meier, Ph.D. (612) 624-1412	Box 390 Mayo Minneapolis, MN 55455
Mayo Clinic Department of Psychiatry	Robert J. Ivnik, Ph.D. (507) 284-2985	Section of Psychology (W9B) Mayo Clinic Rochester, MN 55905
Mediflex Rehab - Camden Institute for Brain Injury Research & Training	Rebecca Cash, Ph.D. (609) 342-7600 (800) 524-2523	Three Cooper Plaza, Suite 518 Camden, NJ 08103
New York Hospital Cornell University Medical College Department of Psychiatry	Steven Mattis, Ph.D. (914) 997-5944	Westchester Division White Plains, NY 10605
University of Cincinnati College of Medicine & Children's Hospital Pediatrics, Division of Psychiatry & Psychology	M. Douglas Ris, Ph.D. (513) 559-4336	Elland & Bethesda Avenue Cincinnati, OH 45229-2899
Cleveland Clinic Foundation Department of Psychiatry and Psychology (P-57)	Gordon J. Chelune, Ph.D. (216) 444-5984	9500 Euclid Avenue Cleveland, OH 44195
Ohio State University College of Medicine Department of Psychiatry Division of Health Psychology	Robert A. Bornstein, Ph.D. (614) 293-4774	Neuropsychology Laboratory Columbus, OH 43210
Ohio State University College of Medicine Department of Pediatrics Division of Psychology	Keith Owen Yeates, Ph.D. (614) 461-2100	700 Children's Drive Columbus, OH 43205

Program	Contact	Address
University of Oklahoma Health Sciences Center Department of Psychiatry and Behavioral Sciences	Russell L. Adams, Ph.D. (405) 271-5639	P. O. Box 26901 Oklahoma City, OK 73190
VA Medical Center Psychology Service (116B)	Diane Howieson, Ph.D. Laurence Binder, Ph.D. (503) 220-8262 ext. 6504	P. O. Box 1034 Portland, OR 97207
Drexel University College of Arts & Sciences Psychology, Sociology and Anthropology	Eric A. Zillmer, Psy.D. (215) 590-8672	Philadelphia, PA 19104
Hahnemann University Department of Mental Health Sciences	Sandra Koffler, Ph.D. (215) 448-4956	Neuropsychology Division M. S. 341 230 North Broad Street Philadelphia, PA 19102
University of Pennsylvania Brain-Behavior Lab. Department of Psychiatry	Andrew J. Saykin, Psy.D. Ruben C. Gur, Ph.D. (215) 662-6094	205 Piersol Building Philadelphia, PA 19104-4283
University of Pittsburgh Western Psychiatric Inst. Dept. of Neuropsychological Assessment and Rehab.	Lynda J. Katz, Ph.D. (412) 624-2866	3811 O'Hara Street Pittsburgh, PA 15213
Brown University Psychology Consortium	Paul Malloy, Ph.D. (401) 455-6355	Butler Hospital 345 Blackstone Blvd. Providence, RI 02906
Brown University Department of Psychiatry and Human Behavior	Thomas J. Guilmette, Ph.D. (401) 277-5027	Rhode Island Hospital APC 608B 593 Eddy Street Providence, RI 02903
University of Texas Southwestern Medical Center Clinical Neuropsychology Lab.	Jim Hom, Ph.D. (214) 688-2886	5323 Harry Hines Blvd. Dallas, TX 75235-9070
Western State Hospital & University of Virginia Medical School Department of Behavioral Medicine & Psychiatry	Jeffrey T. Barth, Ph.D. (703) 332-8391	Box 2500 Staunton, VA 24401
University of Washington Department of Psychiatry and Behavioral Sciences	Brenda D. Townes, Ph.D. (206) 223-5923	325 Ninth Avenue Seattle, WA 98104

Program	Contact	Address
Madigan Army Medical Center Department of Psychiatry	Kenneth Zych, Ph.D. (206) 967-6406	Neuropsychology Fellowship Psychology Service Tacoma, WA 98431
University of Wisconsin Center for Health Sciences Department of Neurology	Charles G. Matthews, Ph.D. (608) 263-5430	Neuropsychology Laboratory U.W.C.H.S.-H4/672 600 Highland Avenue Madison, WI 53792
University of Wisconsin Medical School (MCC) Department of Neurology	Kerry Hamsher, Ph.D. (414) 289-8099	Mount Sinai Medical Center 950 North 12th Street Milwaukee, MI 53201-0342
Medical College of Wisconsin Department of Neurology Section of Neuropsychology	Thomas A. Hammeke, Ph.D. (414) 778-4588	1000 North 92nd Street Milwaukee, WI 53226

The Clinical Neuropsychologist
1987, Vol. 1, No. 1, pp. 9-20.

Continuing Education: An Alternative to Respecialization in Clinical Neuropsychology*

Manfred J. Meier
University of Minnesota Medical School

ABSTRACT

This presentation aims to extend the concept of a Learning and Assessment Center to the establishment and maintenance of competencies for the practice of clinical neuropsychology. The resulting process would begin with an analysis of current practices in the field for the purpose of identifying competencies. After reduction into performance objectives, the necessary knowledge, skills, and attitudes for reaching performance objectives would then be specified. Standardized training protocols and modules would be developed for use at selected sites where necessary supplementary course work can be provided and where the instructional methodology necessary for communicating with individuals in the field is available. The interested trainee in the field would need access to the autotutorial technology required for relating to the central facilities and for processing the sample cases and case simulations necessary for learning. The educational materials would be replicable and exportable to virtually any site that could provide the necessary materials and time/access for the professional in the field. Any resulting modules could be articulated with sponsored conferences and workshops for the purpose of maximizing educational yield, stated in competency-based terms, in what would become a systematic and comprehensive continuing education process. By beginning with the assessment of individual needs or insufficiencies, this model could provide an alternative to respecialization as a means of adding necessary basic scientific knowledge, applied generic core competencies, and specialized clinical neuropsychological competencies for effective practice at an advanced level. The model's flexibility hopefully would serve individuals with the entire range of continuing education needs encountered in a vital and progressive new clinical specialty.

It is almost a decade since serious and deliberate consideration of educational and credentialing issues arose in the neuropsychological community. Beginning

*Presidential Address delivered to the membership of the Division of Clinical Neuropsychology at the meeting of the American Psychological Association, August 1986. The author is indebted to the assistance of Robert Bornstein and Allan Yozawitz in identifying source material for this and future work in this area.

with American Psychological Association (APA) and International Neuro-psychological Society (INS) symposia in 1976 and 1977, and a general report from the now joint APA Division 40/INS Task Force on Education, Accreditation, and Credentialing (1981; 1984), there has been substantial progress toward defining educational guidelines for predoctoral, internship, and post-doctoral programs. Both Division 40 and INS executive bodies have approved these guidelines for publication in their respective newsletters (1983, 1984, 1986). It is somewhat ironic (or perhaps indicative of the conceptual and logistic difficulties inherent in such an effort) that guidelines for continuing education have not as yet been addressed - ironic because the early discussions of education and credentialing were motivated by a growing recognition of shortcomings in the way already degreed psychologists were pursuing competency attainment in clinical neuropsychology. The characteristic mode of competency pursuit at that time was attendance at a few workshops and a (sometimes not so) gradual incorporation of the principles of interpretation being professed by a guru of choice. Reflected against the growing body of knowledge and application in neuropsychology and the clinical neurosciences, including the well-intended efforts of workshop providers, workshops appeared to promise a quick road to success but threatened to destroy the credibility of the new specialty before it was fully evolved. Thus, the educational domain in greatest immediate need of improvement appeared to be continuing education.

The fact that continuing education was not addressed first in our efforts to define educational and credentialing guidelines was due to the vagueness of the task, since guidelines for the educational sequences required to become a fully competent professional were not available. Accordingly, the Task Force focused on the preparation of predoctoral, internship, and postdoctoral program guidelines (1983, 1984, 1986). As such programs increased in number, parallel efforts to establish external credentialing procedures, such as board certification, necessarily proceeded from an incomplete educational base for the typical provider of clinical neuropsychological services. Had a uniform educational base been necessary to embark on the credentialing venture, it probably would have taken a decade before a complete educational product was available for examination.

Assuming that it will take another decade before the guidelines for predoctoral, internship, and postdoctoral programs have been implemented and evaluated, and the subsequent new generation of clinical neuropsychologists appears in practice, continuing education and experience will remain the primary basis for competency development in the near future. If a measure of the impact upon practice of current predoctoral, internship, and postdoctoral activities were available, it seems unlikely that the cumulative result would be equivalent to the impact of continuing education activities. Hopefully, we are all engaged in continuing education to some extent through the resources provided by APA, INS, National Academy of Neuropsychologists, and the various medical and neuroscience organizations engaged in the pursuit of new knowledge and application. Within this neurobehavioral sciences framework, there is ample opportunity for the establishment and maintenance of competency. Information that is relevant for entry level functioning is provided most directly through workshop and conference activities that can be aimed deliberately at practice issues. The quality of workshop activities is assured only indirectly by organizational sponsorship as provided by APA (for a fee and without deliberate review), INS (through its half-day workshops), and other organizations and individuals in an elaborate configuration. Such activities, combined with demonstrated professional experience (with or without supervision), constitutes the current basis for determining eligibility for the American Board of Clinical Neuropsychology/American Board of Professional Psychology (ABCN/ABPP) examination. A majority of individuals sitting for the examination are coming through the continuing education channel. Very few are as yet coming out of formal pre- or postdoctoral programs. Predoctoral programs are likely to produce an increasing number of people, since the 5-year postdoctoral experience board eligibility requirement is just being approached by many individuals who have completed such programs. However, the number of predoctoral programs remains limited. There is a significant increase in the number of postdoctoral programs, but these characteristically handle very few fellows and are not likely to meet the needs of the many individuals in the field who are employed and seek an alternative to formal postdoctoral or predoctoral training. These are people who have been in the field for many years and cannot readily sacrifice the time on-site required for "respecialization" through a pre- or postdoctoral program.

The term "respecialization" has been used to designate the special case of an individual from a nonapplied area, such as experimental, physiological, or developmental psychology, seeking a credential in a traditional applied field such as clinical, counseling, or school psychology. In the context of training in clinical neuropsychology, the term might be apt for describing the movement of an individual in any area into this specialty through a formal predoctoral program. There probably have been a few such instances. The term might also be applied to formal postdoctoral programs: thus, the title "Continuing Education: Alternatives to Respecialization." The term is something of a misnomer, since some individuals are not respecializing but rather specializing for the first time; some are moving into applied roles after formal training in a more basic scientific role; still others have extensive clinical training but lack an adequate scientific foundation for acquiring the competencies of a specialty that requires a background in the neurosciences as well as in basic and applied psychology.

Whatever the sources of knowledge and kinds of supervised experience, it seems reasonable to expect any clinical neuropsychologist to meet the criteria related to knowledge and practice generated by the Joint Division 40/INS Task Force on Education, Accreditation, and Credentialing. It would also seem reasonable that the background and experience requirements conform to ABPP's general requirements and to the projected APA criteria embodied in the principles for the identification and recognition of new specialties that are being developed by the Subcommittee on Specialization (S.O.S.) and the APA Board of Professional Affairs (Sales, Bricklin, & Hall, 1984). S.O.S. has done an extraordinary amount of thinking and work toward formulating the concepts of basic and applied generic cores for professional practice. These principles are integrally related to our Task Force's guidelines for pre- and postdoctoral training and provide an interesting point of departure for designing a continuing education model for individuals in the field. It is the purpose of this presentation to explore this relationship as a first step toward developing a continuing education model.

It should be emphasized at this juncture that APA has no formal policy regarding new specialties or new specialty training requirements. APA has not adopted the proposed designation system for defining educational programs in psychology as distinguished from other disciplines. Similarly, APA has not adopted a formal policy for the recognition of new specialties or for the accreditation of training programs in new areas. (Parenthetically, accreditation is a term applied to program evaluation as contrasted with evaluation of individual professional competencies which is referred to as credentialing. The term credentialing also encompasses degrees and certificates which are credentials bestowed by educational institutions and not by professional organizations and agencies such as credentialing or licensing boards.) Even though the designation system and the S.O.S. principles have not been adopted formally by APA, they have direct implications for defining the necessary knowledge and sets of skills (or competencies) required of a professional psychologist. An appropriate scientific core based on current APA accreditation guidelines for traditional de facto specialty programs and from the designation system document would approximate the following:

* RESEARCH METHODOLOGY
* STATISTICS AND MEASUREMENT
* HISTORY AND SYSTEMS
* REGULALTORY STANDARDS AND ETHICS
* BASES OF BEHAVIOR
  -Biological
  -Cognitive-Affective
  -Individual and Social

It is usually assumed that a Ph.D. in psychology reflects competency and formal coursework in these areas as a foundation for subsequent (i.e., long-term) development as a professional psychologist. Any continuing education model should begin with an evaluation of the individual's educational credentials to help validate this claim. Presumably, licensure assures this basic generic foundation. However, licensure boards vary considerably and often do not have such distribution requirements.

Thus, a first step in continuing education would appear to be the establishment or completion of the scientific core through removal of any basic deficiencies (or insufficiencies). This core would then serve as the basis from which specialized professional practice would evolve. However, as S.O.S. points out, between the scientific core and the ultimate configuration of specialty role competencies lies a combination of knowledge and skills shared by all applied specialties, termed applied generic cores (AGC). The AGC concept leaves open the possibility of a single common generic core that all specialties should demonstrate on an overlapping basis as well as applied generic cores that are shared between one rather than another subset of specialties or between more than one specialty. Ultimately, there might be an applied generic core that is limited (at least in fully developed form) to a specialty (e.g., clinical neurobehavioral science core for clinical neuropsychology). Such a core for clinical neuropsychology might initially be a component of the specialized end product but could well evolve into a AGC if the specialty became more differentiated in the future -- as might occur, for example, between adult and child neuropsychology, areas which at this stage of our development do not appear to warrant fully separate designation (some already argue for separate programs).

The specialized third phase of knowledge and skill development is then conceived in terms of four parameters of practice: client populations served, problems addressed, techniques and technologies utilized, and service settings. S.O.S. attempted to distinguish between specialty and proficiency practice around these four parameters. Thus, full specialty practice would require the knowledge and skills involved in addressing a wide range of problems encountered by the specialty, numerous client populations, a myriad of techniques and technologies, and various service settings. By contrast, proficiency practice would be more limited. For example, a proficiency might be defined as the application of a particular technique or technology in a single setting and to a particular client population and problem. An example of a proficiency in clinical neuropsychology might be the application of the Halstead-Reitan battery in a psychiatric setting to the problem of differentiating between functional and organic determinants of behavior change in affective and ideational disorders. A fully competent specialist would be able to address that problem with a wide range of techniques, in various settings, and to other client populations. The specialist would also be able to address the entire range of problems encountered in an independent practice, applying generic as well as specialized knowledge and skills -- again, across a wide range of neuropsychological referral issues.

The concept of proficiency has certain merits because it allows for the sharing of particular functions by a number of specialties. For example, a clinical psychologist could perform in the more limited proficiency role with full awareness of the boundaries of that role and the bases of competency attainment beyond that role. If proficiencies can be defined and validly achieved, it might avert fragmentation and facilitate mobility across specialties. However, it is first necessary to define the specialty in terms of these four parameters of practice, perform a comparable analysis of other specialties, and determine where overlap legitimately exists. In any case, the distinction is a useful one and should be explored after a given specialty's claim to having defined and fulfilled specialty requirements has been established.

The AGC that is common to all professional specialties will necessarily evolve over time. There appears to be increased agreement between clinical and counseling psychologists relative to a core that is shared by practitioners in these specialties. Some have argued that clinical and counseling are not specialties at all but, rather, are practiced exclusively from the common AGC. However, many would argue that, beyond this core, each of these specialties could (and should) identify their specialized knowledge base and skills for each of the four parameters of practice. In any case, if specialties exist at all, they are expected to emanate from the AGC "as it operates across specific populations, techniques, technologies, problems and settings constituting specialization in psychology" (Sales et al., 1984). The common AGC has not yet been defined formally but would appear to include the following:

* PRINCIPLES AND PRACTICE OF INTERVIEWING
* COGNITIVE AND PERSONALITY ASSESSMENT
* DESIGN AND EVALUATION OF REPRESENTATIVE INTERVENTION
* CLINICAL RESEARCH DESIGN AND IMPLEMENTATION
* STANDARDS AND ETHICS

The importance of the AGC concept may lie in its relevance for resolving a key issue in clinical neuropsychology and for differentiating specialized from generic applied issues in continuing education. Many cognitive, physiological, and developmental psychologists have acquired highly specialized professional role competencies in clinical neuropsychology while functioning as researchers in clinical settings. While their specialized skills are valued, they sometimes lack the applied generic knowledge and skills to function fully independently in private practice, where a broad range of psychopathological and neuro-psychological problems present themselves. An incomplete component of their professional preparation would appear to be the AGC being discussed in the specialization context. Respecialization in a traditional specialty appears to be the only presently available mechanism for them to acquire the necessary generic applied knowledge and skills, an unrealistic or unfeasible option for most individuals. Others whose educational and experiential base lies primarily in a traditional applied area, such as clinical psychology, may have a corresponding insufficiency in scientific core knowledge, both in general psychology and especially in the neurosciences. The more extensive scientific background of cognitive, developmental, and physiological psychologists is desirable but does not offset the need for generic applied preparation, since the roles and responsibilities of the professional are heavily anchored in the AGC. The more extensive background in clinical roles and experience of clinical psychologists is desirable but does not offset the lack of adequate preparation in scientific psychology and the neurosciences.

Examination of the bases of failure to pass the ABPP examination in clinical neuropsychology reveals that basic people without adequate applied background and the applied people with limited neuroscience and basic psychological science background are having the most difficulty (Nik Palo, Executive Secretary, ABPP, Personal Communication). This is not surprising in light of the specialized knowledge and skills identified as necessary by the Division 40/INS Task Force for competency as a clinical neuropsychologist. The Task Force identified competency domains that are the specialized counterparts of the above AGC. Review of these should make it readily apparent what specialized knowledge and skills a continuing education model must provide.

* Differential diagnosis between psychogenic and neurogenic syndromes and disorders (e.g., depression vs. dementia).

* Differential diagnosis between two or more suspected etiologies of cerebral dysfunction (e.g., neoplasm vs. cerebral vascular accident).

* Delineation of spared and impaired functions secondary to an episodic event (e.g., cerebral vascular accident, head trauma, infection).

* Establishment of baseline measures to monitor progressive cerebral disease or recovery processes (e.g., neoplasm, demyelinating disease, head injury).

* Comparison of pre- and postneuropsychological functioning following pharmacologic, surgical, and behavioral interventions (e.g., drug trials, tissue excision, shunts, revascularization, language or cognitive therapy).

* Assessment of cognitive and affective status for the formulation of rehabilitation strategies and the design of remedial interventions.

Competence in clinical neuropsychology requires the knowledge and clinical skills to comprehend and integrate the implications of information in the areas of:

* functional neuroanatomy and pathophysiology

* disorders of attention, sensory, perceptual, conceptual, language, memory, voluntary and involuntary motor, and affective processes

* neurological and related diseases, including their manner of presentation, course, and treatment

* CNS effects of systemic disorders

* child development and ontology of neuropsychological processes

* expected decrements in neuropsychological processes as a function of normal aging

* behavioral pathology and psychopharmacology

* psychophysiological principles underlying behavioral pathology

* social-cultural factors as codeterminants of behavior

* principles of personality assessment and interviewing skills

* principles of test construction and validation

* principles of test administration and interpretation relating to both fixed and flexible neuropsychological batteries

* principles of cognitive remediation and derivation of specific intervention strategies

Eliminating insufficiencies at any of these three levels will require the packaging of multiple procedures and educational opportunities to meet individual needs. Needs or insufficiencies are expected to vary quite widely so that the model should permit a highly individualized continuing education "curriculum" design and evaluation. In order to address such insufficiencies, a strategic focusing of content is necessary to minimize on-campus or on-clinical site participation of the trainee. With the advancement of personal computer technology, and assuming the availability of relevant clinical cases in the individual's own practice, it should be feasible to provide supervision at a distance and combine such experiences with didactic and additional clinical coursework in the educational institutional setting.

It is proposed that the Assessment Center (or Learning and Assessment Center in this context) approach holds promise for obtaining full clinical competency in neuropsychology through continuing education without undergoing a completely formal on-site pre- or postdoctoral program in the specialty. Additionally, this approach could lead to the development of materials that would help already fully competent individuals to maintain and expand their competencies in the future. This is particularly germane for younger neuropsychologists who may well be faced with the need to fulfil specific continuing education requirements for maintaining licenses and diplomate status should the State Boards and the ABPP move in the direction of recredentialing through continuing education. Traditionally, continuing education in professional psychology has emphasized didactic workshops and conferences rather than a competency-based or competency-determined approach. There is rarely an effort to pretest the audience to determine what knowledge or skill each participant brings into the conference so that the conference's impact, if any, is usually unknown. Goals of these activities are characteristically limited to the transmission of new knowledge, but little opportunity for expanding skills or establishing new competencies. Since expertise in clinical neuropsychology depends on both knowledge and competence, bringing the trainee to standard will require approaches that prepare the trainee for full competency as defined in the S.O.S. principles document. A key methodological approach for achieving this goal on a continuing education basis is the Assessment Center approach, modified to incorporate both learning and assessment activities.

The Assessment Center concept originated in the Office of Strategic Services (OSS) during World War II where it was applied to the problem of selecting readiness and competence for special war-time duties by means of situational tests. Applications were subsequently extended into management selection and placement procedures in large multinational corporations (Bray, 1974). As the concept evolved, it became evident that it encompassed more than the application of a circumscribed group of methods in a particular place or facility and that it could be extended as a process into multiple settings, utilizing a variety of techniques and situations for observing and evaluating professional behavior, either those already established or those being learning. Assessment centers can be designed to include learning components and, thereby, facilitate the acquisition of new knowledge and the incorporation of such knowledge into new competencies (Williamson & Schallman, 1980). Thus, a (learning and) assessment center can be characterized as a multimethod resource for transmitting, collecting, reviewing, and integrating information for the development, evaluation, and deployment of competencies in particular settings (Cyrs, 1976). By implication, the knowledge and skills acquired through a learning and assessment center (again considered as a process without specific geographic boundaries) could be directed to the four parameters of practice identified by S.O.S., namely, settings, problems, client populaltions, and techniques/technologies. Assessment center operations have been developed in other contexts (Moses & Byham, 1977) and could be adapted to our needs as follows:

1. The dimensions, attributes, characteristics, or qualities evaluated by this center would be determined by analysis of relevant professional behaviors in accord, for example, with the roles and competencies identified by the Division 40/INS Task Force.

2. Multiple assessment and teaching techniques would be used based on analyses of behaviors relevant to the competencies. Emphasis would be placed on simulations and other autotutorial procedures that parallel or resemble situations in which competencies are applied, including simulations, case problem-solving, and fact-finding exercises. These can be administered be means of personal computer technology to include a wide range of autotutorial exercises as well as dialogues and communications with a clinical supervisor at virtually any distance.

3. The process calls for multiple assessors who receive prior training. Extended to continuing education, such assessors would also serve as supervisors by transmitting information and problems to the trainee, providing feedback, and, ultimately, assessing training outcomes and progress. Any protocols so generated would then be subject to pooling and/or verification by an additional assessor or assessors.

4. Such exercises could be combined with traditional educational activities in an educational institutional setting, though with sharply reduced on-site time, especially when augmented by appropriately sponsored workshops, conferences, and scientific/professional meeting attendance.

5. Exercises could include case materials provided by the trainee in his/her professional setting and devised on the same basis as a simulation to tap the variety of behaviors identified as relevant to the tasks. Pre- to posttesting would be done routinely to determine the effectiveness of the procedures and the individual.

The learning and assessment of multiple skills by means of multiple measurement tools and observations of the individual's behavior by multiple observers distinguishes the center from the traditional learning format. Traditionally, learning (formal or continuing) usually occurs on the basis of a more fragmented and less organized approach. Underlying traditional graduate training is the assumption that all the necessary knowledge and skills will become integrated as a matter of course during the internship and future experience. Conversion of problems involving different client populations, techniques, and settings into cases for simulated and direct application of clinical skills would require the involvement and cooperation of a representative group of educators in clinical neuropsychology and clinical neuropsychologists in the field to accomplish the following:

* describe the required behaviors for effective performance in each of the major roles of a clinical neuropsychologist;

* develop the necessary computer software for linking the practitioner in training in the field to the "central facility";

* incorporate multitrait-multimethod assessment designs for making judgments that the attainment of knowledge and skills across the four targeted parameters has been achieved;
* develop a research design for assessing the quality of resulting measures.

The "central facility" could consist of a consortium of educational institutions committed to developing competency-determined training modules and extending them into the practice setting so that the professional in the field can maintain or expand competencies without lengthy periods of residence at the educational institution (McClelland, 1973). In fully developed form, the center could provide the equivalent of a postdoctoral program without extensive absence from professional practice. Short of such an elaborate goal, the approach appears to have considerable merit for augmenting traditional conference and workshop activities as a means of pursuing continuing education.

Such innovations in instructional methodology have been introduced in other professions (MacKinnon, 1975). Competencies are first defined in the field. Terminal performance objectives then must be defined before professional practice can be translated into modules or self-contained instructional packages for use in the learning and assessment center. The learner can then be subjected to direct tests and be given the necessary supervision for developing the competency in accord with accepted standards of practice. In addition to assisting the professional in the field to achieve additional education, the learning and assessment center, conceived as a methodological resource, can assist the professional to qualify for a new specialty or practice area in which he/she may not have received primary training.

A performance analysis of the roles of clinical neuropsychologists will be needed to generate terminal performance objectives for each competency identified by the Division 40/INS Task Force on Education, Accreditation, and Credentialing. Thus, the necessary further analysis of competencies in the development of self-contained training modules remains to be done. Ultimately, in the United States, such an undertaking will require the cooperation and active participation of APA, state associations, state licensing boards, national credentialing agencies such as ABPP, and the National Register. If successful, the model could be applied to other specialties. Many of the procedures could also be derived from and used in formal predoctoral internship and postdoctoral programs.

Bray, D.W. (1984, August,). Assessment centers for research and application. Psi Chi Distinguished Lecture delivered at the meeting of the American Psychological Association, Toronto.

Cyrs, T.E. (1976). Modular approach to curriculum design using the systems approach. In P.Sleeman & D.M.Rockwell (Eds.), *Instructional media and technology*. New York; Halsted Press.

Mackinnon, D.W. (1975). An overview of assessment centers. Technical report No. 1. Greensboro,NC: Center for Creative Leadership.

McClelland, D.C. (1973). Testing for competence rather than for "intelligence". *American Psychologist, 28*, 1-14.

Moses, J.L., & Byham, W.C. (Eds.) (1977). *Applying the assessment center method*. New York: Pergamon.

Sales, B., Bricklin, P., & Hall, J. (1984). *Manual on specialization: Principles*. Proposed to the Board of Professional Affairs, American Psychological Association, Washington D.C.

Williamson, S.A., & Schaalman, M.L. (1980). The assessment of occupational competence. 2. *Assessment Centers: Theory, practice, and implications for education*. Contract 400-78-0028, U.S. Department of Education, ERIC, Washington D.C.

Report of the Task Force on Education, Accreditation, and Credentialing (1981). *International Neuropsychological Society Bulletin*, 5-10.

Report of the Joint INS/Division 40 Task Force on Education, Accreditation, and Credentialing (1984). *Newletter 40, 2*, 3-8.

Guidelines for internship Programs in Clinical Neuropsychology (1983). *International Neuropsychological Society Bulletin*.

Guidelines for Doctoral Training Programs in Clinical Neuropsychology. (1986). INS/Division 40 Task Force on Education, Accreditation, and Credentialing. *Newsletter 40*, 4, 4.

Guidelines for Postdoctoral Training in Clinical Neuropsychology. (1986). INS/Division 40 Task Force on Education, Accreditation, and Credentialing. *Newsletter 40*, 4, 4.

The Clinical Neuropsychologist
1988, Vol. 2, nr. 1, pp. 25-29

Reports of the Division 40 Task Force on Education, Accreditation, and Credentialing

Subcommittee on Continuing Education

GUIDELINES FOR CONTINUING EDUCATION IN CLINICAL
NEUROPSYCHOLOGY

Robert A. Bornstein
The Ohio State University

INTRODUCTION

The Guidelines for Continuing Education (CE) presented below represent a continuation of the interest in setting forth guidelines at all levels of training and education in clinical neuropsychology. These guidelines follow previous documents from the Task Force which have addressed Doctoral Training Programs, Internships, and Post-Doctoral Training. The latter guidelines were compiled in a previous volume of this journal (Task Force Reports, 1987; Vol. 1, No. 1, pp. 29-34). The current document contains two separate sets of recommendations or guidelines. The first part of the document provides guidelines for *providers* of CE programs, while the second part is directed toward *consumers* of these programs. These guidelines were developed in conjunction with the principles and criteria for CE as set forth by the American Psychological Association. The guidelines both for providers and consumers of CE in clinical neuropsychology incorporate general and specific guidelines. The committee members who prepared this report included R.A. Bornstein (Chair), Lloyd Cripe, Byron P. Rourke, and Alan Yozawitz.

GENERAL PRINCIPLES FOR PROVIDERS OF CONTINUING EDUCATION.

CE programs include a broad range of activities which provide neuropsychologists with knowledge and skills to help them maintain professional competence. *CE is not a method for development of basic competence in the clinical practice of neuropsychology.* Rather, the goal of CE is to enhance the established competence of neuropsychologists by updating previously acquired skills or learning new skills based upon an established knowledge base. These basic principles are pertinent to providers of CE programs and for those who avail themselves of such programs.

GUIDELINES FOR PROVIDERS OF CONTINUING EDUCATION IN CLINICAL NEUROPSYCHOLOGY

1. CE programs should have specific learning objectives derived in response to specific learning needs and interests of the intended audience. The specific learning objectives should be clearly and explicitly defined to assist consumers in the evaluation of the relevance of the program to their particular needs.

Consistent with the previously stated general principles, providers of CE programs should not offer programs that imply, or could be interpreted by consumers to imply, that basic competence in clinical neuropsychology is established through such programs. Programs which suggest acquisition of further specialized skills within neuropsychology based upon attendance at workshops advertised as "advanced" could imply that attendees will assume a useable level of professional competence in neuropsychology. Instead, the message should be clear that such programs are intended to build upon and enhance previously established competencies in neuropsychology. Providers of CE activities should avoid such terminology so as to reduce the likelihod that misunderstandings of the goals of the program will occur.

Providers of multitiered CE programs, such as those which offer some activity predicated on satisfactory completion of a preliminary prerequisite CE program (e.g., advanced workshops, attendance at which requires previous attendance at a basic workshop) should be aware of the implications this may have on consumers' expectations. In these situations, providers should be particularly obligated to emphasize to consumers that the "islands of skill" being offered are an inadequate mechanism for establishment of basic clinical competence.

Introductory workshops designed for psychologists (or others) who do not possess basic competence in neuropsychology should avoid giving the impression that the field of clinical neuropsychology rests solely or largely on the basis of the use of a set of specifically designed procedures. Introductory programs should be developed for a number of purposes which could include (1) general introduction to the origins and applications of neuropsychological assessment procedures, (2) application of clinical neuropsychological procedures in specific settings or contexts, (3) interactions between clinical neuropsychologists and other psychological and nonpsychological specialists, (4) application and implementation of neuropsychological data, (5) development of neuropsychologically oriented skills in regard to tests and procedures with which psychologists may be competent such as Wechsler Intelligence Scales, (6) development of skills related to recognition of appropriate referral problems that can be addressed by neuropsychological data, and the possible implications of the resulting data in the context of treatment or management of those problems.

2. Providers of continuing education programs should be required to evaluate their program in regard to demonstration of learning with respect to stated goals and participant satisfaction. Specific items for evaluation may include (1) attitude and/or behavior change, (2) knowledge and skill improvement, (3) enhancement of technical judgement, (4) acquisition of new ideas, new theoretical developments, tools, techniques, or processes. The participant satisfaction evaluation should include (1) quality and quantity of instruction (presenter, materials, and demonstrations), (2) usefulness of content, (3) level of knowledge and ability of presenter to teach.

3. Instructional personnel must possess the credentials and experience to qualify as *competent and expert* in the topic to be taught and be able to facilitate learning. Examples of documentation of such expertise include but are not limited to (1) prominence in scholarly activity such as publications dealing with clinical neuropsychological topics included in the CE program, (2) board certification by recognized professional credentialling boards (e.g., the American Board of Clinical Neuropsychology), (3) fellowship status in The Division of Clinical Neuropsychology of APA. Presenter's performance may be monitored by the participant satisfaction procedures.

4. Providers of CE activities regularly update the content of their programs and modify the programs where necessary to reflect changes in the supporting empirical data base. CE programs should be designed to be at the postgraduate level, and the curriculum content must be related to the stated learning objectives. The activity must be of sufficient duration (minimum of 3 hours) to explore a subject or group of related subjects in reasonable depth.

5. Participants should be provided written documentation of their participation. That documentation should include the names and dates of the CE program, and should also contain a statement that the document does not represent a credential to be used to document basic competence in clinical neuropsychology.

6. All aspects of the CE program, including content, promotional materials, demonstrations, case materials, and credentials of presenters, must be consistent with APA *Ethical Principles of Psychologists*.

GENERAL PRINCIPLES FOR CONSUMERS OF CONTINUING EDUCATION IN CLINICAL NEUROPSYCHOLOGY

Individuals who lack formal and extensive background in clinical neuropsychology should not approach CE workshops individually or in combination (e.g., basic and advanced workshops) as an acceptable method of obtaining basic competence in clinical neuropsychology. Consumers of CE programs should be suitably informed of the purposes of each program by prospectus, and should seek activities geared to their own level of education, experience, and competence in clinical neuropsychology.

Clinical neuropsychology is a specialized area of practice which entails unique procedures and a body of knowledge specific to the area. Clinical neuropsychology should not be regarded as a subfield of clinical psychology, health psychology, or any other specialty area in applied psychology. In this context, psychologists who may have developed competence in one of these other specialty areas cannot *establish competence* in clinical neuropsychology solely through the use of a self-fashioned program of CE activities. Those psychologists who propose to respecialize or expand their areas of specialty must do so within the context of an institutional program that incorporates the APA guidelines on re-specialization.

GUIDELINES FOR CONSUMERS OF CONTINUING EDUCATION PROGRAMS IN CLINICAL NEUROPSYCHOLOGY

1. Individuals should pursue activities consistent with their level of neuropsychological expertise. Individuals should not engage in CE activities that espouse educational objectives which exceed their own level of training and experience. To facilitate this process, CE providers should present a structured rating form to assist individuals in defining their level of expertise. (This could include relevant experiences or courses that might be viewed as pre-requisites for the CE program.)

2. Individuals should expect clearly defined and explicitly stated educational goals. The materials presented in the program should be appropriate for actualization of the stated goals.

3. The specific goals to be attained are linked to the individual's level of competence. Particular CE activities (or combinations thereof) should not be considered to be a mechanism for attainment of basic competence in clinical neuropsychology. Rather, the educational goals of CE programming should be to broaden the scope of or to refine established skills and competencies.

4. CE activities may be useful supplements to the educational experiences of formal institutionally based training programs. Individuals with established basic competencies in clinical neuropsychology may broaden their competencies through the refinement of existing skills or the development of new skill applications.

5. Providers of CE experiences should be recognized experts in the area addressed by the CE program. Examples of documentation of such expertise include but are not limited to (1) prominence in scholarly activity such as publications dealing with clinical neuropsychological topics included in the CE program, (2) board certification by recognized professional credentialling boards (e.g., the American Board of Clinical Neuropsychology), (3) fellowship status in The Division of Neuropsychology of APA.

REFERENCE

Reports of the INS-Division 40 Task Force on Education, Accreditation, and Credentialing. (1987). *The Clinical Neuropsychologist, 1,* 29-34.

The Clinical Neuropsychologist
1987, Vol. 1, nr. 1, pp. 21-28.

American Board of Clinical Neuropsychology: Policies and Procedures

Linas A. Bieliauskas   and   Charles G. Matthews

Rush-Presbyterian-St. Luke's
Medical Center

University of Wisconsin-
Clinical Science Center

ABSTRACT

The policies and procedures for obtaining a diplomate in Clinical Neuropsychology from the American Board of Clinical Neuropsychology-American Board of Professional Psychology are briefly described. A brief historical background and rationale for the diplomate process is provided.

BACKGROUND

In June, 1981, several members of the Joint APA Division 40/International Neuropsychological Society (INS) Task Force on Education, Accreditation, and Credentialing in Clinical Neuropsychology met in Minneapolis to discuss the need for formulation of board procedures to credential competency in clinical neuropsychology. These members included Linas Bieliauskas, Edith Kaplan, Muriel Lezak, Manfred Meier, Charles Matthews, Steven Mattis, and Paul Satz.

The Joint Task Force had just completed a document describing training in clinical neuropsychology and its practice (INS/APA, 1984). During the course of its work, the task force had come to the realization that training in clinical neuropsychology was far from standardized and that there was an increasing number of individuals who claimed competency in this area without indication of effective background or training. There was no credential which was recognizable to the public as assuring confidence that a given individual had indeed demonstrated competence in clinical neuropsychology.

This small group agreed that the time had come for establishment of a board procedure which would recognize the competent practice of clinical neuropsychology. It was agreed that the members of the initial board should be individuals who would, by consensus, have attained national visibility in clinical neuropsychology. It was also agreed that no member of the initial board would be "grandfathered." All initial members would agree to be examined by each other and passed before being seated on the board. Accordingly, the American Board of Clinical Neuropsychology (ABCN) was incorporated in the state of Minnesota in August, 1981 with the following members who were subsequently examined in August-September, 1983:

Arthur Benton	Charles Matthews, Secretary
Linas Bieliauskas	Steven Mattis, Vice President
Thomas Boll	Manfred Meier, President
Nelson Butters	Allan Mirsky
Louis Costa	Oscar Parsons
Leonard Diller	Homer Reed
Gerald Goldstein	Byron Rourke
Harold Goodglass	Paul Satz
Edith Kaplan	Aaron Smith
Muriel Lezak, Treasurer	Otfried Spreen
Joseph Matarazzo	Barbara Wilson

Charles Golden joined the board in 1984.

The purpose of the ABCN was to provide a procedure which screened the credentials of potential applicants, evaluated work samples, and conducted examinations of basic and applied knowledge of clinical neuropsychology and examples of its practice. From the time of the initial formation of the board, it was decided to pursue an affiliation with the American Board of Professional Psychology (ABPP) as the only recognized body which had historically assessed competency in applied areas of psychology. A formal affiliation with ABPP was formalized in 1983 and the first ABCN/ABPP diplomates were awarded at the ABPP convocation in August, 1984.

Since 1984, ABPP has assumed, in addition to its responsibilities for other areas of applied psychology, administrative responsibility for the processing of applications for the Diplomate in Clinical Neuropsychology. ABCN has continued to screen credentials, evaluate work samples, and conduct examinations under the auspices of ABPP.

PURPOSE OF THE EXAMINATION

The examination for the diplomate is designed to assess advanced competence in the practice of clinical neuropsychology. As can be seen below, it is intended not just as a measure of fund of knowledge, but also as a tool to determine the effectiveness of application of neuropsychological principles in the clinical setting and the promotion of the welfare of the patient. The examination is designed to provide a standard by which competence to practice clinical neuropsychology is judged. Success or failure in taking the examination alone neither affirms nor denies academic preparation, neuroscience expertise, or clinical skills in other areas. Rather, it is designed to assess the ability to integrate appropriate neuropsychological and clinical knowledge in the care of patients.

At the time the diplomate was created, there was no set, clear, recognized qualification for the practice of clinical neuropsychology. Today, the routes to becoming a clinical neuropsychologist are varied and numerous (Report of the Task Force, 1981). An additional advantage to creation of the diplomate was to provide a credential which the lay public, attorneys, educators, and other consumers of clinical neuropsychological services could recognize. As with a diplomate in any other area of professional practice, the granting of a diplomate in clinical neuropsychology indicates that the individual has undergone and passed examination, by his/her peers, on the ability to practice in a competent fashion.

ADMINISTRATIVE STRUCTURE FOR APPLICATION AND
EXAMINATION

Application and Credentials Review
In applying for the Diplomate in Clinical Neuropsychology the potential applicant first writes a letter of interest to the Executive Secretary of ABPP. ABPP will send necessary application materials to the candidate. The completed applications are then sent back to ABPP where a file is created and the materials reviewed to insure they meet ABPP standards. Once ABPP standards are met, the file is sent to the credentialing committee of ABCN, currently headed by Charles Matthews, where each file is screened to meet the standards of ABCN. Once passed, the file is returned to ABPP which notifies the candidate that his/her credentials do or do not meet standards.

Work Sample Evaluation
Upon notification that credentialing standards have been met, the candidate is instructed to prepare two work samples for evaluation. These work samples are to reflect the clinical work of the candidate and typically include clinical neuropsychological assessments with some indication of follow-up interven-

tions. The interventions may include treatment by the candidate, recommendations for treatment by others, consultation to other health professionals, follow-up assessment, etc. Both work samples must include raw data as part of the submission. In addition, it is expected that complete historical and demographic information of relevance will be included in each work sample. The candidate is expected to have a thorough knowledge of the patients and to be aware of their current status. The candidate is given 1 year to prepare and submit the work sample.

The candidate is instructed to send the work sample to ABPP Central Office which, in turn, sends it to one of three "time-zone" coordinators - eastern, midwestern, or western. The time-zone coordinator to whom the work samples are sent should be the one in the region where the candidate wishes to have the oral examination, not necessarily where the candidate resides. Oral examinations are typically conducted in major cities in each region: typically, Boston or Washington in the eastern zone, Chicago in the midwestern zone, and Los Angeles in the western zone.

The time zone coordinators acknowledge receipt of the work samples and send them to three examiners for evaluation. Examiners for the work sample are chosen, at random, from across the nation, not necessarily from the same time zone to which the work sample was submitted. Each of the three examiners rates the work samples as "pass" or "fail" on the basis of demonstrated competency, including use of appropriate neuropsychological and psychological instruments, accurate interpretation of results, and provision of meaningful reports. Specific comments are provided for each work sample whether it is passed or failed, for the purpose of creating a list of questions to be asked in the oral examination or to help the applicant prepare and resubmit a more satisfactory work sample.

If two of the three examiners pass the work samples, the candidate is informed that he/she has been admitted to the oral examination and is instructed as to potential dates and place for the exam. Typically, dates for the oral examination are set only after enough candidates have been admitted to make the examination feasible, though not less than once per year.

If two examiners fail the work samples, the candidate is informed that he/she will not be admitted to the oral examination and that he/she may reapply for candidacy according to ABPP guidelines. Thus, in all cases, two "passes" or "fails" are required when a decision regarding admittance to the oral examination is made.

Oral Examination

Once the dates for the oral examination are determined, the candidate is expected to appear at the designated time and place. Transportation and lodging are at the candidate's own arrangement and expense. Suggestions as to lodging are usually provided by the time-zone coordinators.

The oral examination is designed to assess the clinical competence of the candidate. While fundamental neuropsychological, neurological, and neuroscience knowledge are expected, the candidate must also demonstrate an advanced degree of clinical knowledge and skills in the care of patients. It has been the experience of the Board to date that those candidates who have not passed the oral examination have had either solid neuroscience knowledge without adequate clinical knowledge and skills, or have shown good clinical knowledge and skills without adequate neuroscience knowledge. For example, the candidate is expected to demonstrate an adequate neurological/neurophysiological understanding of the injury or disease about which he/she is being questioned, the neuropsychological procedures employed, and the effect of affective, character, or other personality/social variables that may have had a bearing on symptom presentation and test performance. The ABCN exam is designed to determine advanced competency in all of these areas as they relate to evaluation and care of patients.

The oral examination is broken down into three parts, each lasting about 1 hour. Each phase is conducted by one examiner. Each examiner rates each candidate in the following areas: Evaluative Skills, Intervention Knowledge and Skills, Scientific and Professional Knowledge, Ethics and Social Responsibility, and Professional Commitment. Any of the three examiners may ask questions regarding these areas at any time.

The first part of the examination is called the "Work Sample". The examiner quizzes the candidate about the nature of the patient, the presenting symptoms and illness or injury, the nature of and rationale for the procedures employed, justification for the conclusions reached, and rationale for the recommendations made. It is imperative that the candidate have thorough and complete knowledge of the patients and their current status. As with other parts of the oral examination, the critical element here is the ability to demonstrate a reasonable, rational, and defensible approach to patient evaluation, treatment, and a high level of report-writing skill.

The second part of the examination is called "Fact Finding". The examiner will present a one paragraph vignette on a case which has been thoroughly prepared by one of the examiners. The candidate will have a choice of either a child or adult case. After examining the vignette, the candidate must extract all further demographic, medical, historical, and test information about the case from the examiner by questioning the examiner. In other words, the candidate conducts a "mock" evaluation of the case by asking for the above information which the examiner has available. Based on the information, the candidate is required to reach conclusions as to the nature of the neuropsychological and psychological deficits and strengths of the patient being presented, the behavioral diagnosis and/or implications for the patient, the relationship between measured behavior and/or test results and the patient's injury, illness, and/or presenting symptoms, and recommendations to be made. Again, a relevant and systematic method for approaching the case is critical.

58

It is not crucial that the same conclusions about the case be reached by the candidate as by the preparer of the case; it is crucial that the conclusions reached by the candidate be reasonable and defensible.

The third part of the exam is termed "Ethics". The candidate is presented with a neuropsychologically related vignette, usually about 3/4 of a page in length. Issues of professional practice, behavior, and ethics are embedded in the vignette. After reviewing the vignette, the candidate is asked to address those issues which present ethical or professional conflicts, what actions should be taken regarding them, and how he/she would improve on the situation or behave under similar circumstances. The APA *Ethical Principles of Psychologists* (APA,1981) is required background for this portion of the examination. After discussing the vignette, the examiner asks the candidate about his/her own professional practices, professional involvement, and research activities. For this portion, demonstration of an advanced level of clinical and research practice, a firm grasp of professional ethics, and commitment to the field are the major areas of examination.

At the end of the three parts of the exam, the examiners meet and reach an overall decision of pass or fail. As with the work sample, the decisions of two of the three examiners determine the outcome of the examination.

Objective Examination

At the present time, the oral examination, as described above, is the only basis for determining diplomate status in clinical neuropsychology. A 200 item, multiple-choice, objective examination has also been developed, which all candidates are required to take. The objective examination is presently being given to gather normative data and does not count toward achieving or failing to achieve the diplomate. The multiple-choice exam is taken during the other half of the day on which the oral examination is conducted. The 200 items are divided into five basic areas: neuropsychological testing, neuroanatomy, clinical neurology, child neuropsychology, and general clinical psychology. Eventually, the exam will be used as the primary vehicle for determining the candidate's fund of basic knowledge in areas relevant to the practice of clinical neuropsychology.

HOW TO APPLY FOR THE EXAMINATION

An individual is eligible to receive the diplomate in any area recognized by ABPP at the end of his/her fifth year postdoctorate practice. However, an individual may apply for examination at the end of his/her fourth year of postdoctorate practice.

Application is initiated by writing to:
Executive Secretary
American Board of Professional Psychology, Inc.
2100 East Broadway, Suite 313
Columbia, Missouri 65201-6082.

Applicants should specify in their application that they are interested in applying for candidacy for the diplomate in Clinical Neuropsychology. The Executive Secretary of ABPP will then forward descriptive materials and an application to the applicant as soon as possible.

On completion of the application, the applicant's file is forwarded to the eligibility committees of ABBP and of ABCN. The potential applicant should meet the following criteria, at a minimum, before applying for diplomate status:

1. Doctoral degree in psychology from a regionally accredited university.
2. Membership in APA or, where appropriate, CPA.
3. Licensed at the level of independent practice in some state or province.
4. Training and experience in basic neurosciences, functional neuroanatomy, neuropathology, clinical neurology, psychological assessment, clinical neuropsychological assessment, psychopathology, and psychological intervention.
5. Five years (at least 4 years) of postdoctoral experience in psychology which may include research, teaching, clinical services, and/or administration.
6. Three or more years of clinical neuropsychological experience at either pre- or postdoctoral levels.

More specific eligibility criteria will be forwarded once the application is initiated.

CONCLUDING REMARKS

The creation and maintenance of the diplomate in Clinical Neuropsychology has been a timely and rewarding, but difficult, experience. To fully meet its potential to serve as a benchmark of competent practice, the good will, dedicated services, and willingness to submit to examination by the practioners in our field is an ongoing necessity.

This brief description of the ABCN/ABPP diplomate process in clinical neuropsychology is intended not to be a fixed or final statement, but to explain the development and evolution of the examination process thus far. The diplomate process will continue to develop and change as new individuals join in this worthwhile quest for improvement and maintenance of standards of practice in clinical neuropsychology.

REFERENCES

APA. (1981). Ethical Principles of Psychologists. *American Psychologist, 36*, 633-638.

INS/APA. (1984). Report of the Task Force on Education, Accreditation and Credentialing in Clinical Neuropsyhology. *The INS Bulletin*, 5-10. *Newsletter 40*, 1984, *2*, 3-8.

The Clinical Neuropsychologist
1990, Vol. 4, No. 4, pp. 337-343

61

The American Board of Clinical Neuropsychology Update 1990

Linas A. Bieliauskas   and   Charles G. Matthews
Ann Arbor VAMC/University of   University of Wisconsin-
Michigan Medical Center   Clinical Science Center

ABSTRACT

Changes that have taken place in the policies and procedures for obtaining a diplomate
in Clinical Neuropsychology from the American Board of Clinical Neuropsychology-
American Board of Professional Psychology are reviewed. Instructions for application
and obtaining further information are provided.

The American Board of Clinical Neuropsychology (ABCN), incorporated in 1981, has continued to develop and improve its procedures for examination in the practice specialty of clinical neuropsychology. Since the first published description of ABCN policies and procedures (Bieliauskas & Matthews, 1987), there have been a number of changes in the makeup and operations of ABCN and it is the purpose of this paper to provide an update for potential candidates and others interested in the diplomate process.

ABCN was legally incorporated in 1981 and was formally incorporated as part of the American Board of Professional Psychology (ABPP) in 1984, under whose auspices ABCN has conducted examinations ever since. In 1989, ABPP decided that the different specialties within which diplomate credentials are provided would now be termed Specialty Councils, each of which was primarily responsible for developing and maintaining examination procedures in the specialty.

ABCN is, thus, now the ABPP Specialty Council for Clinical Neuropsychology, formalizing its traditional responsibility for the diplomate examinations in the specialty.

Changes in Bylaws

The ABCN bylaws were revised in 1988 to incorporate several significant changes. First, ABCN became a membership organization rather than exclusively a directing board. This was done to further the goals of ABCN in developing the credentialing process and to involve more thoroughly those who had successfully undergone the examination requirements. This meant that all who had received their diplomate in Clinical Neuropsychology from ABPP were eligible to be members of ABCN, Inc. The actual "Board" was redesignated as the "Board of Directors" (BOD) of ABCN and reduced to 15 members, all of whom were to be elected for five-year terms by the membership. The members of the original founding board drew lots to rotate off the BOD, three at a time at yearly intervals, until the entire BOD was elected by the membership at large. The BOD chooses its own officers. The first elections were held in 1989; the members and officers of the BOD for 1990 are:

Kenneth Adams	Joseph Matarazzo
Linas Bieliauskas, Treasurer	Charles Matthews, Vice President
Thomas Boll	Steven Mattis, President
Nelson Butters	Manfred Meier, Representative to ABPP
Charles Golden	Homer Reed
Gerald Goldstein	Byron Rourke, Secretary
Kathleen Haaland	Barbara Wilson
Kerry Hamsher	

Three new members will be elected in 1991.

Second, in order to enable a membership organization to function, resources were necessary. The bylaws were changed to enable the BOD to collect dues from its members. The dues were to be collected only as a cost of maintaining membership in ABCN and did not affect one's diplomate status. The primary reason for collecting dues was to build resources for developing an objective examination in Clinical Neuropsychology which would supplement the oral examination process. Other reasons included the need to finance mailings for elections, newsletters, and general correspondence. Dues were set at $25.00 for 1989 and 1990, and 80-90% of diplomates have elected to pay the dues and remain members of the organization. The collection of dues and subsequent revenue also will permit ABCN to maintain and distribute a directory of its members to those potentially wishing consultation with diplomates.

Third, the rights and requirements for members of ABCN were spelled out in the bylaws. The requirements to be a member included: (1) passing the examination for diplomate in Clinical Neuropsychology by ABPP, (2) maintaining diplomate status as to legal and ethical standards, and (3) payment of annual dues to ABCN. The primary purpose of being a member of ABCN was clearly to lend support to maintaining the quality of the examination process. The rights of members included: (1) listing in the ABCN directory, (2) voting for members of the BOD, (3) eligibility to be a member of the BOD and hold office, (4) eligibility to serve on various committees of ABCN, and (5) eligibility to be an examiner in the oral examination process and to participate in continuing development of examination procedures.

Procedural Changes

At several workshops during the Midwestern examinations, ABCN delegates worked on methods to increase the standardization and reliability of the examination procedures. As a result, three documents were produced.

First, "Guidelines for Work Samples in Clinical Neuropsychology" was developed as an aid to the candidate in preparing the work samples. In addition to specific instructions, these guidelines include a checklist that is used by reviewers of the work samples so that the candidate knows the general standards to which the work sample will be held. All candidates for the diplomate in Clinical Neuropsychology receive a copy of these guidelines. In brief, the work sample needs to include original copies of neuropsychological reports, expansion of those reports to include relevant background material, and supporting copies of raw data. More detailed descriptions can be found in the guidelines.

Second, a "Candidate's Manual for Oral Examinations in Clinical Neuropsychology" was developed to aid the candidates in preparing for the oral examinations. The basic procedures are similar to those described by Bieliauskas and Matthews (1987): these include oral examination on the Work Sample, Fact Finding, and Ethics. In brief, the examination on the *Work Sample* includes questions about the procedures used, the reasons for conclusions drawn, and purpose of the reports. It is crucial that the candidate have a thorough knowledge of the information in the Work Sample, including clinically relevant information about the patients, a thorough understanding of the procedures used, and in-depth knowledge about the neuropsychological aspects of the disease/dysfunction with which they are dealing. *Fact Finding* involves a candidate being given a brief vignette of an adult or child who has undergone neuropsychological assessment; the candidate is then required to extract all necessary information from the examiner. In capsule form, the candidate conducts a mock neuropsychological evaluation and is required to reach logical, systematic, and defensible conclusions about the case in question. During the *Ethics* portion, the candidate is also presented with brief vignettes involving ethical issues and asked to identify and discuss their implications for patient welfare and professional conduct. During this portion of the examination, candidates also discuss their own professional practice, methods, and procedures used, ways of involvement with the profession of neuropsychology, etc. As with other areas, sound judgment and defensible practices need to be demonstrated.

The three examiners meet following these specific exam sessions and discuss the candidate's performance. A positive vote of two out of the three is required to pass the overall examination. It should be noted that a candidate does not pass or fail on any single part of the examination but rather on the examination as a whole following discussion among the examiners. Thus, it is conceivable that a candidate could do well on Work Sample and Fact Finding portions and then demonstrate insensitivity to unethical practices during the third portion of the exam; that candidate would likely be failed by the examiners when this issue became known. All the examiners judge the candidate on Evaluative Skills, Intervention Knowledge and Skills, Scientific and Professional Knowledge, Ethics and Social Responsibility, and Professional Commitment. By ABPP standards, serious deficiencies in any of these areas can be cause for failure to award the diplomate. The procedures for oral examination are described in more detail by Bieliauskas and Matthews (1987) and in the "Candidate's Manual" that all candidates receive prior to the oral examination.

Third, the workshops developed the "Examiner's Manual for Oral Examinations in Clinical Neuropsychology." This manual was prepared to make examiners thoroughly familiar with all aspects of the examination and procedures for arriving at decisions regarding a candidate's competency. Checklists were devised for each aspect of the examination to enable different examiners to conduct their inquiries in a more standardized fashion and to provide for more reliable comparison between candidates and between examiners. All examiners receive a copy of this manual and necessary forms and checklists prior to the oral examination.

These documents have significantly improved the reliability and quality of the examination procedures and they will continue to be reviewed and improved in the continuing process of providing the fairest and most accurate examinations for determination of competence to practice Clinical Neuropsychology. A review of the examination process by ABCN takes place at least once a year and committees are designated to work on various aspects of the examination for as long as is necessary.

Administrative Changes

ABCN oral examinations have traditionally been administered in Eastern, Midwestern, and Western time zones. Because of varying numbers of candidates per time zone and difficulties with coordination of work samples, reviewers, and examiners, the BOD decided to centralize all examinations and ABCN administration, beginning in 1990. Henceforth, all oral examinations will take place in Chicago, currently at Rush-Presbyterian-St. Luke's Medical Center where Robert Wilson has agreed to manage local arrangements. The examinations will take place on at least an annual basis, though more examinations will be scheduled if sufficient candidates are available.

To insure that different regions of the country as well as different clinical neuropsychological approaches continued to be represented in the examination process, an Examination Committee was formed. The committee is chaired by Kerry Hamsher, and includes as members Nelson Butters, Lloyd Cripe, Susan Filskov, Gerald Goldstein, Kathleen Haaland, and Robert Hart. The Examination Committee is charged with: (1) selection of examiners for each oral examination, (2) selection of diplomates for training as examiners, and (3) development of the objective examination (see below).

All administration for ABCN was centralized in Ann Arbor, and Linas Bieliauskas was appointed as Executive Director. The centralization of ABCN administration now provides one office for all correspondence, receipt of work samples, maintenance of records, mailing of newsletters, keeping of a database, etc. It has also enabled ABCN to have a central working phone and FAX number for information. Since the centralized administration became effective, ABCN has also begun publication of its annual Membership Directory, which is to be distributed to its members and other interested parties. Copies of the directory or other information can be obtained by contacting ABCN at its new address:

American Board of Clinical Neuropsychology, Inc.
Department of Psychiatry,
University of Michigan Medical Center
1500 E. Medical Center Drive
Ann Arbor, MI 48109-0704
Phone: (313) 936-8269, FAX: (313) 936-9761

Objective Examination
ABCN has long wished to develop an objective examination to assess depth of basic knowledge in Clinical Neuropsychology. The oral examinations certainly accomplish this to some degree, but it is not possible to cover the necessary breadth of knowledge during questioning which is, by nature, limited by the types of cases presented and evaluated. In addition, the validity of an objective evaluation of knowledge base will generally be superior to judgment by a single examiner. In the past, a 200-item examination has been administered during the oral examinations for standardization purposes only, and has not counted in any decisions regarding the awarding of the diplomate thus far. The major drawback to further development, which would assure the examination to be valid and legally defensible, has been the required expenditure of time and financial resources that ABCN did not have.

Several developments have led to progress in this area. First, in 1988, the Division of Clinical Neuropsychology (40) of the American Psychological Association generously awarded a grant of $10,000 to ABCN for development of the objective examination. In 1989, ABPP agreed to match this amount. With these resources and the dues support of ABCN members, the necessary finances are now in place and the objective examination is currently under development in consultation with the Professional Examination Service. It is anticipated that the examination will be ready for use by January, 1992.

The objective examination is to be used as a screening instrument for basic knowledge. It will consist of 200-multiple choice questions covering five domains: Child Neuropsychology, Adult Neuropsychology, Neuroscience, Behavioral Neurology, and General Clinical Psychology. The questions will all be referenced and contained in an item pool that will provide for alternate forms of the examination for those who may need to take it more than once. The score for passing will be determined by standard, objective procedures during test development with the Professional Examination Service.

The objective examination will be administered annually, in several cities across North America that should be convenient to almost any candidate. It will be supported by a separate fee and it will be required to pass this examination in order to be admitted to the oral examination.

Application Procedures

An individual is eligible to receive the diplomate in any area recognized by ABPP at the end of his/her fifth year of postdoctorate practice. However, since the interval between initial application and final examination may last one to two years, application at the end of the third year of postdoctoral practice would be appropriate. This gives ample time for receiving and filling out necessary application materials, obtaining and forwarding letters of recommendation, graduate transcripts, internship certificates, etc., taking the objective examination, preparing a work sample, and sitting for the oral examination.

The process is open and all interested individuals are welcomed and encouraged to apply for examination in Clinical Neuropsychology. Application is initiated by writing to the following:

Executive Secretary
American Board of Professional Psychology, Inc.
2100 East Broadway, Suite 313
Columbia, Missouri 65201-6082.

Applicants should specify that they are interested in applying for the examination for the diplomate in Clinical Neuropsychology. After necessary application materials are completed and returned to ABPP, the eligibility committees of ABPP and ABCN will review the credentials. Minimal eligibility criteria for applying for the examination in Clinical Neuropsychology are further described in Bieliauskas and Matthews (1987).

Once eligibility has been determined and approved by ABPP, the remainder of the examination procedures are administered from the ABCN central office. The candidate will be informed of the time for the next objective examination and will be required to pay the examination fee. After the objective exam is passed, candidates will be given up to one year to prepare their work samples and will be informed of the time and date of the next oral examination. Once the candidate commits to the examination, he/she will be expected to appear at the designated time and place. Transportation and lodging are at the candidate's own arrangement and expense, although suggestions as to lodging are usually provided. Chicago was chosen as the central site of examinations because of its easy and relatively inexpensive access, public transportation, and lodging.

Current Developments

It is expected that the development of the objective examination, increased standardization of instructions to candidates and methods of oral examination, and centralized examinations will provide improved access for prospective candidates and heightened validity for the process. We anticipate that the centralization of ABCN administration will make it easier to answer questions from members and candidates, to more easily track candidates through the examination process, and increase the efficiency and reduce the time between initial application and final examination. Members of ABCN are currently developing methods for monitoring the continued quality, reliability, and validity of the examinations. We expect the maturing of the examination process to continue. In all these areas, it is our judgment that ABCN has progressed far ahead of any other board procedure in applied psychology.

As of this writing, there are 169 individuals who have been awarded the diplomate in Clinical Neuropsychology by ABPP. It has been exciting and rewarding to see the growth of ABCN and its positive influence on the development of the profession of Clinical Neuropsychology. Prior to the establishment of ABCN, our field has been lacking in clear designation of professional credentials for specific competencies and skills to deal with the multi-faceted problems presented by patients with injury/disease of the central nervous system. We believe that the continued development of a specialty is best served by self-examination to assure the quality and standards of the profession in the interest of best serving the public. To have achieved diplomate status in any specialty simply means that one's credentials have been reviewed and that one has been examined by one's peers and found competent to practice in that specialty. To that end, the continued support of ABCN members and the voluntary submission to examination by colleagues bespeaks confidence in the meaningfulness and value of the specialty of Clinical Neuropsychology within the general field of health care.

REFERENCES

Bieliauskas, L.A., & Matthews, C.G. (1987). American Board of Clinical Neuropsychology: Policies and Procedures. *The Clinical Neuropsychologist, 1*, 21-28.

The Clinical Neuropsychologist
1991, Vol. 5, No. 4, pp. 381-382

Diplomates in Clinical Neuropsychology
American Board of Clinical Neuropsychology (ABCN)
American Board of Professional Psychology (ABPP)

TCN publishes regularly the names of candidates succesfully completing examinations for the ABCN-ABPP Diplomate, courtesy of ABPP. In addition, a cumulative list appears in the last issue of each volume.

Adams, Kenneth M.
Adams, Russell L.
Artiola, Lydia
Auerbach, Vivian A.
Baade, Lyle E.
Bach, Gale W.
Barkley, Russell A.
Baron, Augustine
Baron, Ida S.
Barrett, Edwin T.
Barth, Jeffrey T.
Becker, Bruce C.
Becker, James T.
Beniak, Thomas E.
Benton, Arthur L.
Berent, Stanley
Bernard, Larry C.
Bieliauskas, Linas A.
Bigler, Erin D.
Binder, Laurence M.
Blackwood, H. Daniel
Bleiberg, Joseph
Boll, Thomas J.
Bornstein, Robert A.
Borod, Joan C.
Brandt, Jason
Brooker, Alan E.
Brown, Gregory G.
Bryant, Ernest T.
Buchholz, Dennis J.
Butters, Nelson M.
Caplan, Bruce M.
Chelune, Gordon J.
Clement, Pamelia F.
Clionsky, Mitchell L.
Costa, Louis D.
Craig, Paul L.
Cripe, Lloyd L.
Crosson, Bruce A.

Davidovicz, Herman M.
Delaney, Richard C.
Diller, Leonard
Dodrill, Carl B.
Doiron, Richard G.
Elliott, Robert W.
Faibish, George M.
Fein, Deborah A.
Fennell, Eileen B.
Filskov, Susan B.
Fischer, Mariellen
Fishburne, Francis J.
Fisk, John L.
Fletcher, Jack M.
Freides, David
Furst, Charles J.
Garron, David C.
Gillen, Robert W.
Goldberg, Elkhonon
Golden, Charles J.
Goldstein, Gerald
Goodglass, Harold
Gordon, John E.
Gordon, Wayne A.
Guilmette, Thomas J.
Gur, Ruben C.
Haaland, Kathleen Y.
Hammeke, Thomas A.
Hamsher, Kerry DeS.
Harris, Milton E.
Hart, Robert P.
Hayden, Mary E.
Heaton, Robert K.
Heck, Edward T.
Hermann, Bruce P.
Hollis, Roy E.
Honor, Stephen
Hopewell, C. Alan
Howieson, Diane B.

Incagnoli, Theresa M.
Ivnik, Robert J.
Jacobsen, L. Dee
Johnson, Judy W.
Jones, Barbara P.
Kane, Robert L.
Kaplan, Edith F.
Karzmark, Peter
Kaszniak, Alfred W.
Kelly, Mark P.
Klusman, Lawrence E.
Knights, Robert M.
Koffler, Sandra P.
Kovner, Richard
Kurlychek, Robert T.
Kutner, Kenneth C.
Laplant, Robert
Larrabee, Glenn J.
Lee, Gregory P.
Leli, Dano A.
Levin, Harvey S.
Levine, Maureen J.
Lezak, Muriel D.
Logue, Patrick E.
Loring, David W.
Lorinstein, I. Barry
Lorr, Joan A.
Lundgren, Sandra
Lynch, William J.
MacDonald, G. Wayne
Mack, James L.
Majovski, Lawrence V.
Malec, James F.
Manning, Alexander A.
Marlowe, Wendy B.
Matarazzo, Josph D.
Matarazzo, Ruth G.
Mateer, Catherine A.
Matthews, Charles G.

Mattis, Steven
McSweeny, Austin J.
Meier, Manfred J.
Melendez, Fernando
Mendoza, John E.
Millis, Scott R.
Mirsky, Allan F.
Mitrushina, Maura N.
Morgan, Steven F.
Moses, James A.
Newby, Robert F.
Norton, James C.
Novack, Thomas A.
Parker, Raymond A.
Parker, Rolland S.
Parsons, Oscar A.
Patterson, Marian B.
Peck, Edward A.
Petrucci, Ralph J.
Powel, Jeffrey
Prigatano, George P.
Purisch, Arnold D.
Pusakulich, Robert L.
Rao, Stephen M.
Rausch, Helen R.

Reed, Homer B.
Reed, James C.
Rhodes, John M.
Ris, M. Douglas
Rothke, Steven E.
Rourke, Byron P.
Ryan, Joseph J.
Satz, Paul
Sbordone, Robert J.
Schaeffer, Jeffrey
Schenkenberg, Thomas
Schneider, Anne S.
Schwartz, Melvin L.
Sherr, Rose Lynn
Shonkoff, Alan D.
Smith, Aaron
Snow, William G.
Sobota, Walter L.
Souheaver, Gary T.
Spellacy, Frank J.
Spreen, Otfried
Stuss, Donald T.
Sweet. Jerry J.
Swirsky-Sacchetti, Thomas C.

Taylor, Gerry
Theye, Frederick W.
Thies, Armin P.
Townes, Brenda D.
Tranel, Daniel
Tucker, David M.
Tureen, Robert G.
van Gorp, Wilfred G.
van Mastrigt, Robert L.
Varney, Nils R.
Venezia, Daniel J.
Walker, Preston J.
Walter, Marc S.
Weintraub, Sandra
White, Roberta F.
Wilkening, Greta N.
Wilson, Barbara C.
Wilson, Robert S.
Young, Ted W.
Youngjohn, James
Yozawitz, Allan
Zapf, Richard F.
Zerfas, Philip G.
Zych, Kenneth A.

The Clinical Neuropsychologist
1989, Vol. 3, No. 1, pp. 3-21

Neuropsychology Technicians in Clinical Practice: Precedents, Rationale, and Current Deployment

John W. DeLuca
Hawthorn Center

ABSTRACT

The practice of employing neuropsychological technicians dates back to the very establishment of clinical neuropsychology as a profession. The utilization of technicians affords the neuropsychologist with optimal standardization, reliability, and validity of the assessment process. Moreover, the practice is highly cost-effective and efficient. However, recent efforts by some state psychology associations, state psychology boards, and third-party health care providers have attempted to supplant or eliminate this practice. The purposes of this paper are as follows: (1) to review the historical, professional, and legal precedents for utilizing technicians; (2) to delineate the rationale for their deployment; (3) to examine current deployment patterns; and, (4) to provide some working professional guidelines for the training and utilization of neuropsychology technicians.

As do members of the medical profession, psychologists often ruminate over professional issues such as the scope of practice and the delegation of services. At a very basic level, these concerns translate as a continual struggle over issues of "turf", control, and power among various health care professions. With respect to interprofessional jostling regarding the scope of practice, many psychologists are concerned with attempts to allow social work practice to include independent

The author would like to thank Drs. Kenneth M. Adams, Homer B.C. Reed, Jr., and Ralph M. Reitan for providing unpublished information. Also, the author is very grateful to Hawthorn Center Librarian Delphine Sefcik for her expertise and persistence in obtaining some rather obscure reference material. This paper is dedicated to the three expert NTs who were my teachers: Marilyn Chedour, Cathleen McDonald, and Lois Robinson.

diagnosis and treatment of mental illness (Howard, 1987). Incredible as it may seem, similar struggles occur on a more limited scale within the profession of psychology.

For example, there are those psychologists who object to the practice of delegating the administration and scoring of psychological tests to sub-Master's degree level personnel. As a case in point, some members of the Michigan Psychological Association (MPA) clinical division have raised objections to the use of such technicians by neuropsychologists (Howard, 1987). This group of psychologists would seek to restrict the administration of psychological tests to licensed psychologists (Howard, 1987). In fact, the official MPA newsletter, *The Michigan Psychologist* (1988), has even gone so far as to refuse to accept advertisements for positions seeking unlicensed sub-Master's level personnel to function as psychometrists (i.e., psychological technicians, psychological assistants, psychological aides).

Although the MPA clinical division aims to protect testing as a unique feature of psychology, it has not yet decided whether the use of neuropsychological technicians (NTs) is a violation of this principle (Howard, 1987). At present, the Michigan Public Health Code (Act 368 of 1978) permits licensed psychologists to delegate test administration to nonlicensed individuals (Howard, 1987). While the delegation of services to technicians can be limited by the Michigan Board of Psychology (i.e., the Department of Licensing and Regulation), there are no restrictions at present.

The move to restrict and even eliminate the use of NTs is not limited to Michigan. For instance, Bornstein (personal communication, April 25, 1988) indicated that the Ohio Board of Psychology is considering a similar stance. In Massachusetts, Blue Cross-Blue Shield (BCBS) has sought to disallow payments to health care providers using sub-Master's degree level NTs (H.B.C. Reed, personal communication, April 6, 1988). In the latter case, BCBS has agreed to let the Massachusetts Psychological Association decide the matter. No doubt this issue has been or will be raised by other state Psychology boards and state Psychological associations.

In some cases, psychologists have reacted in a conservative manner to the notion of employing sub-Master's level personnel. A very common stance among such psychologists is to maintain that such a practice would lower professional standards (Holt, 1967). In fact, Holt (1967) indicated that similar reactions very likely occurred in the field of medicine when dentistry and nursing became separate professions. Cohen (1969, p. 181) summarized the nature of this resistance quite succinctly:

> It was fascinating to note the heated arguments offered by a number of psychologists about the validity of the procedures being followed. There was no question about the skill that the psychological assistants were able to demonstrate, or about their effectiveness in the roles to which they had been assigned, or about the value to the psychologist of having an assistant. What was at issue was whether the standards of the profession were being downgraded.

Some degree of resentment from skeptical and/or insecure professionals is not uncommon when introducing the use of nonprofessional assistants (Grosser, Henry, & Kelly, 1969). However, health care professionals

> ...in all fields must be convinced that the use of workers, without credentials, as their aides – far from being a threat to their status, integrity, and professional stature – enables them to dedicate their time and skills more fully to their own professional functions of healing and educating, while other persons, with less professional training, can assume the more routine tasks. (Grosser et al., p. xi, 1969).

It may be that some of the hesitancy surrounding the deployment of technical personnel is related to the novelty of the practice. At least in one instance (Arnhoff & Jenkins, 1969), it was shown that professionals having a great deal of contact with subdoctoral personnel were found to have much higher opinions of the technicians' work performances than did persons with little experience or contact.

As radiologists have learned, x-ray technicians are not a threat to their profession. Rather, the technicians provide an invaluable form of assistance (Holt, 1967). In psychology, the technician could perform numerous useful tasks to facilitate the management of a clinic. For example, technicians could provide assistance in scheduling patients, in handling clients, in providing quality assurance data, and so forth. Moreover, the employment of technical staff could help free psychologists from the image of being merely technicians themselves.

As recently as the late 1960's, psychologists in mental retardation facilities and state mental hospitals had very limited professional roles; they were viewed essentially as psychometricians (Baumeister, 1967; Wellner, 1968). Undoubtedly, there remain isolated bastions of ignorance operating under these archaic convictions as though they were caught up in some sort of "time warp". However, L'Abate (1964, p. 172) contends that the utilization of technicians could assist the psychologist in overcoming such limited roles and in achieving

> ...a greater degree of professional integration and usefulness. If we wish to be true consultants and professionals, we cannot waste our time performing time-consuming technical tasks.

PRECEDENTS

Historical

The delegation of services to appropriately trained technical personnel serves several purposes. Not only does this approach provide for a more efficient delivery of services, it also assists in meeting the public's ever-increasing demand for quality health care (Grosser et al., 1969; McGee & Pope, 1975).

This model of professional practice has been proven successful in several health care professions (Gentry, 1974; McGee & Pope, 1975; Kadish, 1969; L'Abate, 1964). In fact, the utilization of paraprofessionals is fast becoming an integrated part of the medical/health care delivery system (Pope, McGee, & Nudler, 1983). For example, physicians have long benefited from the services provided by psychiatric (i.e., registered) nurses, military corpsmen or medics, paramedics and, more recently, pediatric nurse practitioners and physician's assistants. In some instances, technical support staff merely assist the professional (as in the case of dental hygienists). In other instances, x-ray technicians assist the radiologist as well as handle the patient contact arrangement (Cohen, 1969). This practice frees the radiologist to interpret the results and consult with other medical professionals about the results (Cohen, 1969).

U.S. Federal government programs, such as the Allied Health Professional Personnel Training Act of 1966, have supported the development of a "team concept" in providing health care services (Kadish, 1969). In this case, the goal was to improve both the opportunities for training and the quality of educational programs directed at the technician and technologist levels (Kadish, 1969).

Kadish (1969, p. 240) contends

> It is increasingly recognized that the vast health needs of our country cannot be met by traditional methods. New approaches to meeting manpower needs are being considered along with the application of newer technology in health care services, new methods of financing health care, and experiments in systems of delivery of services.

Albee (1968) addressed the problem of manpower shortages by urging a reconceptualization of the entire practice of psychology. More specifically, Albee did not view psychology as a care delivery field per se. Rather, he called for professional psychologists to create and demonstrate the applications of theories; this would allow Bachelor's level personnel to provide direct care (Albee, 1968). Rotter (1973) echoed a similar view; he felt that the utilization of subdoctoral personnel would fulfill the demand for increased clinical services. Rotter suggested that the psychologist take a more controlling or administrative role. That is, the psychologist would diagnose the patient's problem, determine who could best deal with it and what method should be utilized, and then evaluate the effectiveness of the prescribed treatment or intervention. He contended that this process would increase efficiency, improve outcome, and assist in the development of better clinical methods (Rotter, 1973).

A similar stance was promoted in the late 1950s by the Joint Commission on Mental Illness and Health. This commission recommended a drastic change in the training and use of mental health personnel to address manpower shortages (McGee & Pope, 1975). This was iterated in a mid-1960's report entitled "Action for Mental Health" (Holt, 1967). The commission "...recommended the judicious use of subprofessionals specifically trained for limited and supervised functions..." (Holt, 1967, p. 461). Also, the National Commission on Community Health Services (Kadish, 1969) indicated that the employment of technical personnel was the single most promising method of providing adequate health care manpower. More specific to the issue at hand, both the Miami Conference on Graduate Education in Psychology held in 1958 and the Chicago Conference on the Professional Preparation of Clinical Psychologists held in 1965 suggested the training of subprofessional personnel at the pre-Bachelor's, Bachelor's, and Master's level to work in the mental health field and to engage in diagnostic testing (Holt, 1967; Matarazzo, 1973).

Actually, the notion of employing technicians to administer and score psychological tests is not new to psychology. Reitan (H.B.C. Reed, personal communication, April 6, 1988) indicated that the deployment of technicians to administer psychological tests dates back to the early 1940s. Although Russell, Neuringer, and Goldstein (1970) wrote that the utilization of trained testers was an innovation of Ward C. Halstead, the procedure was actually first introduced by the late William A. Hunt, Ph.D. in the Navy during World War II (R.M. Reitan, personal communication, August 21, 1987). The method was used by Halstead during the 1940s at the University of Chicago; by Ralph M. Reitan in the Army at Mayo General Hospital in 1945; and, by Reitan at the inception of the Neuropsychology Laboratory, Indiana University Medical School circa 1950-1951 (H.B.C. Reed, personal communication, April 6, 1988). In the latter instance, the functions of technicians were identical to those of today. That is, NTs were employed to administer and score the Wechsler Scales, the Halstead-Reitan Test Batteries, and other allied procedures.

In the practice of clinical psychology, L'Abate (1964) established a diagnostic laboratory employing technicians to assess children and adults. Other programs utilizing technicians included the Nebraska Psychiatric Institute and the University of Florida (Gentry, 1974a). Affleck, Strider, and Helper (1968) described the goals of the Nebraska Psychiatric Institute's program to train and deploy technicians. The goals were as follows: (1) to train Bachelor's level personnel to administer and score a wide range of psychological tests; (2) to structure the clinical psychologist's duties regarding the supervision of technicians and patient contact; and, (3) to maximize the evaluative and report writing activities of the psychologists by delegating data gathering duties to assistants.

Gentry (1974a) also described in detail several established programs for training psychology assistants: (1) the Family Clinic, Department of Behavioral Medicine, West Virginia University Medical Center; (2) the Oak Ridge Regional Mental Health Center, Oak Ridge, Tennessee; and, (3) the Psychodiagnostic Laboratory, Duke University Medical School. In each case, sub-Master's level personnel were employed quite successfully to engage in test administration and scoring. In addition to these specialized training programs, Pope et al. (1983) indicated that several colleges and universities offered specific undergraduate degree programs aimed at developing mental health and psychology assistants. The latter included Knox College (Gaylesburg, IL), University of Missouri, Yale University, DePaul University, Michigan State University, and Hahnemann Medical College and Hospital.

With respect to the evaluation of technician performance in a clinical psychology setting, Musante (1974) surveyed the faculty and interns of the three programs described by Gentry (1974a). He reported that several psychologists felt that technicians performed the psychological testing more efficiently than did faculty and staff. In fact, technicians were often viewed as invaluable. While there was some truth to the concern about decreased patient contact for the professional, these procedures actually allowed psychologists to see greater numbers of patients and/or to become more involved in therapy and consultation (Musante, 1974).

Sloop and Quarrick (1974) found that faculty and staff often felt that the performances of technicians were of high quality and, in some cases, surpassed their own skills. These authors also assessed the actual performances of technicians in an empirical fashion. The results indicated that technicians and students performed quite well as test administrators; their performances were found to be both reliable and valid.

Both productivity and technician performance were evaluated at the Nebraska Psychiatric Institute (Affleck et al., 1968). Affleck et al. (1968) reported that, in a comparable 4-month period, the number of assessments increased from 69 to 145 following the deployment of technicians. Three independent psychologists evaluated the training program after the first 8 months of operation. They reported technician performance to be both acceptable and satisfactory. The technician's skill in attending to detail and care in scoring were found to be quite good. However, the evaluators did feel that further training and experience would assist the technicians in becoming more relaxed and less mechanical and in increasing their level of interpersonal sensitivity. The evaluators also recommended the practice of assigning specific technicians to specific staff members.

K.M. Adams (personal communications, May 5 and December 18, 1987) stated that the use of technicians in the practice of clinical neuropsychology "...is a very frequent, wide-spread, and well-accepted practice." In fact, Reitan (H.B.C. Reed, personal communication, April 6, 1988) indicated that NTs, under the direct supervision of competent neuropsychologists, are now used world-wide to administer and score psychological tests. For the most part, such personnel have received inservice training in Neuropsychology laboratories (Meier, 1983). There are numerous presentations in books and manuals that outline neuropsychological assessment procedures that either expound or allude to the deployment of technicians (e.g., Boll, 1981; Heaton & Heaton, 1981; Matthews, 1981; Parsons, 1986; Reitan, 1966; Rourke, Bakker, Fisk, & Strang, 1983; Swiercinsky, 1978; Trites, 1981).

Professional

According to K.M. Adams (personal communication, December 18, 1987), the American Psychological Association Division 40 (Clinical Neuropsychology) Executive Committee contends that...

"The use of technicians is a sound and acceptable practice producing good results when the supervising psychologist maintains and monitors high standards of quality assurance suggested for such work in the *General Guidelines for Providers of Psychological Services* (APA, 1987a); *Specialty Guidelines for the Delivery of Services by Clinical Psychologists* (APA, 1981a); and *Ethical Principles of Psychologists* (APA, 1981b).

Furthermore, the APA Division 40 Executive Committee affirmed several principles with respect to the use of NTs as follows: (1) training and performance of NTs are the sole responsibility of the supervising psychologist; (2) the professional relationship is between the patient and the psychologist, with the psychologist billing for work encompassed by subprofessional personnel; and, (3) there is no necessary requirement for postbaccalaureate training in order to engage in neuropsychological assessment.

Moreover, Russ Newman, APA's Director of Legal and Regulatory Affairs for the Practice Directorate, further clarified APA's stance regarding the regulation of NTs by state licensing boards. In correspondence sent to Kenneth Adams (personal communication, August 5, 1988), Newman addressed the concerns raised by neuropsychologists in Kentucky regarding the use of NTs. Upon discussion with the Kentucky Board of Psychology, Newman was able to clarify their position with respect to the utilization of NTs. Newman states that it was not the intention of the Kentucky Board

> ...to prohibit technicians from doing those activities for which they have traditionally and appropriately been utilized. Rather, the Board's concern is with respect to unlicensed individuals who are inappropriately, and without adequate supervision, performing activities which require either a license or the close supervision of a licensed individual. This would include not only the activities of technicians but the activities of psychology trainees, graduate students, and the like. Specifically as to the regulation of technicians, the Kentucky Board indicates that the clerical function of technicians in the *administration* of psychological instruments is not prohibited. The Board's concern in such situations is that technicians not be inappropriately utilized for analysis, interpretation, and integration of test data, or that technicians not be used for administration of tests without supervision.

The Board expressed similar concerns regarding the use of psychological trainees. According to Newman, the Kentucky Board is not concerned with the reasonable use of NTs; the Board is concerned only with those instances in which there occurs a flagrant abuse in the utilization of personnel. "Reasonable use" involves providing adequate supervision, monitoring high standards of quality assurance, and utilizing NTs for appropriately delegated activities.

Furthermore, Newman was clear to state that APA is interested in being apprised of any situation in which the Kentucky Board regulatory practice is not consistent with the above, or when regulation in other states is not based on the reasonable use standard. More specifically, he stated that

...APA would be interested in being informed of the specifics as there are a variety of alternative courses of action which could be undertaken.

Furthermore, several APA guidelines and ethical principles support the use of sub-Master's level technical personnel. For instance, in the Specialty Guidelines for the Delivery of Services by Clinical Psychologists (APA, 1981a) the definitions of providers of service are clearly defined. According to these Guidelines, there are two categories of service providers: the first being the professional clinical psychologist who has earned a Ph.D. from an accredited program in Psychology; the second refers to...

All other persons who are not professional clinical psychologists and who participate in the delivery of clinical psychology services under the supervision of a professional clinical psychologist. Although there may be variations in the titles of such persons, they are not referred to as clinical psychologists. Their functions may be indicated by the use of the adjective *psychologists.* Their functions may be indicated by the use of the adjective *psychological* preceding the noun, for example, *psychological associate,* services are rendered under the supervision of a professional clinical psychologist, who is responsible for the designation given them and for quality control. To be assigned such a designation, a person has the background, training, or expertise that is appropriate to the functions performed. (APA, 1981a, p. 642).

Included in the realm of clinical psychological services are assessment and intervention functions (APA, 1981a). However, the Guidelines are clear to point out that...

Providers of clinical psychological services who do not meet the requirements for the professional clinical psychologist are supervised directly by a professional clinical psychologist who assumes professional responsibility and accountability for the services provided. The level and extent of supervision may vary from task to task so long as the supervising psychologist retains a sufficiently close supervisory relationship to meet this Guideline (APA, 1981a, p. 643).

The General Guidelines for Providers of Psychological Services (APA, 1987a, p. 714) indicate that support personnel may be utilized in health care settings provided that they are assigned tasks commensurate with their level of competence and training. Although the subprofessional personnel are responsible for their functions and behavior when assisting in providing services of a psychological nature, the ultimate responsibility rests with the supervising psychologist (APA, 1987a).

Principle 8 of the Ethical Principles of Psychologists (APA, 1981b) further stresses the importance of using personnel with the proper training and qualifications. Persons who are improperly trained or otherwise unqualified should not be utilized (APA, 1981b). The latter does not preclude the use of sub-Master's level personnel. In fact, the APA Model Act for State Licensure (APA, 1987b) is quite clear about the role of persons engaged in the delivery of psychological services who are exempted from licensure. Exemption J of the Model Act states that "Graduate students, interns, post-doctoral trainees, and applicants for licensure are permitted to function under the supervision of licensed psychologists, as are assistants not eligible for licensure in some states" (APA, 1987b, p. 700). More specifically, the Model Act states...

> Nothing in this act shall be construed to prevent persons from engaging in activities defined as the practice of psychology, provided that such persons shall not represent themselves by the title *psychologist.* Such persons may use the terms *psychological trainee, psychological intern, psychological resident,* and *psychological assistant* and provided further that such persons perform their activities under the supervision and responsibility of a licensed psychologist in accordance with regulations promulgated by the Board. (APA, 1987b, p. 700).

The latter applies specifically to graduate students in psychology, persons persuing postdoctoral training in psychology, and qualified technicians employed by or accountable to licensed psychologists. As with the use of technicians in research, those employed in clinical settings should be fully cognizant of the Ethical Principles for Psychologists (APA, 1981b) and other guidelines associated with the delivery of clinical services.

In its administration of the federally funded Medicare reimbursement program, Blue Cross-Blue Shield of Michigan (BCBS) has specific provisions regarding the utilization of technical personnel. In a memorandum regarding physicians' billings for diagnostic tests, BCBS clarified the Medicare reimbursement rules stated in Section 4051 of the Provisions of the Omnibus Budget Reconcilliation Act of 1987 (OBRA). According to this provision, diagnostic tests include, but are not limited to x-rays, EKGs, EEGs, cardiac monitoring, and ultrasound. "Global Billings" for combined professional and technical services will only be allowed when the physician personally performs or supervises the test. Billings are not accepted if the physician purchases the diagnostic test(s) from an outside supplier.

The supervision must involve the physician's own employees. Furthermore, though the physician need not be in the same room with the employee, he/she must be "...within the premises and immediately available to provide assistance and direction throughout the duration his/her employee is performing the test."

Obviously, as in the case of x-ray or EEG technicians and neurologists, the requirement to be "on the premises" is loosely enforced. However, according to Adams (personal communication, August 10, 1988), the "availability issue" as it applies to NTs and neuropsychologists is only reasonable. That is, Adams contends that there must be recourse for NTs with problems exceeding their training and/or assigned authority.

Legal

The legal precedent for using NTs was established in a case heard by the Court of Appeals of Indiana (*Indianapolis Union Railway v. Walker*, 1974). In this case, Dr. Ralph M. Reitan testified as an expert witness on behalf of the plaintiff. The plaintiff underwent two neuropsychological evaluations in Reitan's laboratory over a period of 2½ years following a head injury sustained in a motor vehicle accident. One of the objections raised in this case contended that Reitan, a nonmedical professional, was not competent to testify about the state of Walker's brain. This objection was found to be without merit due to Dr. Reitan's extensive clinical experience. However, more important to our present discussion was a second objection to Reitan's testimony. The Railway argued that Reitan's testimony was erroneous since the opinions he expressed were based on the results of tests administered by third-party technicians. Moreover, the Railway questioned the element of judgement involved in test administration on the part of the technician.

The court ruled that Reitan's testimony was not hearsay evidence just because the tests were administered by a third party. The court took into account Reitan's testimony about the nature of the professional/technician relationship. Reitan indicated that the tests were administered under his supervision by examiners trained in his laboratory. He also elaborated on the rationale of this procedure; that is, it ensures the objectivity of the data collection in that the examiner follows prescribed written formats and directions. While Reitan admitted that some element of judgement is involved in any test administration due to its dyadic nature, he emphasized two important points. The first being that the tests were designed for a procedure of objective data collection and, second, that the assessment process merely represents data collection and not interpretation. That is, that the test procedures are sufficiently specified and the technicians follow clear enough rules so that they are not responsible for the way the results turn out. Although the technician administered the tests, it was Reitan who rendered the interpretation of the results. The Appelate court concluded that the trial court had properly overruled all the objections to Dr. Reitan's testimony.

RATIONALE

Neuropsychological Assessment
Although the aim of neuropsychology remains the study of brain/behavior relationships, the clinical practice of neuropsychology has grown far beyond a simple unidimensional approach to assessment and diagnosis. No longer are the diagnostic categories of organicity, encephalopathy, or organic brain syndrome adequate. Rather, the most common approach to neuropsychological assessment employs a set battery of standardized tests (e.g., the Halstead-Reitan Neuropsychological Test Batteries and allied procedures) administered by highly trained

examiners to all clients. The aim of such an approach is to produce a reliable and valid "picture" of the individual's brain/behavior relationships (Rourke & Adams, 1984). According to Rourke and Adams, an adequate description such as this requires a reliable "sample" of the structural systems of the brain involved in the mediation of the major components of behavior. This involves obtaining adequate "coverage" of the person's adaptive ability levels (Rourke & Adams, 1984). The battery approach to neuropsychological assessment affords one of the best means to obtain sufficient coverage in that it assesses many of the ability areas necessary for adequate functioning in school, at work, and in other day-to-day activities. In this way, one can delineate the pattern of strengths and weaknesses for a particular individual. Such information is critical in determining current levels of adaptive functioning and in treatment planning (Rourke, Fisk, & Strang, 1986).

Use of Neuropsychological Technicians
While the battery approach is often considered superior to others (e.g., "flexible" approaches) in the sense that it provides a comprehensive picture of the person as a whole, it is both a time-consuming endeavor and labor-intensive (e.g., approximately 4-6 hours to complete in many cases). However, procedures have been developed to circumvent these apparent shortcomings and to make the practice of this type of clinical neuropsychology cost-effective. The most common approach to neuropsychological assessment using a battery of tests involves the deployment of highly trained sub- Master's level NTs. The NTs are trained extensively by a neuropsychologist in test administration and scoring, in the recording of behavioral observations, and in application of age-appropriate normative data. The NT makes behavioral observations, as opposed to clinical interpretations, regarding the patient's levels of attention and motivation during the testing session. The NT also notes any other pertinent activities and behaviors.

With respect to the use of NTs, it should be stressed that they provide a means for objective data collection that is thought to be the bedrock upon which much of the validity of neuropsychological testing rests (K.M. Adams, personal communication, May 5, 1987). According to R.M. Reitan (personal communication, August 21, 1987; 1966), this method is critical in order to retain the objectivity of the data collection and to avoid biases resulting from the possible influences of "clinical observations" on the test results and their interpretation. Conducted in this manner, the neuropsychological assessment can be an objective, rigorously standardized procedure that provides maximal reliability and validity (Reitan, 1966; Rourke, 1976; Rourke et al., 1986).

This method differs greatly from the traditional "clinical" approach to psychological assessment. In the latter case, both the data collection and interpretation phases involve clinical interpretive skills. In the battery approach, the data collection is objective; clinical interpretive skills are employed only in the analysis of the data. This procedure, in conjunction with the use of "blind analysis", yields maximal objectivity, consistency, and standardization of the neuropsychological assessment process.

The process of blind assessment involves the initial interpretation of the neuropsychological test results without prior knowledge of the patient's medical, educational, developmental, or socio-emotional histories (with the exception of information pertaining to the age, sex, and grade level of the patient). Rourke (1976) contends that this approach to neuropsychological assessment and interpretation has the merit of being completely independent and unbiased. Moreover, it allows one to assess the nature of the assessment process itself (Rourke, 1976). Naturally, once the assessment and initial interpretation are completed, the neuropsychologist integrates the test findings with data from the patient's known medical, socio-emotional, educational, and environmental histories in the final written report. Also, there may be other instances in which the neuropsychologist undertakes additional and/or more specialized assessment procedures.

In order to avoid contamination of the assessment or data collection phase by clinical observations and interpretations, sub-Master's level personnel are sought to fill NT positions. The latter also ensures optimal cost-effectiveness. Bachelor's level persons are preferred not only because they can be paid a lower salary than a Ph.D. level psychologist, but because they do *not* become involved in any aspect of the clinical interpretation, analysis, or report writing functions. The use of Master's-level persons could tend to undermine both aspects of this approach. Moreover, Raimy (1957) noted some of the disadvantages of training technicians at the graduate level. These were as follows: (1) the need to appropriate sufficient financial support; (2) the devotion of 2 years of time to complete the Master's degree; and, (3) the fact that the PhD degree is generally coming to be accepted as the minimum necessary level to define a psychologist.

Since the assessment process is highly labor-intensive, the use of NTs allows the neuropsychologist to utilize his/her skills and time in a more efficient manner. That is, he/she is freed to complete more important tasks that include the following: clinical interpretation; providing feedback to parents, teachers, therapists, and other health care professionals; report writing; neurocognitive remediation and therapy; and research.

In short, there are several advantages to the employment of NTs in a clinical neuropsychology service. First, the practice allows for a completely objective and comprehensive assessment of brain/behavior relationships leading to the formulation of individualized treatment recommendations. It also affords a much more efficient use of the professional's time, and it is quite economical.

DEPLOYMENT PATTERNS

Serenty, Dean, Gray, and Hartlage (1986) conducted a survey of clinical neuropsychology practice in the United States. They sent questionnaires to members of APA Division 40 and the National Academy of Neuropsychologists.

Although the purpose of this survey was to delineate other professional issues regarding clinical practice, some information was provided about the use of NTs. According to Serenty et al., the mean number of NTs used per respondent was 1.6. Moreover, approximately one-half of the respondents employed NTs, a figure Serenty et al. contend has been consistent over the past 5 years.

In a survey of clinical neuropsychological services within the Veteran's Administration (VA) Service, McMordie (1984) found that, in 1980, 64 psychologists were assigned primarily to neuropsychological functions. There were also 25 NTs and/or aides. Overall, the 158 VA centers employed 513.3 full-time employees (FTEs) as psychological technicians, including 24.1 (or 4.7 % of the total) in neuropsychology. Although there were no neuropsychological aides, there were 41.3 psychological aides.

In order to ascertain in greater detail the rationale, minimum job requirements, training procedures, job functions, salary levels, workloads, and quality assurance practices associated with the use of NTs, I conducted an informal survey. This open-ended survey was sent to 45 neuropsychologists who were thought to employ NTs; 18 (or 40 %) of the persons responded.

The types of services of the respondents are listed in rank order (from most to least): medical schools, general hospitals, psychiatric units, VA hospitals, children's hospitals, and one school board. The average length of operation of the neuropsychological services was 16.5 years, with a range from 5 to 37 years. Staff ratios of psychologists to NTs (both full- and part-time employees) across all services was approximately 1.77 to 1. However, when interns were included as NTs, the ratio was 1.06 to 1.

The rationale for using NTs included the following: allowing the neuropsychologist more free time to focus on clinical work such as interpretation, report writing, treatment, training, and research (72%); providing a more reliable and accurate collection of data with less intertester variance (56%); cost effectiveness (50%); providing more objective and higher quality assessment standards (44%); allowing for standardized assessment procedures (26%); utilizing Bachelor's-level persons to assure a lower turn-over rate and a higher level of motivation because the position is viewed as an end-goal rather than as a stepping-stone to other positions (11%).

Approximately 89% of the respondents required a Bachelor's degree as a prerequisite; only a few persons specified requiring a major in psychology. Thirty-three percent required previous experience and 11% required completion of only a 2-year college degree. Only one respondent required Master's-level persons; the neuropsychology service in this instance was part of a metropolitan school board. Some of the other qualities required in NTs included the following: good judgement and decision-making skills; the ability to work with difficult patients; the ability to work independently and to take initiative; computer literacy; an eye for detail; intelligence and the ability to learn quickly; high frustration tolerance; accuracy; and adaptability. Job screening procedures generally included interviews (92%); checking school credentials (50%); checking work credentials (33%) and recommendations (33%); and, clinical assessment (8%).

The average time to complete training was 4.6 months; the range was from 1 to 10 months. Training generally included the following: memorization of test directions and scoring procedures; individualized training; observation of assessments; observation of the trainee by a trainer; background readings; and, attendance at related workshops and lectures. Quality assurance procedures included the following: general supervision and guidance (often on a case-by-case basis); observation; cross-checking of scoring; regularly scheduled staff meetings; continuing education; and, recalibration of equipment.

NTs were found to test an average of 3.5 patients per week; the range was from 1 to 5 patients per week. The average time required per assessment was 5.77 hours; the range was from 2 to 8 hours. The following assessment batteries were used: Halstead-Reitan (56%); portions of the Halstead-Reitan (12.5%); and, a combination of the Halstead-Reitan and Luria-Nebraska procedures (31%). Job duties included the following: administration and scoring of neuropsychological test data (100%); recording behavioral observations (50%); providing general information to clients, scheduling, and managing referrals (44%); coding data on computer files (38%); collecting and organizing background data (38%); assisting in quality assurance and checking procedures (31%); participating in research projects (31%); restocking test materials (31%); maintaining files (25%); training of new personnel (19%); writing portions of reports (e.g., background data) (19%); interviewing patients and their families (6%); and, providing feedback to staff (6%).

Classification or job titles included psychometrist, psychology assistant, neuropsychology technician, neuropsychometrist, and psychology aide. The average salary for a B.A.-level position was approximately $20,133 (ranging from $13,520 to $31,000) per annum. Several institutions had two levels of psychometrists at the B.A. level (e.g., an introductory level position and a coordinator or supervisory level position). There were also slightly higher salary ranges for Master's level persons. However, most institutions favored using B.A.-level staff. Of the total number of NTs employed by the 18 respondents, 14% had Associate Degrees, 58% had Bachelor's degrees, and 28% had Master's degrees. Although the results of this survey are by no means exhaustive, the preliminary data do provide some interesting and useful information regarding the utilization and functions of psychometrists in clinical practice.

SUMMARY AND IMPLICATIONS

The purpose of this exposition was to elucidate the importance of deploying NTs in clinical practice. In a general sense, the utilization of NTs was shown to be an extension of the professional/technician model. The latter is a well-established practice that pervades much of the medical and health care system. The practice of employing technicians in psychology in general and, more specifically in clinical neuropsychology, was reviewed. A discussion of the rationale for the deployment of NTs in neuropsychological practice was accompanied by a summary of the historical, professional, and legal precedents associated with this practice. In addition, many of the advantages of this procedure were outlined. These included the following: (1) better standardization, reliability, and validity of the assessment process; (2) cost-effectiveness; and, (3) allowing the neuropsychologist to utilize his/her expertise and time in a more efficient manner.

The concerns expressed by some psychologists regarding the delegation of services to paraprofessional personnel appear to be unfounded. As Cohen (1974, p. 223) suggests, many of the tasks "...could be done more effectively by a specialist psychology technician than by the generalist Ph.D. clinical psychologist." However, there are many questions and practices that must be addressed. Problems involving recruitment, retaining quality personnel, and training/ educational opportunities are some of the more obvious practical issues. Also, there are other important concerns regarding minimum educational requirements, the training process, quality assurance, supervision, the ratios of professionals to technicians, and the limits of job functions (Blau, 1969).

L'Abate (1964) addressed some of these concerns by providing methods for structuring the employment of technicians. These included the construction of clear and concise manuals outlining clinical rules, the types of desirable behavior on the part of the technician during testing, standardized shortcuts for recording patient responses, and clear instructions for test administration. Also, there are several formal training programs and specialized undergraduate degree programs developed to train psychological technicians. As of yet, however, there are no professional guidelines for the training and deployment of psychology technicians as they are deployed in the practice of clinical psychology or clinical neuropsychology.

The following is an attempt to outline some of the key areas that must be addressed in the establishment of professional guidelines for the training and utilization of NTs.

Minimum Educational Requirements
The minimum educational level would be a Bachelor's degree, preferably in psychology. Courses in testing would also be an asset. There is clearly a need to restructure undergraduate training to include a track aimed at developing technicians. Although the latter would not provide specific training and experience in testing, it should prepare the individual to enter an apprentice-like position to receive on-the-job-training. College courses in ethics, testing/ psychometrics, general clinic practice and procedures, and a course specific to the experience of technicians could be developed as part of the required curriculum. Cohen (1974) observed that two such technician training programs were being developed at Georgia College at Milledgeville and at Georgia State University in Atlanta.

Training

On-the-job-training following the current apprentice model would be the primary method for training technicians in neuropsychological assessment, scoring, and patient-management procedures. The following approach is modeled after the method employed at the Regional Children's Center in Windsor, Ontario under the direction of Byron P. Rourke and his chief psychometrist, Marilyn Chedour.

A specific sequential process was developed and applied to the teaching of each assessment measure separately. This method included the following steps: reading manuals and memorizing test instructions; observing experienced examiners; one-to-one training with examiners; observation by experienced examiners (first with the examiner as subject, then with less impaired patients); practice and discussion of scoring procedures with experienced examiners; and, periodic observation and scoring checks. Training in a more general sense could also include seminars and related readings on the assessment process, ethics, and guidelines on handling special and/or problem cases.

Job Functions

NTs could be employed to complete the following tasks: test administration and scoring; keeping referral logs; scheduling patients for assessments and feedback conferences; parent and other caretaker interviews (including the explanation of services and assistance in completing behavioral questionnaires); collection of previous medical and psychological reports; maintaining files; computer coding of data; training new NTs; research; neurocognitive remedial training; and, assisting in parent training groups.

Supervision

At the intermediate level, NTs could be supervised by a senior or chief NT. However, the clinical neuropsychologist is ultimately responsible for the direct supervision of all technical support personnel. In addition, it would be extremely beneficial to the functioning of the clinical service for NTs to attend and participate in general staff meetings.

Quality Assurance

Quality assurance procedures could include the following: checking of scoring; checking of data coded in computer databases; recalibration of equipment; and, scheduled roundtable discussions among NTs and professional staff regarding assessment issues, scoring problems, and means for handling special and problem cases.

Licensing

It may be quite difficult to establish testing procedures for NTs, given the diversity of the assessment procedures employed in various centers. However, licenses could be granted to individuals after the completion of a 12-month full-time

training/work period at a center following the established professional guidelines. Another option would be to provide a limited license in the latter case and a
full license after the completion of an additional 12 months of on-the-job
experience.

Special Topics

It may be useful for technicians to be represented by Division 40 or to establish
their own independent association. Finally, in order to attract and retain qualified
personnel, NTs must be provided with job satisfaction, adequate remuneration
and benefits, and some type of career ladder.

In short, neuropsychologists themselves are responsible for the continuation
and proliferation of the NT position. This includes the changing of the attitudes of
other psychologists, the recognition of the significance and dignity of the NT's
contribution, and the continued enhancement of the NT's skill level and
professional effectiveness (Cohen, 1974). As Gentry (1974b) so aptly noted, we
must assist in developing a stable and attractive career for bright and competent
individuals who either do not have the inclination or opportunity to persue higher
professional levels. The practice of employing technical staff should benefit the
individuals who fill these positions as well as the professionals who guide them
and are the "consumers" of their work.

REFERENCES

Affleck, D.C., Strider, F.D., & Helper, M.M. (1968). A clinical psychologist-assistant
    approach to psychodiagnostic testing. *Journal of Projective Techniques and
    Personality Assessment, 32,* 317-322.
Albee, G.W. (1968). Conceptual models and manpower requirements in psychology.
    American Psychologist, 23, 317-320.
American Psychological Association. (1981a). Specialty guidelines for the delivery of
    services by clinical psychologists. *American Psychologist, 36,* 640-651.
American Psychological Association. (1981b). Ethical guidelines of psychologists.
    American Psychologist, 36, 633-638.
American Psychological Association. (1987a). General guidelines for providers of
    psychological services. *American Psychologist, 42,* 712-723.
American Psychological Association. (1987b). Model act for state licensure of psycholo-
    gists. *American Psychologist, 42,* 696-703.
Arnhoff, F.N., & Jenkins, J.W. (1969). Subdoctoral education in psychology: A study of
    issues and attitudes. *American Psychologist, 24,* 430-443.
Baumeister, A.A. (1967). A survey of the role of psychologists in public institutions for the
    mentally retarded. *Mental Retardation, 5,* 2-5.
Blau, T.H. (1969). Psychologist views the helper. In C. Grosser, W.E. Henry, & J.G. Kelly
    (Eds.), *Nonprofessionals in the human services* (pp. 183-192). San Francisco:
    Jossey-Bass.
Boll, T.J. (1981). The Halstead-Reitan neuropsychology battery. In S.B. Filskov & T.J. Boll
    (Eds.), *Handbook of clinical neuropsychology* (pp. 577-607). New York: Wiley.
Cohen, L.D. (1969). Training psychologists. In C. Grosser, W.E. Henry, & J.G. Kelly (Eds.),
    Nonprofessionals in the human services (pp. 174-182). San Francisco: Jossey-
    Bass.

88

Cohen, L.D. (1974, May). Overview Past, present, future. *Professional Psychology*, 222-226.

Gentry, W.D. (1974a, May). Three models of training and utilization. *Professional Psychology*, 207-214.

Gentry, W.D. (1974b, May). Technicians views of training and function. *Professional Psychology*, 219-221.

Grosser, C., Henry, W.E., & Kelly, J.G. (1969). *Nonprofessionals in the human services*. San Francisco: Jossey-Bass.

Heaton, S.R., & Heaton, R.K. (1981). Testing the impaired patient. In S.B. Filskov & T.J. Boll (Eds.), *Handbook of clinical neuropsychology* (pp. 526-544). New York: Wiley.

Holt, R.R. (1967). Diagnostic testing: Present status and future prospects. *Journal of Nervous and Mental Disease, 144*, 444-465.

Howard, R.C. (1987, July-August). Clinical division news. *The Michigan Psychologist*, 9.

Indianapolis Union Railway v. Walker, 162 Ind. App. 166, 318 N.E. 2d. 578 (1974).

Kadish, J. (1969). Programs in the federal government. In C. Grosser, W.E. Henry, & J.G. Kelly (Eds.), *Nonprofessionals in the human services* (pp. 228-242). San Francisco: Jossey-Bass.

L'Abate, (1964). Innovations for training. In L. Blank & H.P. David (Eds.), *Sourcebook for training in clinical psychology* (pp. 157-174). New York: Springer.

Matarazzo, J.D. (1973). Some national developments in the utilization of nontraditional mental health manpower. *American Psychologist, 26*, 363-372.

Matthews, C.G. (1981). Neuropsychology practice in a hospital setting. In S.B. Filskov & T.J. Boll (Eds.), *Handbook of clinical neuropsychology* (pp. 645-685). New York: Wiley.

McGee, J.P., & Pope, B. (1975, Feb.). Baccalaureate program for mental health workers. *Professional Psychology*, 80-87.

McMordie, W.R. (1984, August). Clinical neuropsychology in the Veterans Administration. *VA Practitioner*, 61-66.

Meier, M.J. (1983). Education and credentialing issues in neuropsychology. In C.J. Golden & P.J. Vicente (Eds.), *Foundations of clinical neuropsychology* (pp. 459-482). New York: Plenum.

Musante, G.J. (1974, May). Staff evaluations of the technician role. *Professional Psychology*, 214-216.

Parsons, O. (1986). Overview of the Halstead-Reitan battery. In T. Incagnoli, G. Goldstein, & C.J. Golden (Eds.), *Clinical application of neuropsychological test batteries* (pp. 155-192). New York: Plenum.

Pope, B., McGee, J.P., & Nudler, S. (1983). *Paraprofessionals in mental health*. New York: Irvington.

Raimy, V. (1957). "Submasteral" psychologists. *American Psychologist, 12*, 516-517.

Reitan,. R.M. (1966). Problems and prospects in studying the psychological correlates of brain lesions. *Cortex, 2*, 127-154.

Rotter, J.B. (1973). The future of clinical psychology. *Journal of Consulting and Clinical Psychology, 40*, 313-321.

Rourke, B.P. (1976). Issues in the neuropsychological assessment of children with learning disabilities. *Canadian Psychological Review, 17*, 89-102.

Rourke, B.P., & Adams, K.M. (1984). Quantitative approaches to the neuropsychological assessment of children. In R.E. Tarter & G. Goldstein (Eds.), *Advances in clinical neuropsychology*, Vol. 2. (pp. 79-108). New York: Plenum.

Rourke, B.P., Bakker, D., Fisk, J.L., & Strang, J.D. (1983). *Child neuropsychology: An introduction to theory, research, and clinical practice*. New York: Guilford Press.

Rourke, B.P., Fisk, J.L., & Strang, J.D. (1986). *Neuropsychological assessment of children: A treatment-oriented approach*. New York: Guilford Press.

Russell, E.W., Neuringer, C., & Goldstein, G. (1970). *Assessment of brain damage: A neuropsychological key approach.* New York: Wiley-Interscience.

Serenty, M.L., Dean, R.S., Gray, J.W., & Hartlage, L.C. (1986). The practice of clinical neuropsychology in the United States. *Archives of Clinical Neuropsychology, 1,* 5-12.

Sloop, E.W., & Quarrick, E. (1974, May). Technician performance: Reliability and validity. *Professional Psychology,* 216-218.

Staff. (1988, January-February). Organizational developments. *The Michigan Psychologist,* 6.

Swiercinsky, D. (1978). *Manual for the adult neuropsychological evaluation.* Springfield: C.C. Thomas.

Trites, R.L. (1981). *Neuropsychological test manual.* Montreal, Quebec: Technolab.

Wellner, A.M. (1968). Survey of psychologists in state mental hospitals. *American Psychologist, 23,* 377-380.

Editor's Note:

As of December, 1988, the assistant attorney general for the state of Kentucky has found that the applicable Kentucky statutory law (KRS 319.010(3)) "defines the practice of psychology in Kentucky to include the construction, administration, and interpretation of tests designed to measure mental abilities, aptitudes, emotions, and motivation". Further definition and clarification will be forthcoming.

The Clinical Neuropsychologist
1989, Vol. 3, No. 1, pp. 23-24

REPORT OF THE DIVISION 40 TASK FORCE ON
EDUCATION, ACCREDITATION, AND CREDENTIALING

Guidelines Regarding the Use of Nondoctoral Personnel in Clinical Neuropsychological Assessment

INTRODUCTION

The guidelines regarding the use of nondoctoral personnel in clinical neuropsychological assessment represent a continuation of previous documents from the Task Force (Task Force, 1987, 1988). The document below presents a general position regarding the use of nondoctoral personnel, and delineates the role of such personnel in the general context of clinical neuropsychological assessment. The committee members who participated in the development of this document included R.A. Bornstein (Chair), Linas Bieliauskas, Lloyd Cripe, James Hom, Edith Kaplan, Roberta White, Alan Yozawitz.

USE OF NONDOCTORAL PERSONNEL IN NEUROPSYCHOLOGICAL ASSESSMENT

The practice of Clinical Neuropsychology involves the integration of data derived from a variety of sources which may include clinical or diagnostic patient interviews, clinical histories, and interpretation of data from various neuropsychological measures. There is a broad range of practice in regard to the use of neuropsychological measures in the assessment of behavioral consequences of impaired brain function. In the use of neuropsychological assessment techniques, individual psychologists may elect to perform their own assessment (in whole or in part) in order to directly observe specific aspects of behavior. However, there is no obligation for all psychologists to perform their own assessments in this manner. One practice in Clinical Neuropsychology includes the supervised participation of nondoctoral personnel (technicians, psychometrists, psychometricians, psychological assistants, etc. depending on the venue). The use of such technicians is a common and accepted practice when the supervising psychologist maintains and monitors high standards of quality assurance as suggested for such work in the *General Guidelines for Providers of Psychological Services,* (American Psychological Association, 1987); *Specialty Guidelines for the Delivery of Psychological Services by Clinical Psychologists*, American Psychological Association, 1981); and *Ethical Principles of Psychologists*, (American Psychological Association, 1981).

ROLES FOR TECHNICIANS IN
CLINICAL NEUROPSYCHOLOGICAL ASSESSMENT

The neuropsychological technician occupies a critical role in the assessment process (for those psychologists who elect to use technicians). No neuropsychologist can interpret improperly obtained data, and it has been suggested that "excellent examination technique is the sine qua non of neuropsychological evaluation" (Boll, 1981). However, technicians have a very narrowly defined and highly specific role in the overall process. These technicians are responsible only for the administration and scoring of neuropsychological tests under the supervision of a neuropsychologist who must be a licensed psychologist in that state or province. The selection of tests, interpretation of those tests, clinical interviewing of patients or family members, and communication of test results and their implications *is the sole and exclusive responsibility of the licensed (neuro)psychologist.* Experienced or "senior" technicians may be involved in the training of new technicians or in the monitoring of testing procedures; however, the ultimate responsibility for testing procedures and training remains with the licensed supervising (neuro)psychologist. The professional relationship in clinical neuropsychology is between the patient and the licensed (neuro)psychologist. Fees for service and accountability for the quality of professional work are exclusively the purview of the licensed (neuro)psychologist.

REFERENCES

American Psychological Association. (1981). Ethical guidelines of psychologists. *American Psychologist, 36*, 633-638.
American Psychological Association. (1981). Specialty guidelines for the delivery of services by clinical psychologists. *American Psychologist, 36*, 640-651.
American Psychological Association. (1987). General guidelines for providers of psychological services. *American Psychologist, 42*, 712-723.
Boll, T.J. (1981). The Halstead Reitan Neuropsychology Battery. In T.J. Boll & S.B. Filskov (Eds.). *Handbook of clinical neuropsychology* (pp. 577-607). New York: John Wiley & Sons.
Reports of the INS-Division 40 Task Force on Education, Accreditation, and Credentialing. (1987). *The Clinical Neuropsychologist, 1*, 29-34.
Reports of the Division 40 Task Force on Education, Accreditation, and Credentialing. (1988). *The Clinical Neuropsychologist, 2*, 25-29.

This statement reflects the official position of the Division of Clinical Neuropsychology and should not be construed as either contrary to or supraordinate to the policies of the APA at large.

The Clinical Neuropsychologist
1991, Vol. 5, No. 1, pp. 20-23

REPORT OF THE DIVISION 40 TASK FORCE ON EDUCATION,
ACCREDITATION AND CREDENTIALING

Recommendations for Education and Training of Nondoctoral Personnel in Clinical Neuropsychology

The use of nondoctoral personnel (at both the Bachelor's degree and Master's degree level) is a common, recognized, and accepted practice in many areas of psychology when supervised by a qualified licensed psychologist who maintains and monitors high standards of quality assurance. In all such situations, these individuals represent the extension of the licensed psychologist, and fulfil limited and clearly circumscribed roles. The use of such nondoctoral personnel is consistent with the policies and procedures defined by the American Psychological Association (*General Guidelines for Providers of Psychological Services*, APA, 1987; *Specialty Guidelines for the Delivery of Psychological Services by Clinical Psychologists*, APA, 1981; and *Ethical Principles of Psychologists*, APA, 1981). In addition, the use of nondoctoral personnel in the area of clinical neuropsychological assessment has been previously addressed (Division 40 Task Force on Education, Accreditation and Credentialing, 1989). That document endorses the use of such personnel in neuropsychological assessment, and defines the roles and responsibilities of psychologists who elect to utilize such personnel. Discussion has arisen in several constituencies regarding the requisite training and educational qualifications for nondoctoral personnel involved in neuropsychological assessment. The current document sets forward some recommended areas of education and training for these personnel (hereafter termed psychometrists). The committee members who contributed to the development of this document included R.A. Bornstein (chair), Roberta White, and James Hom.

Education

Psychometrists should have a Bachelor's degree from a regionally accredited college or university, preferably with a major in Psychology. This basic educational background provides individuals with the necessary background in the science of psychology, and provides the basic academic coursework which serves as a foundation upon which further training in neuropsychological test administration can be based. This coursework typically includes instruction in Abnormal Psychology, Personality, Statistics, and Psychological Testing. Individuals who have completed degrees with non-Psychology majors may also have completed coursework in this area. Individuals who do not have this academic background should be provided with specific information to supplement their training in neuropsychological test administration.

Training

In addition to formal university- or college-based preparation, individuals require training and instruction in numerous areas that pertain to their role as a psychometrist. In addition to the learning of specific test procedures (see below), the psychometrist-trainee must become aware of the goals of neuropsychological examination and his/her specific role in achieving that end. The psychometrist-trainee should also receive training in ethical issues, methods of dealing with situations that arise in the context of assessment, and specific instruction in regard to the limits of his/her role, and relationships with the supervising neuropsychologist in addition to other psychometrists. Each of these topics are considered below.

Administration and Scoring of Neuropsychological Tests

Without question the competence of the examiner is a critical aspect of all assessment (Boll, 1981). In most settings, the most demanding technical requirement for the psychometrist-trainee is to be thoroughly trained in the specific assessment techniques advocated by the supervising neuropsychologist. Psychometrists should be provided with manuals for each test which explicitly define the instructions for administration and scoring. Many neuropsychologists require that standardized test instructions be completely memorized. This complete memorization enhances the efficiency of test administration, permits the psychometrist to focus his/her attention on the patient, and may enhance patient motivation and cooperation. Psychometrists should not be permitted to administer any test to any patient until their mastery of instructions for that specific procedure has been documented by the supervising neuropsychologist (or in some cases a senior level psychometrist).

Extensive early practice administering tests to persons other than patients is essential. In many cases, psychometrist-trainees learn the various procedures in sequence so that they may begin to administer a limited number of tests (on which their mastery has been documented) to the patients being examined by other psychometrists while they learn additional tests. In all cases, the administration of tests to patients by new technicians should be closely supervised and monitored by the neuropsychologist or a senior psychometrist with extensive experience in administration of these procedures. At the completion of the training period, the supervising neuropsychologist should provide written documentation for the psychometrist's file which indicates the nature and duration of training, and which indicates that the psychometrist has satisfactorily completed the training program. For all psychometrists regularly scheduled follow-up supervisory sessions should occur to ensure that standardized administration and scoring procedures are maintained.

Psychometrist's role in achieving the goals of assessment

One typical goal of neuropsychological assessment is to determine a patient's optimal level of performance on a particular battery of tasks. It is important that the psychometrist-trainee understand the philosophical goal of the examination procedures. In addition to test administration, it is typically the role of the psychometrist to establish rapport with the patient, and to structure the assessment session to motivate the patient in order to facilitate accomplishing the goal of the examination. Psychometrist-trainees and new psychometrists should meet regularly with more experienced psychometrists and/or the supervising neuropsychologist to discuss effective procedures for establishing rapport and facilitating patient motivation and performance.

Ethics

It is the responsibility of the supervising neuropsychologist to provide explicit guidance regarding ethical issues that pertain to their activities in neuropsychological examination. These issues include (but are not limited to) protection of patient confidentiality, protection of the confidentiality of test information regarding patients, maintenance and protection of test security, and constraints about dual relationships with patients (or supervisors). The supervising neuropsychologist should provide access to the appropriate APA documents, and may also find it helpful to develop a document describing various ethical issues and the associated constraints these place on the psychometrist.

Situations Arising in the Context of Assessment Sessions

Psychometrists may be working with patients who have a variety of neurological or other medical conditions. It is important for the psychometrist to be aware of appropriate institutional emergency procedures to deal with various medical emergencies such as heart attack, respiratory arrest, seizures, and so forth. In addition to medical emergencies, psychometrists should be aware of recommended procedures for dealing with incompetent or adjudicated patients who attempt to leave the testing setting without authorization. Psychometrists must be trained to be sensitive to subtle or overt suicidal or homicidal threats or innuendoes made during testing. Psychometrists may also be exposed to aggressive or sexually inappropriate behavior on the part of patients, and should be provided with specific instructions on how to handle these situations. The very nature of the assessment situation often elicits requests for information and reassurance by the patient in regard to the adequacy of their performance. It is critical that psychometrists understand the distinction between offering support or encouragement (which is within their role) and evaluative feedback (which is solely within the perview of the supervising neuropsychologist).

Limitation of the Psychometrists Role

It is essential that psychometrists have an explicit understanding of the limited nature of their role in neuropsychological examination. The supervising neuropsychologist must clearly delineate the lines of authority between him/herself and the psychometrist. The psychometrist should be made aware at the time of their employment that their role in the overall process is important, but nonetheless, by definition, is narrowly defined. As stated in a previous Task

Force Report, the role of the psychometrist is strictly limited to the administration and scoring of certain test procedures that are selected, interpreted, and communicated by the licensed neuropsychologist. Similarly, psychometrists should be explicitly instructed not to present him/herself to patients in a manner that implies any independent professional prerogatives.

Some prospective psychometrists may inappropriately view employment as an entry into the professional practice of neuropsychology. It is the responsibility of the supervising neuropsychologist to correct any misperceptions about the potential for growth in the roles and responsibilities of psychometrist. It should be specifically stated that test selection, interpretation, or communication of results are professional activities performed only by the supervising neuropsychologist. It should be further stipulated that these roles are not, nor will they ever be the responsibility of the psychometrist. Psychometrists may make notes during the examination of a patient's behavior, but the interpretation of those behaviors, and the incorporation into a report is strictly the responsibility of the licensed psychologist.

Professional Relationships With Others

The psychometrist should be provided with an organizational structure of the setting in which he/she works. This should include clear delineation of lines of authority, and directions regarding to whom the psychometrist is responsible for various aspects of his/her performance. Some settings employ more senior psychometrists with supervisory responsibilities over the daily conduct of the laboratory. These senior psychometrists may have Master's degrees, or may have several years of experience (following a Bachelor's degree). In any case, the supervising neuropsychologist has the ultimate and legal responsibility for supervising all aspects of work by the psychometrist.

REFERENCES

American Psychological Association. (1981). Ethical guidelines of psychologists. *American Psychologist, 36,* 633-638.

American Psychological Association. (1981). Specialty guidelines for the delivery of services by clinical psychologist. *American Psychologist, 36,* 640-651.

American Psychological Association. (1987). General guidelines for providers of psychological services. *American Psychologist, 42,* 712-723.

Boll, T.J. (1981). The Halstead Reitan Neuropsychology Battery. In S.B. Filskov & T.J. Boll (Eds.). *Handbook of clinical neuropsychology* (pp. 577-607). New York: John Wiley & Sons.

Reports of the Division 40 Task force on Education, Accreditation, and Credentialing. (1989). Guidelines regarding the use of nondoctoral personnel in clinical neuropsychological assessment. *The Clinical Neuropsychologist, 3,* 23-24.

The Clinical Neuropsychologist
1987, Vol. No. 2, pp. 161-184.

Division 40: Task Force Report on Computer-Assisted Neuropsychological Evaluation

Early in 1984, the Executive Committee of Division 40 of the American Psychological Association established a task force on the use of computer technology in testing and remediation/retraining programs in neuropsychology. Composed of a nucleus of Division 40 members suggested by the Executive Committee, plus a larger group of Division 40 members who responded to an open invitation to participate in the development of these guidelines, the task force assembled, reviewed, and discussed a large number of pertinent documents and the broad range of opinion that characterizes this controversial subject.

Fortunately, during the same time period in which the Division 40 Task Force was addressing this topic, a set of guidelines for computer-based tests and interpretations was under development by APA's Committee on Professional Standards and Committee on Psychological Tests and Measurements. This set of guidelines, ratified by the APA Council of Representatives in February, 1986, was carefully reviewed by the Division 40 Task Force. The APA statement was judged to be sufficiently comprehensive, balanced, and rigorous to serve admirably as the basic Division 40 guideline document. The only changes in the APA guidelines suggested by the Task Force and subsequently approved by the Division 40 Executive Committee are in the nature of minor additions designed to focus the reader's attention upon the specific applicability of the guidelines to the practice of clinical neuropsychology.

Permission has been received from APA to re-print the February, 1986 APA guidelines in The Clinical Neuropsychologist. *The Division 40 modifications of the APA document are indicated by brackets in the re-printed text. The original APA guidelines document is available from APA Central Office.*

The Task Force is now initiating Phase II of its mandate, namely, the development of guidelines for the use of computer-assisted retraining/remediation procedures in neuropsychology. Division 40 members interested in contributing to this project are invited to contact Charles G. Matthews, Ph. D., Neuropsychology Laboratory, University of Wisconsin Center for Healthy Sciences, 600 North Highland Avenue, Madison, WI, 53792 (608-263-5430) or J. Preston Harley, Ph. D., Neuropsychology Department, Braintree Hospital, 250 Pond Street, Braintree, MA, 02184 (617-848-5353).

Charles G. Matthews,
Task Force Chairman

Guidelines for Computer-Based Tests and Interpretations*

Committee on Professional Standards (COPS)
and
Committee on Psychological Tests and
Assessment (CPTA)

INTRODUCTION

The use of computers in psychological testing and assessment is not a recent development. With the introduction of user-friendly microcomputers and software within the economic grasp of the individual practitioner, however, the variety of such uses has increased at a hitherto unequaled rate. These uses include computer administration of psychological tests, computerized test scoring, and computer-generated interpretations of test results and related information. The rapid increase in the availability and use of these applications of computer technology has served as the impetus for the writing of this document.

In addition, the market is swiftly expanding for automated test scoring services, computerized test interpretations, computer-administered tests, and software to perform these functions. It is essential that the users, developers, and distributors of computer-based tests, scoring services, and interpretation services apply to these technological innovations the same ethical, professional, and technical standards that govern the development and use of traditional means of performing these functions.

The American Psychological Association (APA) first adopted interim standards on "Automated Test Scoring and Interpretation Practices"many years ago (Newman, 1966, p. 1141). The 1974 *Standards for Educational and Psychological Tests* (APA) included several references to computerized assessment. The 1985 *Standards for Educational and Psychological Testing* (Standards, 1985) contains even more. The guidelines that follow are a special application of the revised *Testing Standards* and relate specifically to the use of computer administration, scoring, and interpretation of psychological [and neuropsychological] test. These guidelines are advisory in nature and are intended to provide a frame of reference for addressing relevant issues arising from the use of computer technology in testing.

Purpose
In January 1984 the APA Board of Directors instructed the Committee on Professional Standards (a committee of the Board of Professional Affairs) and the Committee on Psychological Tests and Assessment (a committee of the Board of Scientific Affairs) to develop guidelines for computer-based test administration, scoring, and interpretation. During the development of these Guidelines the Committee on Professional Standards has consisted of Susan R. Berger, William Chestnut, LaMaurice H. Gardner, Jo-Ida Hansen, Carrie Miller, Marlene Muse, Lyle F. Schoenfeldt, William Schofield (chair), and Barbara Wand. The Committee on Psychological Tests and Assessment has consisted of Wayne F. Cascio, Fritz Drasgow, Richard Duran, Bert F. Green (chair, 1984), Lenore Harmon, Asa Hilliard, Douglas N. Jackson (chair, 1985), Trevor Sewell, and Hilda Wing. Central Office staff assistance was provided by Debra Boltas and Rizalina Mendiola.

These Guidelines were written to assist professionals in applying computer-based assessments competently and in the best interests of their clients. The Guidelines were designed also to guide test developers in establishing and maintaining the quality of new products.

Specific reference is made to existing APA standards of particular relevance to computerized testing, which are abbreviated as follows: the *Ethical Principles of Psychologists (Ethical Principles;* APA, 1981); the *Standards for Educational and Psychological Testing (Testing Standards*; APA, 1985); and the *Standards for Providers of Psychological Services (Provider Standards*; APA, 1977). In addition, use has been made of selected sections of *Standards for the Administration and Interpretation of Computerized Psychological Testing* (Hofer & Bersoff, 1983).

The general purpose of these Guidelines is to interpret the *Testing Standards* as they relate to computer-based testing and test interpretation. They are intended to indicate the nature of the professional's responsibilities rather than to provide extensive technical advice, although some technical material of particular relevance to computer-based assessment has been included. The *Testing Standards* provide complete technical standards for testing. Technical guidance in computerized adaptive cognitive testing can be found in Green, Bock, Humphreys, Linn, and Reckase (1982, 1984). [These guidelines are particularly relevant to persons engaging in the clinical practice of psychology, e.g., clinical psychologists and clinical neuropsychologists, but have relevance to all psychologists in applied settings.]

When the circumstances of computer testing are essentially equivalent to those of conventional tests, it is presumed here that the issue is covered in the *Testing Standards*. For example, test security is essential to the integrity and meaning of scores on any test, whether the test is administered conventionally or by computer. Users should guard computer software for a test as diligently as they would booklets of a conventional test, so no special mention was deemed necessary.

The Guidelines are deliberately slanted toward personality assessment and the migration of conventional tests to the computer form of presentation. Many new tests are now being developed specifically for computer presentation, including many tests requiring novel responses. In general, the *Testing Standards* provides pertinent guidance for the development of such tests and should be considered to take precedence over these Guidelines.

In preparing these Guidelines, the Committee on Professional Standards (COPS) and the Committee on Psychological Tests and Assessment (CPTA) were aware that the sale and use of computerized test scoring and interpretive services extends beyond the membership of APA and that the guidelines may be of some relevance to others. Nevertheless as an APA document, it has been appropriate to refer to APA documents throughout, even though they are binding only on APA members.

The Committees were further aware that APA standards refer to the obligations of individual members, whereas computerized testing services are usually the products of incorporated companies. The purpose of these Guidelines is to offer guidance to APA members as professional psychologists when they use, develop, or participate in the promotion or sale of computerized test scoring or interpretive services, either alone or as an agent or director of a company. The Guidelines apply particularly to the administration and use of tests for individual decision making. However, the Guidelines also are relevant when the test results are to be used in research or in general group evaluation. In all cases, it is expected that professional judgement will determine the relevance of a particular guideline to a particular situation.

Participants in the Testing Process

Test Developer

The *Testing Standards* identifies the test developer as an individual or agency who develops, publishes, and markets a test. For puposes of this document it is useful to distinguish among the following: (a) the *test author*, who originally develops a test; (b) the *software author*, who develops the algorithm that administers the test, scores the test and, in some cases, provides interpretative statements; and (c) the *test or software publisher*, who markets the computer software and accompanying documentation for the test.

Test User

The professional who requires the test results for some decision-making purpose. In some cases the test user provides the scores or an interpretation of the results to some separate decision maker, such as a probation officer or a director of college admissions. In that case, both parties bear responsibility for proper test use.

Test Taker

The individual who takes the test. In some cases, such as in a self-directed guidance system, the test taker may be the ultimate consumer and is in this sense both test taker and test user. When the test taker is the ultimate consumer, special care is needed in providing an appropriate context for understanding the test results.

Test Administrator

The individual who actually supervises and has professional responsibility for administering the test. In cases where the test administrator delegates the proctoring of test administration to another person, the administrator retains responsibility for adherence to sound professional practice.

Responsible actions of these various parties all contribute to the effective delivery of services to clients. Many of these responsibilities have been set forth in the *Ethical Principles* and *Provider Standards*. Reference is made here to these documents even though it is recognized that the parties might not be psychologists in all cases. Although binding only on psychologists, these documents provide sound advice for any person responsible for developing and offering computer-based administration, scoring, and interpretation of psychological [and neuropsychological] tests.

THE USER'S RESPONSIBILITIES

Some aspects of testing can be carried out advantageously by a computer. Conditions of administration of some tests can be better standardized and more accurately timed and controlled when the test is administered by a computer. Test scoring can be done more efficiently and accurately by a computer than it can by hand. Test score interpretation based on complex decision rules can be generated quickly and accurately by a computer. However, none of these applications of computer technology is any better than the decision rules or algorithm upon which they are based. The judgment required to make appropriate decisions based on information provided by a computer is the responsibility of the user.

The test user should be a qualified professional with (a) knowledge of psychological measurement; (b) background in the history of the tests or inventories being used; (c) experience in the use and familiarity with the research on the tests or inventories, including gender, age, and cultural differences if applicable; and

(d) knowledge of the area of intended application. For example, in the case of personality inventories, the user should have knowledge of psychopathology or personality theory.

The responsibilities of users are expressed by the following clauses from the *Ethical Principles* and *Provider Standards.*

Ethical Principle 1: Responsibility
In providing services, psychologists maintain the highest standards of their profession. They accept responsibility for the consequences of their acts and make every effort to ensure that their services are used appropriately.

Interpretation:
Professionals accept personal responsibility for any use they make of a computer-administered test or a computer-generated test interpretation. It follows that they should be aware of the method used in generating the scores and interpretation and be sufficiently familiar with the test in order to be able to evaluate its applicability to the purpose for which it will be used.

Ethical Principle 2: Competence
Psychologists recognize the boundaries of their competence and the limitations of their techniques. They only provide services and only use techniques for which they are qualified by training and experience. They maintain knowledge of current scientific and professional information related to the services they render.

2e. Psychologists responsible for decisions involving individuals or policies based on test results have an understanding of psychological or educational measurement, validation problems, and test research.

Provider Standards 1.5 and 1.6 further underscore the nature of the professional's responsibility:

Provider Standard 1: Providers
1.5. Psychologists shall maintain current knowledge of scientific and professional developments that are directly related to the services they render.

1.6. Psychologists shall limit their practice to their demonstrated areas of professional competence.

Interpretation:
Professionals will limit their use of computerized testing to techniques with which they are familiar and competent to use. [They will not attempt to use computerized testing as a substitute for expertise or training.]

Ethical Principle 6: Welfare of the Consumer
Psychologists fully inform consumers as to the purpose and nature of an evaluative ... procedure

---

Ethical Principle 8: Assessment Techniques
8a. In using assessment techniques, psychologists respect the right of clients to have full explanations of the nature and purpose of the techniques in language the clients can understand, unless an explicit exception to this right has been agreed upon in advance. When the explanations are to be provided by others, psychologists establish procedures for ensuring the adequacy of these explanations.

8c. In reporting assessment results, psychologists indicate any reservations that exist regarding validity or reliability because of the circumstances of the assessment or the inappropriateness of the norms for the person tested. Psychologists strive to ensure that the results of assessments and their interpretations are not misused by others.

Interpretation:
The direct implication of Principles 8a and 8c for the user of computer-based tests and interpretations is that the user is responsible for communicating the test findings in a fashion understandable to the test taker. The user should outline to the test taker any shortcomings or lack of relevance the report may have in the given context.

GUIDELINES FOR USERS OF COMPUTER-BASED TESTS AND INTERPRETATIONS

The previous references to the *Ethical Principles, Provider Standards,* and *Testing Standards* provide the foundation for the following specific guidelines for computer-based tests and interpretations.

Administration

Standardized conditions are basic to psychological testing. Administrative procedures for tests are discussed in Chapters 15 and 16 of the 1985 *Testing Standards*. The main technical concern is standardization of procedures so that everyone takes the test under essentially similar conditions. Test administrators bear the responsibility for providing conditions equivalent to those in which normative, reliability, and validity data were obtained. The following guidelines are of particular relevance to the computerized environment.

1. Influences on test scores due to computer administration that are irrelevant to the purposes of assessment should be eliminated or taken into account in the interpretation of scores.

2. Any departure from the standard equipment, conditions, or procedures, as described in the test manual or administrative instructions, should be demonstrated not to affect test scores appreciably. Otherwise, appropriate calibration should be undertaken and documented (see Guideline 16).

Comment:
A special problem with computerized administration may arise with the use of different equipment by different professionals or use of equipment different from that for which the system originally was intended. Where equipment differences are minor it may be determined on the basis of professional judgment that test scores are unlikely to be affected. In other cases, users should demonstrate empirically that the use of different equipment has no appreciable effects on test scores.

3. The environment in which the testing terminal is located should be quiet, comfortable, and free from distractions.

Comment:
The overall aim is to make the environment conducive to optimal test performance for all test takers. Ideally, a separate cubicle for each terminal is recommended. If this is not possible, at a minimum, terminals should be located in a comfortable, quiet room that minimizes distractions. Users should be prepared to show that differences in testing environments have no appreciable effect on

performance.

The test administrator should be careful to ensure that the test taker is free from distraction while taking the test and has adequate privacy, especially for tests or inventories involving personal or confidential issues. The environment should be quiet, free of extraneous conversation, and only the test administrator and test taker should be in a position to see either the test items or the responses. In addition to maintaining consistency in the testing environment, this helps to prevent inadvertent item disclosure.

4. Test items presented on the display screen should be legible and free from noticeable glare.

Comment:
(*See Testing Standards*, 1985, 15.2) The placement of the equipment can introduce irrelevant factors that may influence test performance. Proper design and position of the display screen will avoid reduction in the legibility of the test materials by reflections from windows, ceiling lights, or table lamps.

5. Equipment should be checked routinely and should be maintained in proper working condition. No test should be administered on faulty equipment. All or part of the test may have to be readministered if the equipment fails while the test is being administered.

Comment:
Proper equipment design and optimum conditions do not ensure against malfunctioning equipment. To prevent disruptions such as sticky keys or dirty screens that may adversely affect test performance, there should be a schedule of regular and frequent maintenance, and the equipment should be checked for each test taker prior to its use.

6. Test performance should be monitored, and assistance to the test taker should be provided, as is needed and appropriate. If technically feasible, the proctor should be signaled automatically when irregularities occur.

Comment:
Monitoring test performance is important so that the user can remedy any problem that might affect the psychometric soundness of the eventual score or interpretation. For users who test a few individuals, this can be done by simply looking in on the test taker; users who regularly test large numbers of people may

wish to monitor automatically. This can be done by using computer programs that notify the test proctor if a test taker is responding too quickly or slowly or outside the range of response options. Peculiar responses might generate a warning to the proctor that the test taker does not understand the test directions, is not cooperating, or that the terminal is malfunctioning. In most cases, help should be immediately available to the test taker. In the case of self-administered tests for guidance and instruction, help may not be urgently needed, but some provision should always be made for assisting the test taker.

---

7. Test takers should be trained on proper use of the computer equipment, and procedures should be established to eliminate any possible effect on test scores due to the test taker's lack of familiarity with the equipment.

Comment:
It is important to ensure that test takers are so familiar with the equipment and procedures that they can devote their full attention to the substance of the test items. Adequate training should be given to those who need it. This may require an ample store of sample items. It is very likely that such practice will reduce anxiety, increase confidence, and improve the reliability and validity of test results.

---

8. Reasonable accommodations must be made for individuals who may be at an unfair disadvantage in a computer testing situation. In cases where a disadvantage cannot be fully accommodated, scores obtained must be interpreted with appropriate caution.

Comment:
Computerized testing may facilitate testing persons with some physical disabilities by providing especially large type or especially simple response mechanisms. In other cases, the computer may place persons who have certain handicapping conditions at a disadvantage. Chapter 14 of the 1985 *Testing Standards* addresses the testing of persons who have handicapping conditions.

Although tests have been successfully administered by computer to large numbers of both younger and older adults, some older people may need special reassurance and extended practice with the equipment and can be expected to respond more slowly than younger test takers. Of course, no accommodation is appropriate when the disadvantage is what is being tested. A person with poor eyesight is at a disadvantage in a test of visual acuity; it is precisely that disadvantage that is being assessed.

Interpretation

9. Computer-generated interpretive reports should be used only in conjunction with professional judgment. The user should judge for each test taker the validity of the computerized test report based on the user's professional knowledge of the total context of testing and the test taker's performance and characteristics.

Comment:

A major concern about computer-generated reports is that they may not be as individualized as those generated in the conventional manner. Some information, such as demographic characteristics of the test taker, can be included in interpretation programs so that the computer will use more appropriate norms or base rates, if they exist, and qualify interpretations to take into account the particular test taker's characteristics. But no assessment system, whether computer based or conventional, can, at this time, consider all the unique relevant attributes of each individual.

A test user should consider the total context of testing in interpreting an obtained score before making any decision (including the decision to accept the score). Furthermore, a test user should examine the differences between characteristics of the person tested and those of the population for whom the test was developed and normed. This responsibility includes deciding whether the differences are so great that the test should not be used for the person (*Testing Standards*, 1985, 7.6). These, as well as other judgments (e.g., whether conditions are present that could invalidate test results), may be ones that only a professional observing the testing situation can make. Thus, it is imperative that the final decision be made by a qualified professional who takes responsibility for overseeing both the process of testing and judging the applicability of the interpretive report for individual test takers, consistent with legal, ethical, and professional requirements. In some circumstances, professional providers may need to edit or amend the computer report to take into account their own observations and judgments and to ensure that the report is comprehensible, free of jargon, and true to the person evaluated.

A long history of research on statistical and clinical prediction has established that a well-designed statistical treatment of test results and ancillary information will yield more valid assessments than will an individual professional using the same information. Only when the professional uses more information than the statistical system will the professional be in a position to improve the system's results. Therefore, if the system has a statistical, actuarial base, the professional should be wary of altering the system's interpretation. Likewise, if the system represents the judgments and conclusions of one or more skilled clinicians, the professional must recognize that changing the computerized interpretation means substituting his or her judgment for that of the expert. The final decision must be that of a qualified provider with sensitivity for nuances of test administration and interpretation. Altering the interpretation should not be done routinely, but only for good and compelling reasons.

THE DEVELOPER'S RESPONSIBILITIES

Developers of computerized test administration, scoring, and interpretation services are referred to the *Testing Standards* (1985), which provides standards for test development. The following general principles from the *Ethical Principles* and the *Provider Standards* also are relevant.

Ethical Principle 8: Assessment Techniques
8b. Psychologists responsible for the development and standardization of psychological tests and other assessment techniques utilize established scientific procedures and observe the relevant APA standards.

8d. Psychologists recognize that assessment results may become obsolete. They make every effort to avoid and prevent the misuse of obsolete measures.

8e. Psychologists offering scoring and interpretation services are able to produce appropriate evidence for the validity of the programs and procedures used in arriving at interpretations. The public offering of an automated interpretation service is considered a professional-to-professional consultation.
Psychologists make every effort to avoid misuse of assessment reports.

8f. Psychologists do not encourage or promote the use of psychological assessment techniques by inappropriately trained or otherwise unqualified persons.

Provider Standard 1: Providers
1.5 Psychologists shall maintain current knowledge of scientific and professional developments that are directly related to the services they render.

Provider Standard 3: Accountability
3.4 Psychologists are accountable for all aspects of the services they provide and shall be responsive to those concerned with these services.

When advertising and selling computer-based testing services, the following are relevant.

Ethical Principle 4: Public Statements
Public statements, announcements of services, advertising, and promotional activities of psychologists serve the purpose of helping the public make informed judgments and choices. Psychologists represent accurately and objectively their professional qualifications, affiliations, and functions, as well as those of the institutions or organizations with which they or the statements may be associated. In public statements providing psychological information or professional opinions or providing information about the availability of psychological products, publications, and services, psychologists base their statements on scientifically acceptable psychological findings and techniques with full recognition of the limits and uncertainties of such evidence.

4b. Public statements include, but are not limited to, communication by means of periodical, book list, directory, television, radio, or motion picture. They do not contain (i) a false, fraudulent, misleading, deceptive, or unfair statement; (ii) a misinterpretation of fact or a statement likely to mislead or deceive because in context it makes only a partial disclosure of relevant facts; (iii) a testimonial from a patient regarding the quality of a psychologist's services or products; (iv) a statement intended or likely to create false or unjustified expectations of favorable results; (v) a statement implying unusual, unique, or one-of-a-kind abilities; (vi) a statement intended or likely to appeal to a client's fears, anxieties, or emotions concerning the possible results of failure to obtain the offered services; (vii) a statement concerning the comparative desirability of offered services; (viii) a statement of direct solicitation of individual clients.

4e. Psychologists associated with the development or promotion of psychological devices, books, or other products offered for commercial sale make reasonable efforts to ensure that announcements and advertisements are presented in a professional, scientifically acceptable, and factually informative manner.

4g. Psychologists present the science of psychology and offer their services, products, and publications fairly and accurately, avoiding misrepresentation through sensationalism, exaggeration, or superficiality. Psychologists are guided by the primary obligation to aid the public in developing informed judgments, opinions, and choices.

4j. A psychologist accepts the obligation to correct others who represent the psychologist's professional qualifications, or associations with products or services, in a manner incompatible with these guidelines.

4k. Individual diagnostic and therapeutic services are provided only in the context of a professional psychological relationship. When personal advice is given by means of public lectures or demonstrations, newspaper or magazine articles, radio or television programs, mail, or similar media, the psychologist utilizes the most current relevant data and exercises the highest level of professional judgment.

Provider Standard 2: Programs
2.3.1 Where appropriate, each psychological service unit shall be guided by a set of procedural guidelines for the delivery of psychological services. If appropriate to the setting, these guidelines shall be in written form.

GUIDELINES FOR THE DEVELOPERS OF COMPUTER-BASED TEST SERVICES

The Testing Standards (1985) and the previous cited sections of the *Ethical Principles* and *Provider Standards* provide the foundation for the following specific guidelines for the developers of computer-based test services.

Human Factors
10. Computerized administration normally should provide test takers with at least the same degree of feedback and editorial control regarding their responses that they would experience in traditional testing formats.

Comment:
For tests that involve a discrete set of response alternatives, test takers should be able to verify the answer they have selected and should normally be given the opportunity to change it if they wish. Tests that require constructed responses (e.g., sentence completion tasks) typically require more extensive editing facilities to permit test takers to enter and modify their answers comfortably. Tests that involve continuous recording of responses (e.g., tracking tasks) can make use of a variety of visual, auditory, or tactile feedback sources to maximize performance and minimize examinee frustration.

---

11. Test takers should be clearly informed of all performance factors that are relevant to the test result.

Comment:
Instructions should provide clear guidance regarding how the test taker is to respond and the relative importance of such factors as speed and accuracy. If changes are permitted, directions should explain how and when this is to be done. Before the actual test begins, the testing system itself or the proctor should check that these instructions are understood and that the examinee is comfortable with the response device.

The availability of screen prompts, an on-line help facility, or a clock display (in the case of timed performances) may be used advantageously to guide the examinee through the test instructions, test practice, and possibly the test itself. If used during the test, such devices become a part of the test itself, and cannot be changed without recalibrating the test.

---

12. The computer testing system should present the test and record responses without causing unnecessary frustration or handicapping the performance of test takers.

Comment:
Advances in hardware and software design have provided a wide range of ways to transmit information to the computer. Computer test design should explore ways that are most comfortable for test takers and allow them to perform at their best. For example, a touch-sensitive screen, light pen, and mouse may all be perceived as being significantly less confusing than a standard computer keyboard. When a standard keyboard is used, it may be appropriate to mask (physically or through software control) all irrelevant keys to reduce the potential for error.

The type of test and test item may create special design problems. Speed tests must have especially quick and uniform time delays between items to minimize frustration. Tests that require reading of long passages or that have complicated directions to which test takers may want to refer occasionally require procedures that allow display changes and recall. Diagrams with fine detail require displays with greater resolution capacity than normal. If such modifications are not possible, the test takers should be provided with the diagrams or instructions in booklet form.

---

13. The computer testing system should be designed for easy maintenance and system verification.

Comment:
When teleprocessing is involved, reasonable efforts should be made to eliminate transmission errors that could affect test scores. Software design should permit ways of checking that scoring and interpretive parameters recorded on a disk, for example, remain intact and accurate.

---

14. The equipment, procedure, and conditions under which the normative, reliability, and validity data were obtained for the computer test should be described clearly enough to permit replication of these conditions.

---

15. Appropriate procedures must be established by computerized testing services to ensure the confidentiality of the information and the privacy of the test taker.

Comment:
Several services that provide computerized administration of clinical instruments maintain confidentiality by avoiding any use of test takers' names. (See Chapter 16 of the 1985 *Testing Standards*.)

Psychometric Properties
16. When interpreting scores from the computerized versions of conventional tests, the equivalence of scores from computerized versions should be established and documented before using norms or cutting scores obtained from conventional tests. Scores from conventional and computer administrations may be considered equiva-

lent when (a) the rank orders of scores of individuals tested in alternative modes closely approximate each other, and (b) the means, dispersions, and shapes of the score distributions are approximately the same, or have been made approximately the same by rescaling the scores from the computer mode.

Comment:
If individuals obtain equivalent scores from both conventional and computer administration, computer-specific factors will have been shown to have no appreciable effect, and the computer version may legitimately be used in place of the conventional test. If condition (a) is not met, the tests cannot be claimed to be measuring the same construct and should not be used interchangeably. If (a) is met but (b) is not, then one set of scores can be rescaled to be comparable with scores from the other test. If conventional norms are being used, then the computer test scores should be rescaled. If condition (b) is met but (a) is not, then scaling will produce similar distributions, but test equivalence has not been demonstrated. If the tests are not equivalent, new norms should be established. Chapter 4 of the *Testing Standards* (1985) concerns norming and score comparability. Testing Standard 4.6 states that data on form equivalence should be made available, together with detailed information on the method of achieving equivalence. (See also the comment on Standard 2.11, pp 22-23).

A number of research designs can be used to study equivalence. Differences in the means, dispersions, or shapes of computer and conventionally obtained test score distributions all indicate a lack of strict equivalence when equivalent groups are tested. Although perfect equivalence may be unattainable (and unnecessary), the following condition should be satisfied if one wishes to use norms from a conventionally developed test to interpret scores from a computerized test. Computer-obtained test scores should preserve, within the acceptable limits of reliability, the ranking of test takers. If ranking is maintained, then scale values can be transformed through such procedures as linear or equipercentile equating so that test takers receive the same score as they would have obtained through conventional administration. In this way, cutting scores, validity estimates, norms, and other data generated from the conventional scale can be applied to the computer-obtained scores. The same considerations would apply (with the obvious changes) to a test developed entirely in the computer medium that was later printed in paper-and-pencil format. The equivalence of the forms should be established before norms developed for the computer version are used in interpreting the derivative paper-and-pencil format.

The present Guidelines are conservative in suggesting empirical information about equivalence for each test that is rendered in a different presentation mode. At present some tests in some situations show differences; others do not. As the literature expands, generalizations presumably will permit accurate expectations of the effect of presentation mode.

114

17. The validity of the computer version of a test should be established by those developing the test.

Comment:
Procedures for determining validity are the same for tests administered conventionally and by computer (see Chapter 1 of the 1985 *Testing Standards*). A new computer test should be validated in the same way as any other test. If equivalence has been established between the conventional and computer-administered forms of a test, then the validity of the computer version can be generalized from the validity of the conventional version. If equivalence has not been established, the validity and meaning of the computer version should be established afresh. At present, there is no extensive evidence about the validities of computerized versions of conventional tests. Until such evidence accumulates, it will be better to obtain new evidence of predictive and construct validity.

---

18. Test services should alert test users to the potential problems of nonequivalence when scores on one version of a test are not equivalent to the scores on the version for which norms are provided.

Comment:
This will most often be a problem when comparing a computer version of a test with a conventional paper-and-pencil version, but it can also be a problem when comparing tests presented on two different computer systems. Screens of very different size, or special responding devices such as a light pen, could in some circumstances affect test norms. This is especially an issue with timed responses, which are known to vary in speed for different types of required responses. Until enough information accumulates to permit generalization about the relevance of equipment variation, caution is prudent. When a test is offered on different equipment the offerer should provide assurance of comparability of results, and the accompanying manual should reflect the different equipment.

---

19. The test developer should report comparison studies of computerized and conventional testing to establish the relative reliability of computerized administration.

---

20. The accuracy of computerized scoring and interpretation cannot be assumed. Providers of computerized test services should actively check and control the quality of the hardware and software, including the scoring, algorithms, and other procedures described in the manual.

---

21. Computer testing services should provide a manual reporting the rationale and evidence in support of computer-based interpretation of test scores.

Comment:
The developer is responsible for providing sufficient information in the manual so that users may judge whether the interpretive or classification systems are suited to their needs. Chapter 5 of the 1985 *Testing Standards* summarizes the information that should be presented in the manual.

Classification
Certain classification systems depend on the determination of optimal cutting scores. The determination of the cutting score is, in turn, dependent on a number of statistical and practical variables including (a) the base rate of the characteristic to be inferred, (b) the error of measurement at various points along the test score scales, (c) the validity of the tests for the inference to be made, and (d) the costs of errors of classification. Balancing all these considerations is as difficult in making computerized test interpretations as it is in making clinical interpretations.

---

22. The classification system used to develop interpretive reports should be sufficiently consistent for its intended purpose (see Chapter 2 of the 1985 *Testing Standards*. For example, in some cases it is important that most test takers would be placed in the same groups if interested (assuming the behavior in question did not change).

Comment:
There is a trade-off between consistency and precision. The more classification decisions the test is asked to make, the less consistent will such assignments be. Making too few classifications may lead test users to ignore meaningful differences among test takers; too many may lead test users to overestimate the precision of the test.
    Classification systems should be sufficiently consistent so that most test takers

116

would be placed in the same groups and given the same interpretations if retested, and sufficiently precise to identify relevant differences among test takers. Consistency depends upon both the reliability of the test and the size of the score intervals in each class. Precision requires that the test be capable of discriminating meaningfully among test takers. Cutting scores and decision rules should take into account the discriminability of the test at different points of the measurement scale and the purposes for which the interpretations will be used. At a minimum, classification categories must represent rational decisions made in the light of the goals users have in mind. The more important the consequences for the test taker, the more assurance there should be that the interpretation and ultimate decisions are fair and accurate. Developers of interpretive systems should exercise discretion in deciding how many and what kinds of classifications will be useful.

---

23. Information should be provided to the users of computerized interpretation services concerning the consistency of classifications, including, for example, the number of classifications and the interpretive significance of changes from one classification to adjacent ones.

Validity of Computer Interpretations
24. The original scores used in developing interpretive statements should be given to test users. The matrix of original responses should be provided or should be available to test users on request, with appropriate consideration for test security and the privacy of test takers.

---

25. The manual or, in some cases, interpretive report, should describe how the interpretive statements are derived from the original scores.

Comment:
Professionals who provide assessment services bear the ultimate responsibility for providing accurate judgments about the clients they evaluate. It should be possible to fulfill these ethical demands without infringing on the testing service's proprietary rights. To evaluate a computer-based interpretation, the test user should know at least two facts: (a) the nature of the relationship of the interpretations to the test responses and related data, and (b) the test taker's score or scores on the relevant measures. (In addition, raw data or item responses often will be very useful). For example, the test developer could describe the organization of interpretive statements according to the scale on which they are

based, otherwise provide references for statements in the report, or provide in the manual all the interpretive statements in the program library and the scales and research on which they are based. Each test taker's test and scale profile can be printed along with the narrative interpretations, together with the original set of responses where appropriate.

26. Interpretive reports should include information about the consistency of interpretations and warnings related to common errors of interpretation.

Comment:
Test developers should provide information that users need to make correct judgments. Interpretive reports should contain warning statements to preclude overrreliance on computerized interpretations. Unusual patterns of item responses can lead to seemingly inconsistent statements within a single report ("the respondent shows normal affect"; "the respondent may have suicidal tendencies"). Either the manual or the introductory comments on the interpretation might indicate that inconsistent statements result from inconsistent test responses, which may indicate that the result is not valid.

27. The extent to which statements in an interpretive report are based on quantitative research versus expert clinical opinion should be delineated.

28. When statements in an interpretive report are based on expert clinical opinion, users should be provided with information that will allow them to weigh the credibility of such opinion.

Comment:
Some interpretations describe or predict objective behavior, whereas others describe states of mind or internal conflicts. Some interpretations are very general, others quite specific. [For example, interpretations of neuropsychological tests typically have implications regarding adequacy of brain functioning, with such interpretations sometimes extended to specific lateralization and localization inferences]. Some make statements about the test taker's present condition; others make predictions about the future. Some make use of well-established, consensually understood constructs, others use terms drawn from ordinary language. The type of interpretation determines the nature of the evidence that should be provided to the user.

29. When predictions of particular outcomes or specific recommendations are based on quantitative research, information should be provided showing the empirical relationship between the classification and the probability of criterion behavior or condition in the validation group.

Comment:
Computerized interpretation systems usually divide test takers into classes. It is desirable to present the relationship among classes and the probability of a particular outcome (e.g., through an expectancy table) as well as validity coefficients between test scores and criteria.

---

30. Computer testing services should ensure that reports for either users or test takers are comprehensible and properly delimit the bounds within which accurate conclusions can be drawn by considering variables such as age or sex that moderate interpretations.

Comment:
Some reports, especially in the area of school and vocational counseling, are meant to be given to the test taker. In many cases, this may be done with limited professional review of the appropriateness of the report. In such cases, developers bear a special burden to ensure that the report is comprehensible. The reports should contain sufficient information to aid the test taker to understand properly the results and sufficient warnings about possible misinterpretations. Supplemental material may be necessary.

Review
31. Adequate information about the system and reasonable access to the system for evaluating responses should be provided to qualified professionals engaged in a scholarly review of the interpretive service. When it is deemed necessary to provide trade secrets, a written agreement of nondisclosure should be made.

Comment:
Arrangements should be made for the professional review of computer-based test interpretation systems by persons designated as reviewers by scholarly journals and by other test review organizations, including the Buros-Nebraska Institute of Mental Measurement. Such reviewers need more information than a regular consumer could absorb, but generally will not need access to the computer code or the entire array of statements from which interpretations are fashioned. At present, there is no established style for reviewing a CBTI system, and different reviewers may want different information. At a minimum, a reviewer

should be able to communicate freely with technically qualified, knowledgeable persons associated with the test developer, who can answer questions about the system. Access to the system should be provided for trying actual or simulated test responses and for exercising the offered components of the system.

In some cases it may be necessary to impart trade secrets to the reviewer, in which case a written agreement should state the nature of the secret information and the procedures to be used to protect the proprietary interests of the test author, the software author, and the test publisher. As a rule, however, it is advisable to make readily available enough information for a reviewer to evaluate the system. This would include the general structure of the algorithms and the basis for transforming test responses into interpretive reports, but it might not extend to the entire library of interpretive statements or to the specific numerical values of the cutting point and other configural definitions. The general size of the statement library or equivalent process of generating interpretations should be provided, along with information about its source. The algorithms can usually be explained in reasonable detail without disclosing trade secrets.

REFERENCES

American Psychological Association. (1981). Ethical principles of psychologists. *American Psychologist, 36(6),* 633-638.

American Psychological Association. (1977). *Standards for providers of psychological services.* Washington, DC: Author.

American Psychological Association, American Educational Research Association, & National Council on Measurement in Education. (1974). *Standards for educational and psychological tests.* Washington, DC: American Psychological Association.

Green, B.F., Bock, R.D., Humphreys, L.G., Linn, R.B., & Reckase, M.D. (1982). Evaluation plan for the computerized Adaptive Vocational Aptitude Battery. Baltimore, MD: Johns Hopkins University, Department of Psychology.

Green, B.F., Bock, R.D., Humphreys, L.G., Linn, R.B., & Reckase, M.D. (1984). Technical guidelines for assessing computerized adaptive tests. Journal of Educational Measurement, 347-360.

Hofer, P.J. & Bersoff, D.N. (1983). *Standards for the administration and interpretation of computerized psychological testing.* (Available from D.N. Bersoff, APA, Suite 511, 1200 Seventeenth St, N.W., Washington, DC 20036)

Newman, E.B. (1966). Proceedings of the American Psychological Association, Incorporated, for the year 1966. *American Psychologist, 21(12),* 1125-1153.

Standards for educational and psychological testing. (1985). Washington, DC: American Psychological Association.

The Clinical Neuropsychologist
1991, Vol. 5, No. 1, pp. 3-19

Guidelines for Computer-Assisted Neuropsychological Rehabilitation and Cognitive Remediation

Charles G. Matthews
University of Wisconsin School
of Medicine, Madison, WI

J. Preston Harley
Consulting Neuropsychologist
Chicago, IL

James F. Malec
Mayo Clinic
Rochester, MN

Early in 1984, the Executive Committee of Division 40 (Clinical Neuropsychology) of the American Psychological Association, established a task force on the use of computer technology in evaluation and rehabilitation in Neuropsychology. Because of the complexity of the topic, the Task Force decided to complete its work in a two-phase report. Phase I titled *Task Force Report on Computer-Assisted Neuropsychological Evaluation* was completed in late 1986 and was published in *The Clinical Neuropsychologist* (1987).

The Phase II report, titled *Division 40 Task Force Report: Guidelines for Computer-Assisted Neuropsychological Rehabilitation and Cognitive Remediation,* has been developed by a committee co-chaired by Charles G. Matthews, Ph.D. and J. Preston Harley, Ph.D. Members of the Phase II Task Force were:

Gregory Brown, Ph.D.
Leonard Diller, Ph.D.
Rosamond Gianutsos, Ph.D.
Ned L. Kirsch, Ph.D.
Robert T. Kurlychek, Ph.D.

William J. Lynch, Ph.D.
A. John McSweeney, Ph.D.
James F. Malec, Ph.D.
Jeri Morris, Ph.D.
Daniel L. Schachter, Ph.D.

The Task Force met for preliminary discussion at the Mid-Winter Division 40 meeting in Washington, DC in February, 1987, when specific committee members were assigned responsibility for separate sections of the report. Some of these preliminary position statements as well as input received from the audience attending were discussed at a Division 40 Conversation Hour at the APA convention on August 30, 1987. Since September 1987, the Task Force has continued to develop and refine these position papers, and submitted a draft to the Division 40

Executive Committee for its review, correction, and further action at the August, 1989, Division 40 meeting in New Orleans.

The Phase I document had its format predetermined by the format used in the *Guidelines for Computer-Based Tests and Interpretations* developed by APA's Committee for Professional Standards and Committee of Psychological Tests and Measurements (1986). This APA statement was judged to be sufficiently comprehensive, balanced, and rigorous to serve as the basic guideline for this report. As noted in the introduction to the Phase I report (1987), the only changes in the APA Guidelines were... *in the nature of minor additions designed to focus the reader's attention upon the specific applicability of the guidelines to the practice of clinical neuropsychology* (p. 161).

The format selected for the Phase II report is illustrated in an article in the 1987 American Psychologist, titled *Resolutions Approved by the National Conference on Graduate Education in Psychology*. This format presents *Issues* followed by a series of *Resolutions* for each issue, and lends itself to a somewhat more extended presentation of the background and controversy involved in the relatively new field of computer-assisted neuropsychological rehabilitation and cognitive remediation than was required for the Phase I document. **The Phase II document has been written to represent the official policy of Division 40 in the matters addressed, but the document has not been reviewed by APA for approval.**

ISSUE 1: DOES COMPUTER-ASSISTED COGNITIVE REHABILITATION HAVE A ROLE IN THE PRACTICE OF CLINICAL NEURO-PSYCHOLOGY ?

The technological aura and enthusiastic claims of efficacy associated with the initial use of computer-assisted rehabilitation programs in the early 1970s have gradually been replaced by a more modest and balanced consensus: (a) that the computer is not a magical instrument and has no inherently unique status as a treatment tool; and, (b) given that caveat, a number of potential benefits can be derived from its proper use.

Computer software can provide a medium to capture and engage the interest of the patient. Because computers are often employed in the repetitive presentation and recording of increasingly complex tasks, properly constructed and presented software programs can minimize the patient's frustration and loss of dignity when working on tasks he or she once could have accomplished with ease. For some patients, the context of learning to use the computer itself – regardless of the software package – can provide the patient with an experience of mastery and a sense of control. Because the computer can collect and store data representing the patient's performance over time, the therapist can be freed to focus on treatment rather than data collection. In fact, the computer can often measure multiple dimensions of performance (latency, strength, and locus of response) at levels not possible for the human observer (e.g., milliseconds, grams, and millimeters). The computer is a particularly efficient medium for tasks that would otherwise require extensive set-up and/or preparation time, (e.g., rapid change of font size for reading tasks, rapid modification of graphic materials) and permits the simultaneous monitoring and recording of many components of patients' responses for later inspection and analysis. Additionally and importantly, use of the computer allows for a precise, reliable, and standardized presentation of materials and is at the same time adaptable for use across theoretical contexts. This has the potential for promoting interdisciplinary team consistency and coordination.

Despite the frequency of the disclaimer that the computer is only a tool, the fact remains that the tool continues to be confused with treatment itself. When claims are made that certain software can remediate cognitive deficits of one kind or another, the implication is that the software itself is the agent of change rather than the organized treatment program in which it is being used. In a similar way, claims for the efficacy of psychological tests presume expert use and oversight by a qualified psychologist. To fail to make this distinction between the computer as tool versus treatment and to imply that the tool determines therapeutic outcome is to discourage the thoughtful use of such software and to encourage and perpetuate unwarranted expectations regarding its efficacy. As Ben-Yishay and Prigatano (1990) suggest, cognitive remediation is meaningful only if it is embedded in and systematically coordinated with other neuropsychological rehabilitation interventions.

RESOLUTIONS:

1.1 Computer-assisted rehabilitation procedures appear to have a sufficient number of practical advantages and potential benefits to encourage their continued experimental investigation, further development, and empirical validation.

1.2 Appropriate clinical use of computer software in rehabilitation is dependent upon maintaining a clear distinction between software being properly viewed as a component in an organized treatment program versus being improperly viewed as treatment itself.

ISSUE 2: WHAT IS THE EVIDENCE FOR THE EFFICACY OF COMPUTER-ASSISTED NEUROPSYCHOLOGICAL REHABILITATION AND COGNITIVE REMEDIATION ?

In order to assess the role of computers in cognitive rehabilitation, it is necessary to consider empirical evidence that bears on the issue. Specifically, we need to know whether there is any evidence that (a) cognitive rehabilitation is effective under any conditions, and (b) use of a computer contributes to or improves the efficacy of a remedial intervention. The answers to these questions depend on the nature and goals of the rehabilitative strategy that is used, and the specific role played by the computer in a particular intervention.

Research studies of memory rehabilitation (Gouvier, Webster, & Blanton, 1987) will be considered first. This priority is dictated not only by the fact that more empirical research is available on memory rehabilitation than on other cognitive functions, but also because the paucity of supportive findings for the efficacy of memory rehabilitation suggests an appropriately prudent approach to the efficacy studies of cognitive rehabilitation efforts in other areas of neuropsychological deficit.

Restoration. One possible goal of memory rehabilitation is to restore memory processes to premorbid or near-premorbid levels through training. In studies in which this has been attempted by exposing patients to repetitive drills and exercises across multiple training sessions, no significant training effects on general mnemonic function have been documented (Batchelor, Shores, Marosszeky, Sandanam, & Lovarini, 1988; Godfrey & Knight, 1985; Prigatano et al., 1984). The null results are perhaps not surprising since the assumptions underlying the restoration approach are theoretically ill-founded (Schacter & Glisky, 1986). The lack of empirical evidence for the efficacy of restoration approaches does not "prove the null hypothesis", but suggests that attempts to use the computer to administer restoration-oriented memory drills or exercises are unlikely to succeed because the computer has no inherent therapeutic powers, as already discussed under Issue 1. The computer is simply a convenient means of presenting training stimuli (O'Connor & Cermak, 1987).

Reduction of Negative Impact. A second approach to memory rehabilitation has explored whether patients can learn to use mnenomic strategies and thereby reduce the negative impact of memory disorders on their everyday lives. Several types of strategies have been investigated, including visual imagery mnemonics (Cermak, 1975; Crovitz, 1979; Crovitz, Harvey, & Horn, 1979; Lewinsohn, Danaher, & Kikel, 1977; Malec & Questad, 1983; Wilson, 1987), verbal organization (Gianutsos & Gianutsos, 1979; Glasgow, Zeiss, Barrera, & Lewinsohn, 1977; Wilson, 1982), and rehearsal (Schacter, Rich, & Stampp, 1985). The general outcome of these studies is that various strategies enhance memory processing, but are not always consistently used by patients on their own in everyday life (Wilson, 1987). The important question of generalization is thus suggested.

Compensatory Aids. A third approach to memory rehabilitation involves providing patients with external aids, such as notebooks, diaries, and alarm clocks, that can serve as helpful reminders and counteract some of the impact of everyday consequences of a memory disorder. There is some evidence that such external aids can be useful in real-life environments (Harris, 1984; Kurlychek, 1983; Parenté & Anderson-Parenté, 1989; Wilson & Moffat, 1984). It has also been suggested that the computer could be used as an external aid for memory-impaired patients (Harris, 1984; Silbeck, 1984). Preliminary evidence exists that patients can use the computer to aid performance of a real-life task (Chute, Conn, Dipasquale, & Hoag, 1988; Kirsch, Levin, Fallon-Krueger, & Jaros, 1987), and further controlled investigations into this possibility should be pursued.

Domain Specific Knowledge and Skills. A fourth approach to memory rehabilitation involves attempting to teach patients domain-specific knowledge and skills that are useful in everyday life (Schacter & Glisky, 1986; Wilson, 1987). Several studies have shown that patients can learn specific new skills, even though memory does not improve in any general sense (e.g., Jaffe & Katz, 1975; Wilson, 1987). The research of Glisky and colleagues (1986 a, b) has demonstrated that memory-impaired patients can learn to operate and interact with computers in the laboratory, and also has shown that a severely amnestic patient could be successfully trained to perform a real-world job involving data entry into a computer (Glisky & Schacter, 1987). These results suggest a rather different role for computers in memory rehabilitation than has been considered previously. It may be useful to attempt to train patients for jobs involving certain uses of computers. However, much more evidence needs to be accumulated before it can be determined what kinds of patients and jobs are appropriate for such training.

EMPIRICAL EVIDENCE: OTHER COGNITIVE DOMAINS

There is some evidence for the efficacy of interventions in the rehabilitation of attentional deficits (Ben-Yishay, Piasetsky, & Rattok, 1987; Sohlberg & Mateer, 1989) and visuoperceptual disorders, (Gianutsos & Matheson, 1987; Gordon et al., 1985; Ruff et al., 1989). Treatments that may involve some computer-assisted procedures are also under investigation to improve reasoning and judgement (Goldstein & Levin, 1987; Prigatano, 1986). Clinical investigators reporting such findings, however, typically note a number of hard-to-control methodological shortcomings in this research. These include (a) lack of appropriate control groups, (b) lack of methods for distinguishing the effects of the computerized intervention from other ongoing rehabilitation the patient is receiving, (c) lack of methods for controlling for the influence of spontaneous recovery, (d) difficulty in evaluating the effect of the intervention in daily life once training has ceased, (e) over utilization of "select" patients or candidates who have high prospects for success, and (f) insufficient acknowledgement of the need for controlling for the Hawthorne effect.

Sohlberg and Mateer (1989) and Malec (1986) have pointed out the importance of regarding cognitive rehabilitation as a set of different procedures used to improve personal functions related to different cognitive domains. Principles for training may be significantly different as applied to different cognitive skills. For instance, although it is now clear that memory cannot be improved by repetitive drills or massed practice as previously discussed, practice may contribute to gains in attentional capacities (Sohlberg & Mateer, 1989). Although the disappointing research literature in memory rehabilitation efforts suggests the need for a cautious approach to evaluating efficacy studies in other cognitive domains (Cicerone & Tupper, 1986; Gordon, Hibbard, & Kreutzer, 1989), the clinical and experimental literature relevant to rehabilitation in these other cognitive domains suggests that interventions being developed hold more promise and should be vigorously and rigorously pursued (Lynch, 1988; Rimmele & Hester, 1987).

RESOLUTIONS:

Ideally, cognitive rehabilitation techniques and procedures should be empirically validated in the manner suggested by Paul (1969) who observes that the ultimate empirical validation question is...*What treatment, by whom, is most effective for this individual, with what specific problem, under which set of circumstances, and how does it come about?* (p. 62). Until such time as Paul's very demanding definition can be achieved, the following guidelines are suggested.

2.1 In view of the absence of evidence for the efficacy of memory drills for the purpose of generalizable memory improvement, there appears to be no empirical justification for clinical use of computers to these ends.

2.2 The use of computers to teach mnemonic strategies, as external aids, and as supports for employment appears to have more realistic and promising prospects, although much more research is needed before confident deployment in the clinical realm is justified (Kurlychek & Levin, 1987).

2.3 The efficacy of cognitive rehabilitation techniques should be evaluated in terms of the specific cognitive domains under study. Thus, negative findings in the domain of memory should not be unfairly generalized to potentially more remediable deficits in other areas (e.g., visuoperceptual disorders, attention). This implies that comprehensive neuropsychological examinations employing reliable and valid tests at strategic points independent of training content are an essential component of such programs of development. Standardized psychological and neuropsychological tests should not be utilized in cognitive remediation exercises or therapy.

2.4 Results of investigations based upon less than ideal research designs should not be subjected to perjorative dismissal if the limitations of such designs are explicitly stated by the investigator and appropriately modest conclusions are offered. Many clinical settings and difficult clinical questions may not lend themselves to rigorous experimental research but such considerations should not limit continuing investigation using other scientific methodologies (e.g., single-case design, systematic clinical observations). At the same time, reports of efficacy based upon uncontrolled case or cohort studies, testimonials, or anecdotal findings are unacceptable evidence of efficacy.

2.5 The Discussion and Resolutions offered under Issue 2 should be reviewed on a regular basis (e.g., every 5 years) and updated as required, based upon new research findings.

ISSUE 3: CONSUMER PROTECTION, RISK/BENEFIT ANALYSIS

As discussed thus far, clinical and research experience in cognitive rehabilitation warrants some degree of optimism about the clinical utility and efficacy of these procedures. Nonetheless, inherent risks appear to be present that must also be considered.

One potential risk of cognitive rehabilitation is that **false hopes may be raised,** and **denial of disability may be reinforced,** for the cognitively impaired individual and his or her family. This can occur because small objective gains in skill with a given training exercise may follow from long hours of interaction with the training task. These small gains become the straw of hope at which the disabled person and family grasp as evidence that further significant improvement will be forthcoming, even when all other evidence indicates future recovery of cognitive ability will be minimal.

A second risk is that the development of an isolated or task-specific skill may serve **as false evidence of general competency** for the cognitively-impaired individual and the family. In this way an inaccurate perception of the disabled individual emerges; this can interfere with rehabilitation efforts and recommendations for safe conduct. Generalization must be demonstrated and not merely presumed.

Thirdly, focusing efforts and time in the use of cognitive rehabilitation software runs the risk of **diverting attention from more problematic concerns** which potentially may be more directly remediable. These would include family problems, social and vocational adjustment issues, emotional disorders, and financial problems. Financial problems can, of course, be exacerbated by professional charges resulting from the interminable and inappropriate employment of cognitive rehabilitation software in treatment.

Fourth, significant time spent working with cognitive rehabilitation software may **perpetuate social isolation** of the cognitively disabled individual. Distractibility may be reduced through the utilization of the computer-patient interface in some cases, but this must be individually assessed.

RESOLUTIONS:

3.1 Risks can be reduced by the use of computer-assisted and other cognitive rehabilitation procedures in the context of an organized treatment program. In most cases, the best treatment program will be identified, implemented, and monitored by an interdisciplinary team of rehabilitation professionals.

3.2 Clinical neuropsychologists can make a unique contribution to cognitive rehabilitation efforts because, by virtue of their training, they are sensitive not only to the patient's cognitive problems, but also to issues related to personality, emotional disorders, family problems, and vocational concerns. It is generally acknowledged that this complex of issues can interact to have an adverse effect on an individual's functioning after brain injury.

3.2.1 In all treatment endeavors by clinical neuropsychologists, including cognitive rehabilitation, risks to the consumer are minimized by rigorous adherence to ethical standards as set forth in APA's *Ethical Principles for Psychologists* (1981).

3.2.2 Risks are minimized by setting standards for training and experience of all providers of cognitive rehabilitation. Issues related to such standards are discussed in Issue 4.

3.3 Risks are reduced by setting and meeting at least minimal standards for publication and dissemination of cognitive rehabilitation software. Proposed standards follow.

STANDARDS FOR PUBLICATION AND DISSEMINATION

3.3.1 Software publishers should support research on efficacy of cognitive rehabilitation computer programs and the academically free dissemination of reports, abstracts, and references.

3.3.2 When the software is sold, the purchasers should be encouraged to notify the publisher of reports of any additional efficacy studies by themselves or others.

3.3.3 The publisher should maintain and circulate a listing of efficacy studies, without regard to their outcome, to purchasers.

3.3.4 In consultation with the psychologist-author, the publisher should encourage research by providing cognitive rehabilitation software at cost to qualified investigators.

3.3.5 A review of existing research on the efficacy of the specific software package should be provided with the software. Studies should be reviewed in two categories: (a) single case, case series, and repeated measures designs; (b) designs including a control group and parametric statistics.

3.3.6 Publishers must avoid actual or implied claims about treatment efficacy that cannot be substantiated. If no studies exist to support the efficacy of the software, this should be clearly stated.

3.3.7 Psychologist-authors should require review and approval of all advertising of products using their name and/or materials, and should provide corrections to misleading or inaccurate statements.

3.3.8 Publishers should discourage the perception of cognitive rehabilitation software as a self-standing treatment and should encourage its perception as a tool to be used in treatment.

3.3.9 Publishers may consider a disclaimer such as the following: No claims for the specific, independent therapeutic value of this product are made. It should be used only with appropriate professional consultation.

3.3.10 Publishers should provide sufficient documentation to permit the purchaser to evaluate and use the software in an appropriate manner.

3.3.11 A statement of the rationale, the theoretical basis, and available normative data for the program should be provided.

3.3.12 A statement of the learning principles to be incorporated with the software should be provided, including suggested methods for (a) cueing/fading of prompts for correct responding, (b) reinforcement of correct responding, (c) shaping of incorrect to correct responses, (d) performance-determined task difficulty levels, (e) the range of compensatory skills or skill areas that the software promotes.

3.3.13 A description of persons for whom the software was designed should be provided, including: (a) age range of appropriate patients, (b) skill deficits that may be considered for treatment (e.g., attention, memory, visuospatial deficits), (c) visual and hearing ability required, (d) manual and bimanual dexterity required, (e) computer and keyboard familiarity required, (f) educational attainment required (e.g., reading ability, mathematics ability).

3.3.14 Information concerning technical aspects of the program should be provided, including a description of (a) input modes, (e.g., joystick, mouse, adapted keyboard, light pen, touch screen, voice activation); and (b) available output, (e.g., data analyses permitted, print-out options, comparisons across sessions).

3.3.15 The publisher should provide for follow-up consultation with the psychologist-author or with another psychologist assuming responsibility for the software, who will be available to consult and respond to inquiries relating to the use of the software. Publishers are urged to take affirmative action to encourage the utilization of this service, and to encourage feedback (not simply endorsements) from users.

3.3.16 Publishers should conform to the relevant guidelines on test development set forth in *Standards for Educational and Psychological Testing* (1985) and to the relevant sections of the *Code of Fair Testing Practices in Education* (1988).

3.4 Appropriate levels of professional consultation would be encouraged by labeling software in three classes as follows:

3.4.1 Class A: This program should be used only under the direct and continuous supervision of a qualified professional. Such programs are too difficult and complex for the majority of patients to use without such supervision. Other programs in this category may be simpler, but are designed for more severely handicapped persons. Both types of programs require a trained professional to explain and augment instructions, offer corrections, and provide appropriate reinforcement.

3.4.2 Class B: This program may be used independently by certain patients in a clinical setting with periodic or moderate professional supervision. Such programs allow some better functioning patients who have mastered more basic programs to participate in a more independent fashion in a controlled setting. The therapist is responsible for selecting difficulty level, responding to questions, and integrating computer rehabilitation with other therapies.

3.4.3 Class C: This program may be used independently by better functioning patients in nonclinical settings (e.g., home) with periodic professional supervision. Programs in this category should present instructions, cues, and feedback sufficient to allow relatively advanced patients to practice independently without daily supervision. With adequate consultation, family members may be able to assist. Regular professional consultation is important to permit the trainer to evaluate the appropriateness, progress, and effectiveness of both specific and general aspects of the cognitive rehabilitation program.

ISSUE 4. STANDARDS FOR SERVICE PROVIDERS: TRAINING AND EXPERIENCE

The employment of computer-assisted cognitive remediation procedures and cognitive rehabilitation is obviously not the sole province of the neuropsychologist. Guidelines proposed for training and experience must therefore strive for an appropriate and realistic balance between two major competing valences. On the one hand is the conceptual and functional premise of those professionals who hold that any applied clinical activity that seeks to acquire professional status, whether it be psychotherapy or computer-assisted cognitive remediation, requires mastery of a coherent, if not unique, body of scientific knowledge acquired through appropriate educational and training experiences. On the other hand is the observation of Hawley and Capshaw (1981) that de-professionalization appears to be gaining momentum throughout the world of work, particularly in the human services.

Tension between these competing views is not resolved but may be attenuated by reference to an interdisciplinary process in which specialized knowledge and skills are not focused in a single "specialist", but are implemented by a team of care providers. Fordyce (1981) offered the following distinction between multidisciplinary and interdisciplinary processes. *Both involve efforts by people from several disciplines, and both require that these people have at least passing familiarity with the knowledge and methods of the other disciplines. But interdisciplinary differs from multidisciplinary in that the end product of the effort - the outcome - can only be accomplished by a truly interactive effort and contributions from the disciplines involved. ...In a multidisciplinary exercise, two or more professions may make their respective contributions, but each contribution stands on its own feet and could emerge without the input of another* (p. 51).

A recurrent theme throughout this document has been that the training, experience, and skill of the service provider is critical to the effectiveness of computer-assisted cognitive rehabilitation. Cognitive rehabilitation is a service that requires a broad base of knowledge and skill. Ideally, cognitive rehabilitation service providers would be knowledgeable about the following: (a) basic relationships between specific brain dysfunction, cognition, behavior, and emotions; (b) basic research regarding specific cognitive processes, such as attention, memory, visuospatial skills, and higher-order abilities; (c) basic research regarding effectiveness of cognitive rehabilitation techniques; (d) behavioral principles for effecting change; (e) instructional methods for teaching individuals with specific cognitive dysfunction and/or learning disabilities; (f) methods for enhancing generalization of the effects of cognitive rehabilitation to the patient's functional abilities and everyday life; (g) basic computer use. Furthermore, the practitioners should have practical experience in cognitive rehabilitation with brain-damaged patients.

With a few isolated exceptions (Frangicetto, 1989), no formal training programs for providers of cognitive rehabilitation exist. No standards for, or system of, credentialing cognitive rehabilitation service providers exist (Kreutzer & Boake, 1987). Into this vacuum, individuals from a number of disciplines have entered to offer cognitive rehabilitation services: psychologists and neuropsychologists, speech pathologists, occupational therapists, and learning disability specialists. Each of these disciplinary groups comes to the enterprise of cognitive rehabilitation with specific knowledge and skill relevant to cognitive rehabilitation as well as with specific deficiencies. As mentioned previously, neuropsychologists are expert in understanding relationships between specific brain dysfunction, cognition, behavior, and emotions, but typically have no systematic training in methods to rehabilitate cognitive deficiencies. Speech pathologists have training in rehabilitating certain cognitive impairments within the language domain. Similarly, learning disability specialists are focused in their training to work with individuals, typically children and not adults, with specific problems that in some cases are similar to the problems of brain-damaged patients and in other cases are not. The training that occupational therapists receive in rehabilitation typically focuses on the development of functional skills, with significantly less emphasis on understanding underlying cognitive, emotional, and behavioral processes.

Thus, cognitive rehabilitation is not clearly the purview of any one discipline. Neuropsychology and other disciplines possess a base of knowledge and skill that is relevant to cognitive rehabilitation. These considerations lead to the following recommendations.

RESOLUTIONS:

4.1 Consideration should be given to the development of a curriculum for cognitive rehabilitation service providers at major universities, preferably taught by an interdisciplinary faculty. The program offered would include training as outlined in paragraphs three and four of this section. Such a program would be available to individuals from any rehabilitative discipline who would take this curriculum as a subspeciality area of their training.

4.2 Were specific standards for credentialing of cognitive rehabilitation service providers to be developed, such standards should include (a) degree requirements, such as, bachelor's degree in an educational, psychological, or rehabilitative discipline from an accredited college or university, educational and training requirements as outlined in the first paragraph of this section, and requirements for a specified time period (e.g., two years) of supervised practice in cognitive rehabilitation. Such standards would be best developed by an interdisciplinary group of rehabilitation specialists, such as the Interdisciplinary Special Interest Group on Head Injury of the American Congress of Rehabilitation Medicine (Harley, 1990), in conjunction with interdisciplinary groups such as the International Neuropsychological Society and disciplinary groups such as the American Speech and Hearing Association, American Occupational Therapy Association, and Divisions 22 (Rehabilitation Psychology) and 40 (Clinical Neuropsychology) of the American Psychological Association.

4.3 Until such time as training and standards for cognitive rehabilitation are developed, appropriate training and supervision of cognitive rehabilitation providers remains the responsibility of individual rehabilitation centers and providers. Systems for supervision of cognitive rehabilitation services should be developed within rehabilitation centers. It would be appropriate that such supervision would, in part, be within individual disciplines. Overall supervision of the cognitive rehabilitation program and of individual providers and trainees would be best offered through an interdisciplinary group consisting, at a minimum, of a neuropsychologist, speech pathologist, and occupational therapist.

ISSUE 5: ETHICAL STANDARDS FOR SERVICE PROVIDERS

Of the 10 guidelines that governed the preparation of the 1985 APA *Standards for Educational and Psychological Testing,* four are particularly germane to the *Guidelines for Computer-Assisted Neuropsychological Rehabilitation and Cognitive Remediation.* First, a statement of technical standards for sound professional practice should be presented rather than a social action prescription. Second, a strong ethical imperative should be embodied, though it was recognized that enforcement mechanisms could not be included. Third, all standards would not be uniformly applicable across a wide range of instruments and uses. Fourth, standards should be presented at a level that would enable a wide range of people who work with tests or test results to use the *Standards.* The *Standards for Educational and Psychological Testing* document was formulated with the intent of being consistent with the APA *Standards for Providers of Psychological Services* (1977) and with the APA's *Ethical Principles of Psychologists* (1981) which are binding on members of APA. The *Standards for Educational and Psychological Testing* Committee suggested that "those who are not members of APA consider the ethical principles to be advisory in general outline if not in detail" (p. vii). This same suggestion obtains with respect to the *Guidelines for Computer-Assisted Neuropsychological Rehabilitation and Cognitive Remediation.*

RESOLUTIONS:

5.1 The clinical neuropsychologist in his/her professional relationships with other professional disciplines who may also be employing cognitive remediation procedures will exercise as a starting point ethical principles 2 and 7 from the APA *Ethical Principles for Psychologists* (1981) namely, the requirement that ...*the psychologist recognizes the areas of competence of related professionals, making full use of the professional, technical and administrative resources that best serve the needs of consumers* (p. 636).

5.2 As with any clinical technique or tool, cognitive remediation procedures should be used in a responsible manner by responsible, skilled, and knowledgeable clinicians.

5.3 Cognitive remediation programs should be used in the context of a treatment plan with a specific rationale to achieve specific goals for a specific individual having specific problems.

5.4 The clinician prescribing the use of cognitive remediation software programs would necessarily have to be knowledgeable about several areas, including rehabilitation generally, brain-behavior relationships, cognitive science, and learning theory, as well as the specific features of the program including the validity evidence or lack thereof (see introduction to Issue 4 above).

5.5 Qualified practitioners should either have specific course work that will assist them in understanding neurobehavioral problems and deficits or have formalized training (such as internships, workshops, or directly supervised work experiences) in brain-behavior relationships sufficient to acquire functional understanding of the impact of specific brain injuries on behavior (see 4.1 and 4.2 above).

5.6 There are, at present, no formal mechanisms either to ratify an individual's credentials as a qualified practitioner or to monitor the compliance of an individual with specific ethical standards. There are no formal mechanisms to assure the regular upgrading of such special proficiency skills through continuing education courses. This being the case, it is, ultimately, the responsibility of the individual clinician to determine if he/she is sufficiently qualified. This determination should be made with consideration of both the welfare of the client and the ethical standards of the practitioner's own professional discipline.

ISSUE 6: EPILOGUE

The Division 40 Task Force adopts no specific position at this time on the question of requiring/adopting certification or licensing criteria for neuropsychologists who desire to be identified as possessing a special competency in cognitive remediation techniques. Were such special competencies deemed to be desirable, possible mechanisms for implementation are offered in 4.1 and 4.2 above.

Predictably, given the mandate from the Division 40 Executive Committee to prepare the present document, the Task Force feels strongly about the need for the Guidelines document offered here. Consequently, the Committee disagrees with Kramer (1985) who, referring specifically to computer-based test interpretation...*remains skeptical about the ultimate need for separate [ethical] guidelines for computer-based test interpretation [or within the present context, computer-assisted cognitive remediation techniques] ...perhaps,as a result of the advent and popularization of (these techniques) we will need to revise the* Standards for Providers of Psychological Services (1977), revamp the Standards for Educational and Psychological Testing (1985) or even redo the Ethical Principles for Psychologists (1981), *but in the final analysis these documents provide clear [procedural and ethical] guidelines for those desiring assistance in the determination of appropriate practices in the use of the techniques. We should*

134

*not saddle computer-based test interpretation [or cognitive remediation] with
separate technical and ethical guidelines simply because it is the application of a
powerful technology* (p. 320).

The Committee, on the contrary, presents the proposed Division 40 Guidelines
as a reasonable and necessary expansion and specific application of the more
generic APA ethical *Principles and Standards* documents cited in the quotation.
It is the Committee's hope that the proposed Guidelines document will, in fact,
be viewed as fully congruent with and entirely supportive of Kramer's conclud-
ing statement: i.e., *as in all our work, we must remain vigilant so that technology
is not abused in a manner that does harm to people or our profession* (p. 320).

REFERENCES

American Psychological Association. (1977). *Standards for providers of psychological
    services.* Washington, DC: Author.
American Psychological Association. (1981). Ethical principles for psychologists.
    American Psychologist, 36, 633-638.
American Psychological Association. (1985). *Standards for educational and psychologi-
    cal testing.* Washington, DC: Author.
American Psychological Association. (1986). *Guidelines for computer-based tests and
    interpretations.* Washington, DC: Author.
American Psychological Association. (1987). General guidelines for providers of psy-
    chological services. *American Psychologist, 42,* 712-723.
American Psychological Association. (1987). Resolutions approved by the national con-
    ference on graduate education in psychology. *American Psychologist, 42,* 1070-1084.
American Psychological Association. (1988). *Code of fair testing practices in education.*
    Washington, DC: Joint Committee on Testing Practices.
Batchelor, J., Shores, E.A., Marosszeky, J.E., Sandanam, J., & Lovarini, M. (1988).
    Cognitive rehabilitation of severely closed-head-injured patients using computer-
    assisted and noncomputerized treatment techniques. *Journal of Head Trauma
    Rehabilitation, 3,* 78-85.
Ben-Yishay, Y., Piasetsky, E., & Rattok, J. (1987). A systematic method of ameliorating
    disorders in basic attention. In M. J. Meier, A. L. Benton, & L. Diller (Eds.),
    Neuropsychological rehabilitation (pp.165-181). New York: Guilford Press.
Ben-Yishay, Y., & Prigatano, G. P. (1990). Cognitive remediation. In M. Rosenthal, E. R.
    Griffith, M. R. Bond, & J. D. Miller (Eds.), *Rehabilitation of the adult and child
    with traumatic brain injury* (pp. 393-409). Philadelphia: F. A. Davis.
Cermak, L. (1975). Imagery as an aid to retrieval for Korsakoff patients. *Cortex, 11,* 163-
    169.
Chute, D.L., Conn, G., Dipasquale, M.C., & Hoag, M. (1988). ProsthesisWare: New class
    of software supporting the activities of daily living. *Neuropsychology, 2,* 41-57.
Cicerone, K. D., & Tupper, D.E. (1986). Cognitive assessment in the neuropsychological
    rehabilitation of head-injured adults. In B.P. Uzzell & Y. Gross (Eds.), *Clinical
    neuropsychology of intervention* (pp. 59-83). Boston: Martinus Nijhoff Publishing.
Crovitz, H. (1979). Memory retraining in brain-damaged patients: The airplane list. *Cortex,
    15,* 131-144.
Crovitz, H., Harvey, M., & Horn, R. (1979). Problems in the acquisition of imagery
    mnemonics: Three brain-damaged cases. *Cortex, 15,* 224-234.
Division 40: Task Force Report on Computer-Assisted Neuropsychological Evaluation
    (1987). *The Clinical Neuropsychologist, 2,* 161-184.

Fordyce, W. (1981). On interdisciplinary peers. *Archives of Physical Medicine, 62,* 51-53.

Frangicetto, T.J. (1989). Northampton Community College-Cognitive Retraining Program. Unpublished paper.

Gianutsos, R., & Gianutsos, J. (1979). Rehabilitating the verbal recall of brain-damaged patients by mnemonic training: An experimental demonstration using single-case methodology. *Journal of Clinical Neuropsychology, 1,* 117-135.

Gianutsos, R., & Matheson, P. (1987). The rehabilitation of visual perceptual disorders attributable to brain injury. In M. J. Meier, A. L. Benton, & L. Diller (Eds.), *Neuropsychological rehabilitation* (pp. 202-241). New York: Guilford Press.

Glasgow, R. E., Zeiss, R. A., Barrera, M., Jr., & Lewinsohn, P. M. (1977). Case studies on remediating memory deficits in brain-injured individuals. *Journal of Clinical Psychology, 33,* 1049-1054.

Glisky, E., & Schacter, D. (1987). Acquisition of domain-specific knowledge in organic amnesia: Training for computer-related work. *Neuropsychologia, 25,* 893-906.

Glisky, E., Schacter, D., & Tulving, E. (1986a). Computer learning by memory-impaired patients: Acquisition and retention of complex knowledge. *Neuropsychologia, 24,* 313-328.

Glisky, E., Schacter, D., & Tulving, E. (1986b). Learning and retention of computer-related vocabulary in amnesic patients: Method of vanishing cues. *Journal of Clinical and Experimental Neuropsychology, 8,* 292-312.

Godfrey, H., & Knight, R. (1985). Cognitive rehabilitation of memory functioning in amnesic patients. *Journal of Consulting and Clinical Psychology, 53,* 555-567.

Goldstein, F. C., & Levin, H. S. (1987). Disorders of reasoning and problem-solving ability. In M. J. Meier, A. L. Benton, & L. Diller (Eds.), *Neuropsychological Rehabilitation.* (pp. 327-354). New York: Guilford.

Gordon, W.A., Hibbard, M.R., & Kreutzer, J.S. (1989). Cognitive remediation: Issues in research and practice. *Journal of Head Trauma Rehabilitation, 4,* 76-84.

Gordon, W., Hibbard, M., Egelko, S., Diller, L., Shauer, M., Lieberman, A., & Ragnarssen, K. (1985). Perceptual remediation in patients with right brain damage: A comprehensive program. *Archives of Physical Medicine and Rehabilitation, 66,* 353-359.

Gouvier, D., Webster, J.S., & Blanton, P.D. (1987). Cognitive retraining with brain-damaged patients. In D. Wedding, A.M. Horton, & J. Webster (Eds.), *The neuropsychology handbook: Behavioral and clinical perspectives* (pp. 278-324). New York: Springer.

Harley, J. P. (1990). Standards for cognitive rehabilitation. Head Injury Interdisciplinary Special Interest Group, American Congress of Rehabilitation Medicine.

Harris, J. (1984). Methods of improving memory. In B. Wilson & N. Moffat (Eds.), *Clinical management of memory problems* (pp.46-62). Rockville, MD: Aspen Systems Corporation.

Hawley, L., & Capshaw, T. (1981). In W. Emener, R. Luck, & S. Smits, (Eds.), *Rehabilitation Administration and Supervision* (pp. 281-303). Baltimore: University Park Press.

Jaffe, P., & Katz, A. (1975). Attenuating anterograde amnesia in Korsakoff's psychosis. *Journal of Abnormal Psychology, 34,* 559-62.

Kirsch, H., Levine, S.P., Fallon-Krueger, M., & Jaros, L. A. (1987). The microcomputer as an "orthotic device" for patients with cognitive deficits. *Journal of Head Trauma Rehabilitation, 2,* 77-86.

Kramer, J. (1985). Epilogue. *Computers in Human Behavior, 1,* 317-320.

Kruetzer, J.S., & Boake, C. (1987). Addressing disciplinary issues in cognitive rehabilitation: Definition, training, and organization. *Brain Injury, 1,* 199-202.

Kurlychek, R. (1983). Use of a digital alarm chronograph as memory aid in early dementia. *Clinical Gerontologist, 1,* 93-94.

Kurlychek, R., & Levin, W. (1987). Computers in the cognitive rehabilitation of brain-

136

injured persons. *CRC Critical Reviews in Medical Informatics, 1,* 241-257.

Lewinsohn, P., Danaher, B., & Kikel, S. (1977). Visual imagery as a mnemonic aid for brain-damaged persons. *Journal of Consulting and Clinical Psychology , 45,* 717-723.

Lynch, W. J. (1988). Microcomputer technology in the rehabilitation of brain disorders. In M. Eisenberg & R. Grzesiak (Eds.), *Advances in clinical rehabilitation* (pp.41-58). New York, NY: Springer.

Malec, J. (1986). A flow chart for cognitive rehabilitation. Paper presented at the Seventh Annual Braintree Conference on Traumatic Head Injury.

Malec, J., & Questad, K. (1983). Rehabilitation of memory after craniocerebral trauma: Case report. *Archives of Physical Medicine and Rehabilitation, 64,* 436-43.

O'Connor, M., & Cermak, L. (1987). Rehabilitation of organic memory disorders. In M. J. Meier, A. L. Benton, & L. Diller (Eds.), *Neuropsychological rehabilitation* (pp. 260 - 279). New York: Guilford Press.

Parenté, R., & Anderson-Parenté, J. K. (1989). Retraining memory: Theory and application. *Journal of Head Trauma Rehabilitation, 4,* 55-65.

Paul, G. L. (1969). Behavior modification research: Design and tactics. In C. M. Franks (Ed.), *Behavior therapy: Appraisal and status* (pp. 29-62). New York: McGraw-Hill.

Prigatano, G.P. (1986). *Neuropsychological rehabilitation after brain injury.* Baltimore: Johns Hopkins University Press.

Prigatano, G., Fordyce, D., Zeiner, H., Roueche, J., Pepping, M., & Wood, B. (1984). Neuropsychological rehabilitation after closed head injury in young adults. *Journal of Neurology, Neurosurgery, and Psychiatry, 47,* 505-513.

Rimmele, C.T., & Hester, R.K. (1987). Cognitive rehabilitation after head injury. *Archives of Clinical Neuropsychology, 2,* 353-384.

Ruff, R.M., Baser, C.A., Johnston, J.W., Marshall, L.F., Klauber, S.K., Klauber, M.R., & Minteer, M. (1989). Neuropsychological rehabilitation: An experimental study with head-injured patients. *Journal of Head Trauma Rehabilitation, 4,* 20-36.

Schacter, D. L., & Glisky, E.L. (1986). Memory remediation: Restoration, alleviation, and the acquisition of domain-specific knowledge. In B. Uzzel & Y. Gross (Eds.), *Clinical neuropsychology of intervention* (pp. 257-282). Boston: Martinus Nijhoff.

Schacter, D., Rich, S., & Stampp, M. (1985). Remediation of memory disorders: Experimental evaluation of the spaced-retrieval technique. *Journal of Clinical and Experimental Neuropsychology, 7,* 79-96.

Silbeck, C. (1984). Computer assistance in the management of memory and cognitive impairment. In B. Wilson & N. Moffat (Eds.), *Clinical management of memory problems* (pp. 112-131). Rockville, MD: Aspen Systems Corporation.

Sohlberg, M.M., & Mateer, C.A. (1989). *Introduction to cognitive rehabilitation.* New York: Guilford Press.

Wilson, B. (1982). Success and failure in memory training following a cerebral vascular accident. *Cortex, 18,* 581-594.

Wilson, B. (1987). *Rehabilitation of memory.* New York: Guilford Press.

Wilson, B., & Moffat, N. (1984). *Clinical management of memory problems.* Rockville, MD: Aspen Systems Corporation.

The Clinical Neuropsychologist
1987, Vol. 1, No. 4, pp. 353-363

Social Security Disability
and
Clinical Neuropsychological Assessment

Antonio E. Puente
University of North Carolina at Wilmington

ABSTRACT

This paper reviews the guidelines for Social Security disability evaluation of mental impairments in general and organic syndromes in particular. The listings of diagnostic categories for application and procedures for evaluation are outlined. The qualifications and roles of the clinical neuropsychologist are discussed. In addition, the special problem of malingering is considered.

According to recent figures (Bowe, 1980), approximately 15% of the population of the United States, or over 35 million people, have some type of physical or mental disability. While a significant percentage of children have disabilities (10%; Asch, 1984), most disabled individuals tend to be adults. The incidence of specific work disability increases with age (3% between 16 and 25 years to 24% between 55 and 64 years; US Bureau of the Census, 1983). Low income, limited education, and minority racial status also appear to be associated with more frequent work disability (US Bureau of the Census, 1983).

Since most disabled individuals are unable to be employed, other financial support is often sought. *Worker's (or workmen's) compensation* is one source of support covering work-related disabilities. This type of support has a ceiling of payments limiting the financial resources available to the disabled individual. Worker's compensation rules and support payments vary by state and are often supplemented by other nonoccupational disability insurance which covers injuries and/or illnesses. For this additional insurance, the injury may be either work- or non-work-related.

A preliminary version of this paper was presented at the meeting of the American Psychological Association in Washington, D.C., 1986. The author acknowledges comments on the manuscript by Michael Glancy and J. Randall Price.

While these types of support are often pursued by the disabled worker, Social Security disability assistance is by far the most common type of disability coverage currently available in the United States. When a worker has been declared totally and permanently disabled, Social Security disability may be requested. It is important to note that disability does not mean impairment. The latter involves anatomical (usually diagnosed by a physician) or functional (often diagnosed by a psychologist) abnormality or loss (American Medical Association, 1984). The assessment of disability is made on a strictly administrative analysis which involves determining the employability of an individual, regardless of the abnormality or loss claimed. Indeed, disability is defined by the Social Security Administration (SSA) as "inability to engage in any substantial activity by reason of any medically determinable physical or mental impairment which can be expected to result in death or which has lasted or can be expected to last for a continuous period of not less than 12 months" (pp. 162, Social Security Administration, 1986).

SOCIAL SECURITY DISABILITY

Of the 2.5 million individuals who receive financial assistance from Social Security, approximately 300,000 were deemed to have mental impairment (Rosenberg, 1986). Mental impairments are exceeded only by circulatory system disorders in prevalence of disability (Social Security Administration, 1985).

In 1985 alone 5,809,785 applications for disability benefits were received by the Social Security Administration (Social Security Administration, 1985). Of these, 1,278,338 persons were found disabled upon initial review by the staff of the Social Security Administration (SSA) at the state levels. About one-half of the 718,991 applications that were denied and underwent appeal reconsideration were decided in favor of the applicant. Of those whose applications were rejected after reconsideration, 245,090 individuals requested a hearing but only 102,130 were considered disabled by the Administrative Law Judge (ALJ) who presided over these nonjuried hearings.

In addition to these first-time applicants for SSA Disability, a large percentage of those already on the disability rolls are reviewed yearly by the SSA to determine whether their disability is still "marked" enough to prevent being gainfully employed. By most major estimates, the number of cases reviewed appear to be doubling yearly (United States Senate, 1982). According to the Committee on Governmental Affairs, 160,000 cases were reviewed in 1980 while 840,000 were reviewed in 1983. It is important to note that these reviews were in addition to the reviews completed at the time of the initial application for disability. Thus, the total number of individuals applying and being reviewed for Social Security Disability is clearly on the increase. Of all Social Security cases, a significant portion are mental impairment cases. Estimates vary according to state as well as region, but in some jurisdictions they may constitute up to 50% of the applicant population. According to Nancy Dapper (1987), Acting Executive Program Policy Officer for the Social Security Administration, over the fiscal years 1984, 1985, and 1986, an average of 348,151 mental impairment cases were reviewed by SSA per year. This represents about 24.3% of the total workload for SSA. Of the total number of mental impairment cases, 146,842 or 41% were organically related syndromes (i.e., organic mental disorder at 6%, mental retardation at 35%). The number of mental retardation cases relative to organic mental disorders may be inflated due to the perceived difficulty by attorneys and legal representatives to meet the SSA organic brain syndrome listing.

Under the new regulations, in order to determine the existence and degree of a functional impairment, SSA will consider evidence from four sources (National Organization of Social Security Claimant's Representatives, 1985). These sources include the claimant, Disability Determination Services (state level employees of SSA) personnel, professional health case workers (psychiatric social workers), and medical professionals (psychiatrists and psychologists). Evidence from significant others and work evaluations (e.g., sheltered workshop vocational evaluations) may also be useful.

Table 1. Social Security Disability Procedure and Appeals Jurisdictions.

---

1. Initial Application at Local District Office
      (obtain vocational and medical history)
         If No Disability Found,

2. State Disability Determination Unit*
      (compare medical documentation to Social Security Listings)
         If No Disability Found,

3. Refile at Local District Office
      (obtain additional information)
         If No Disability Found,

4. Office of Hearings and Appeals*
      (Administrative Law Judge/Hearing)
         If No Disability Found,

5. Appeals Council
      (review of case)
         If No Disability Found,

6. Federal Court*
      (new hearing)

---

*   Stages where neuropsychological evaluation may be requested.

The procedure for determing disability using the aforementioned evidence is found in Table 1. Essentially, disability status cannot be achieved if the individual is employed. If the claimant is not employed, the individual is evaluated based on specified "listings". A listing is a diagnostic category based in large part on DSM-III nomenclature. The claimant must (1) directly meet or fit a listing (in this case organic brain syndrome or mental retardation), (2) have a combination of impairments (e.g., organic brain syndrome and depression), (3) have limited medical improvements related to employment, or (4) not be able to retain previous or other (transferable skills) work. Of these, SSA officials appear to prefer directly meeting or fitting a specific mental impairment listing.

At the present time there are nine separate listings for categorizing mental impairments (Social Security Administration, 1986). These include, organic mental disorders, schizophrenia, paranoid, or other psychotic disorders, affective disorders, mental retardation and autism, anxiety-related disorders, somatoform disorders, personality, and substance addiction disorders. Of particular relevance for neuropsychologists is the organic mental disorder listing. Table 2 provides the definition or listing of organic mental disorder encompassing two separate categories, termed Part A and B. Part A contains many of the classical symptoms of "organicity" (e.g., memory impairment), while Part B (which is shared with the other listings) focuses on the effects of the symptoms of Part A or the functional capacity of the person. However, *both* Parts A and B must be evaluated and met to qualify under a listing.

A typical problem in a neuropsychological evaluation of organic syndromes is the minimizing or overlooking Part B of the listing. It is imperative that the clinical neuropsychologist attempt to translate test findings into everyday functional limitations. For activities of daily living, one might extrapolate to behaviors such as home-related chores (e.g., cooking), handling of own benefits, and using public transportation and communication. Social function involves a patient's "capacity to interact appropriately and communicate effectively with other individuals" (pg. 64, SSA, 1986). The third portion of part B may be easier to address in that it involves concentration, persistence, and pace or the ability to "sustain focused attention" long enough to complete a task in a timely fashion. The final portion of Part B is associated with a claimant's continued failure (i.e., deterioration or decompensation) to successfully engage in or adapt to stressful situations.

Table 2. Organic Mental Disorders Listings.

Organic Mental Disorders: Psychological or behavioral abnormalities associated with a dysfunction of the brain. History and physical examination or laboratory tests demonstrate the presence of a specific organic factor judged to be etiologically related to the abnormal mental state and loss of previously acquired functional abilities.

The required level of severity for these disorders is met when the requirements in both A and B are satisfied.

    A. Demonstration of loss of specific cognitive abilities or affective changes and the medically documented persistence of at least one of the following:
1. Disorientation to time and place; or
2. Memory impairment, either short-term (inability to learn new information), intermediate, or long-term (inability to remember information that was known sometime in the past); or
3. Perceptual or thinking disturbances (e.g., hallucinations, delusions); or
4. Change in personality; or
5. Disturbance in mood; or
6. Emotional lability (e.g., explosive temper outburst, sudden crying, etc) and impairment in impulse control; or
7. Loss of measured intellectual ability of at least 15 IQ points from premorbid levels or overall impairment index clearly within the severely impaired range on neuropsychological testing, e.g., the Luria Nebraska, Halstead-Reitan, etc; AND

    B. Resulting in at least two of the following:
1. Marked restriction of activities of daily living, or
2. Marked difficulties in maintaining social funtioning, or
3. Deficiencies of concentration, persistence or pace resulting in frequent failure to complete tasks in a timely manner (in work settings or elsewhere); or
4. Repeated episodes of deterioration or decompensation on work or work-like settings which cause the individual to withdraw from that situation or to experience exacerbation of signs and symptoms (which may include deterioration of adaptive behaviors).

Note. From *Disability evaluation under Social Security: A handbook for physicians.* Social Security Administration, 1986, Washington, DC: Author.

THE ROLE OF THE CLINICAL NEUROPSYCHOLOGIST IN THE DISABILITY PROCESS

According to recent guidelines of the SSA (1986), the definition of a "qualified" psychologist has been revised. The new revision, which is based in part on the American Psychological Association's recommendation (see Goodstein, 1986), indicates that an examiner must (1) possess a doctoral degree in psychology (rather than just "clinical psychology" as was stated in earlier guidelines) from

142

an educational institution accredited by an organization recognized by the Council of Post-Secondary Accreditation, (2) have 2 years of supervised experience in health services of which one must be postdoctoral, and (3) have a license or certification as a psychologist at the independent practice level of psychology by the state in which he or she resides. Applications for consultant status must be made directly to the state SSA office.

While the definition of "qualified" psychologist is clearly outlined, little or no attention has been paid to determining what constitutes a neuropsychologist. Presumably any "qualified" psychologist could complete a neuropsychological evaluation, but the Divison 40/INS Guidelines (TCN, Volume 1, Number 1, pp. 29-34) make it clear that more than self-scrutiny will be required in the future.

Surprisingly, the neuropsychological evaluation is relatively well-defined by the tests (though not procedures) which are considered acceptable. The procedures are outlined for the general evaluation of mental impairments and not for any of the specific listings. These procedures are found in 416,920a of the Federal Register (1985) but do not address specific guidelines with regard to organic syndromes. In their "Final Report" of August, 1985, the SSA stated "The results of *well-standardized* tests such as the WAIS, MMPI, the Rorschach and the TAT may be useful in establishing the existence of a mental disorder (pp. 36057)." They add "Broad-based neuropsychological assessments using, for example, the Halstead-Reitan or the Luria-Nebraska batteries may be useful in determining brain function deficiencies, particularly in cases involving subtle findings such as may be seen in traumatic brain injuries." However, on May 29, 1986 SSA revised and expanded the original list of acceptable psychological tests to include the following 11 tests; Boston Diagnostic Aphasia Examination, McCarthy Scale of Children's Abilities, the Stanford-Binet Intelligence Scale (3rd ed.), Wechsler Intelligence Scale for Children-Revised, Wechsler Adult Intelligence Scale-Revised, the Peabody Picture Vocabulary Test-Revised, the Luria-Nebraska Neuropsychological Battery, the Millon Behavioral Health Inventory and Adolescent Personality Survey as well as the Clinical Multiaxial Inventory, and the Kaufman Assessment Battery for Children. According to the Federal Register, the Luria-Nebraska is "a better technique because it provides a low cost, portable, relatively brief alternative to the Halstead-Reitan Neuropsychological Battery" (pp 19417). In addition, while not explicitly stated, the SSA does not favorably view customized, flexible, or nonstandardized batteries or tests.

Regardless of the tests used, specific factors are considered by SSA in determining whether a claimant meets the organic listing. These factors must be addressed directly in the neuropsychological evaluation (see Table 2). In turn, the Office of Hearing and Appeals residential staff person, often a psychiatrist or psychologist, completes a residual function capacity questionnaire (RFC). At a higher level, the Office of Health Administration, the RFC may be completed either by an Administrative Law Judge or the Medical Advisor. Table 3 provides the basic RFC and Likert-type scale used to quantify the existence and/or extent of brain dysfunction.

Table 3. Residual Functional Capacity Questionaire for Organic Mental disorders.

—————— No evidence of a sign or symptom CLUSTER or SYNDROME which appropriately fits with this diagnostic category. (Some features appearing below may be present in the case but they are presumed to belong in another disorder and are rated in that category).

—————— Psychological or behavioral abnormalities associated with a dysfunction of the brain ... as evidenced by at least one of the following:

Present-Absent-Insufficient	Evidence
1. ____ ____ ____	Disorientation to time and place
2. ____ ____ ____	Memory Impairment
3. ____ ____ ____	Perceptual or thinking disturbances
4. ____ ____ ____	Change in personality
5. ____ ____ ____	Disturbance in mood
6. ____ ____ ____	Emotional lability and impairment in impulse control
7. ____ ____ ____	Loss of measured intellectual ability of at least 15 IQ points from premorbid levels or overall impairment index clearly within the severely impaired on neuropsychological testing, e.g., the Luria-Nebraska, Halstead-Reitan, etc.
8. ____ ____ ____	Other

One of the most complicated evaluation issues in Social Security work is that of "accident neurosis" and malingering. In his classic article, the neurologist Henry Miller (1961) reviewed 200 cases of head injury of which 47 had "gross and unequivocally psychoneurotic complaints." According to Miller, the less serious the injury, the lower the social status, and the more diffuse the injury, the more likely that nonorganic factors were responsible for the clinical picture. The postconcussional syndrome was really a sign of neurosis, according to Miller. However, this initial finding, while often cited, has not been supported by more recent studies. In his presidential address to the section of Neurology of the Royal Society of Medicine (1981), Kelly provided evidence of a "true" posttraumatic or concussional syndrome with a pool of 800 (compared to Miller's pool of 4,000 subjects of which only 200 cases were actually reviewed). Despite numerous methodological problems with the Miller study and contrary evidence such as that provided by Kelly, SSA Personnel often refer to this study in evaluating the importance of malingering in disability cases.

In a recent review, Binder (1986) evaluated numerous studies and concluded that the effects of compensation are often secondary to the original symptom of mild head injury. However, it is clearly up to the clinical neuropsychologist to address carefully and comprehensively the issue of malingering in dealing with such cases since a finding of malingering is a common reason for denial of compensation in forensic cases (Larson, 1970).

Documentation of malingering in Social Security Disability cases poses special difficulties for the clinical neuropsychologist since it is commonly an issue. According to Resnick (1984), malingerers of mental illness in general overreact, call attention to their plight, have more difficulty imitating form than content of the disorder, often do not fit a clear diagnostic entity, and do not show perseveration. While Resnick's observations do provide a foundation for detecting malingering in mental impairment cases, they do not specifically address faking of organic deficits.

An essential initial step in detecting malingering in organic cases is to obtain extensive premorbid history. Evidence from significant others and employers is considered helpful by the SSA. This history taking is especially critical since Social Security cases usually present little if any well-documented history or records and the claimants are often poor historians.

Besides extensive history taking, the clinical neuropsychologist may look for specific patterns of responding on the psychometric tests accepted by SSA. For example, Gynther (1961) has suggested that the F and K scales may be useful in detecting faking on the MMPI. According to Gynther, the F scale is rarely endorsed by psychiatric patients while the K scale is considered to affect the overall clinical profile. However, Gynther did suggest that the F-K dis-simulation index may be more sensitive than either the F or K scales alone. Initial norms for the F-K index were presented by Gough in 1950 and were recently revised by Osborne, Collegan, and Offord (1986). Using normal subjects, Grow, McVaugh, and Eno (1980) reported that the F-K ≥ 7 was useful for detecting faking bad while F-K ≤ -11 suggested faking good. Using organic and nonorganic subjects, Heaton, Smith, Lehman, and Vogt (1978) suggested that an F-K index exceeding a score of 5 was useful for detecting faking. In a related effort, Greene (1978) developed the Carelessness Scale which helps detect poor attention, lack of interest, or simply the inability to complete the MMPI. Nevertheless, care must be taken in using the MMPI with nonwhite and low SES-educational attainment groups (Gynther, 1972) which comprise a substantial portion of Social Security claimants.

One of the earliest studies addressing malingering in neuropsychological cases was reported by Benton and Spreen (1961). Using the Visual Memory Test, Benton et al. found that faking could be detected quantitatively since fakers did worse than the brain-damage sample on this test. Qualitative analyses indicated that errors of omission were more frequently observed in the faking group. According to Heaton et al. (1978), neuropsychological judges were able to correctly classify between 44-81% of head-injured cases and between 25-81% of malingering cases. The authors concluded that an expert's ability to detect malingering in neuropsychological cases ranged from chance to 20%. Interestingly, experience of the judges was not correlated to the correct detection of faking.

Using a larger sample of subjects but only one neuropsychological judge, Goebel (1983) administered the Halstead-Reitan Neuropsychological Test Battery to both control and damaged subjects. The author reported a hit rate of 94.4% and concluded that it was difficult for an average-IQ, nonimpaired individual to fake brain dysfunction. Mensch and Woods (1986) used more judges and average to above-average IQ subjects who were administered the Luria-Nebraska Neuropsychological Battery on two separate occasions; one time the subjects were instructed to fake and another not to fake brain damage. The author reported that the sensorimotor items of the Motor, Rhythm, and Tactile scales were most often "faked" with errors of speed and intention commonplace. While these studies do address malingering directly, the question of faking in clinical (rather than normal) populations, especially in forensic cases, needs to be addressed further. One useful method for detecting faking appears to be the Symptom Validity Testing of Binder and Pankratz (1987). Using 100 trials of visual or auditory stimuli with distraction, this procedure appeared to reliably reflect faking of memory problems. A common theme of inconsistency of test performance surfaces in each of these findings (Keschner, 1960).

Nevertheless Binder (1986) suggested that "Malingering can only be detected through the use of clinical judgment, as there are no empirically validated objective criteria for the identification of malingering on neuropsychological testing" (pp 332). This view is consonant with earlier studies (e.g., Heaton et al., 1978) indicating that clinicians could detect protocols "faked" the bad neuropsychologically.

IN CLOSING

Revisions of Federal Guidelines in recent years have made it possible for psychologists to render consultation in Social Security disability cases. The qualifications and procedures regulating this type of practice are likely to undergo further development. For example, the General Accounting Office (GAO) has been closely monitoring the implementation of the new mental impairment criteria and has strongly advocated a more accurate interpretation of the criteria as well as of medical (e.g., psychological) evidence, and for more mental health resources (GAO, 1986). Neuropsychologists can bring special skills to bear in cases involving brain-behavior impairment and related disability. Those practitioners providing such opinions may help to improve the accuracy and quality of disability determinations *via* ongoing education and communication with patients, officials, and other clinical neuropsychologists.

146

REFERENCES

American Medical Association. (1984). *Guides to the evaluation of permanent improvement.* Washington, DC: Author.

Asch, A. (1984). The experience of disability. *American Psychologist, 39,* 529-536.

Benton, A.L., & Spreen, O. (1961). Visual memory test: The simulation of mental incapacity. *Archives of Clinical Psychiatry, 4,* 79-83.

Binder, L.M. (1986). Persisting symptoms after mild head injury: A review of the postconcussive syndrome. *Journal of Clinical and Experimental Neuropsychology, 8,* 323-346.

Binder, L.M., & Pankratz, L. (1987). Neuropsychological evidence of a factitious memory complaint. *Journal of Clinical and Experimental Neuropsychology, 9,* 167-171.

Bowe, F. (1980). *Rehabilitating America.* New York: Harper and Row.

Committee on Governmental Affairs of the United States Senate (1982). *Oversight of the Social Security Administration review.* Washington, DC: US Government Printing Office.

Dapper, N.J. (1987, February 18). (Selected Social Security Disability determination data concerning mental impairments, FY 84 - FY 86.) Unpublished data. (Available from the Social Security Administration, Baltimore, MD 21235).

Department of Health and Human Resources. (1985). *Evaluation of mental impairments. Federal Register,* August 28, *5,* 167, 35038-35070, Part V, Department of Health and Human Services, 20 CFR Part 404.

General Accounting Office (1986). Social Security: Implementation of new mental impairment criteria for disability benefits. (GAO) HRD-86-75BR). Washington, DC: U.S. Government Printing Office.

Goebel, R.A. (1983). Detection of faking on the Halstead-Reitan Neuropsychological Test Battery. *Journal of Clinical Psychology, 39,* 731-742.

Goodstein, L. (1986, February 10).Letter to Martha A.McSteen, Acting Commissioner of the Social Security Administration. (Available from the American Psychological Assocation, 1200 Seventeenth Street, N.W., Washington, DC 20036.)

Gough, H.G. (1950). The F-K dissimulation index for the MMPI. *Journal of Consulting Psychology, 14,* 408-413.

Greene, R.C. (1978). An empirically derived MMPI Carelessness Scale. *Journal of Clinical Psychology, 34,* 408-410.

Greene, R.C. (1980). *MMPI: An interpretive manual.* New York: Grune and Stratton.

Grow, R., McVaugh, W., & Eno, T.P. (1980). Faking and the MMPI. *Journal of Clinical Psychology, 36,* 910-917.

Gynther, M. (1961). The clinical utility of invalid MMPI F scores. *Journal of Consulting Psychology, 25,* 540-542.

Gynther, M. (1972). White norms and black MMPI's: A prescription for discrimination. *Psychological Bulletin, 78,* 386-396.

Heaton, R.K., Smith, H.H., Lehman, R.A.W., & Vogt, A.T. (1978). Prospects for faking believable deficits in neuropsychological testing. *Journal of Consulting and Clinical Psychology, 25,* 486-491.

Kelly, R. (1981). The post-traumatic syndrome. *Journal of the Royal Society of Medicine, 74,* 243-245.

Keschner, M. (1960). Simulation (malingering) in relation to injuries. In S. Brock (Ed.) *Injuries to the brain, spinal cord and their coverings.* New York: Springer.

Larson, A. (1970). Mental and nervous injury in workmen's compensation. *Vanderbilt Law Review, 23,* 1243-1263.

Mensch, A.J., & Woods, D.J. (1986). Patterns of feigning brain damage on the Luria-Nebraska Neuropsychological Battery. *International Journal of Clinical Neuropsychology, 8*, 59-63.

Miller, H. (1961). Accident neurosis. *British Medical Journal, April 1, 1961,* 919-928.

Osborne, D., Collegan, R.C., & Offord, K.D. (1986). Normative tables for the F-K Index of the MMPI basd on a contemporary normal sample. *Journal of Clinical Psychology, 42,* 593-595.

National Organization of Social Security Claimant's Representatives (1985). New listings of impairment. *Social Security Forum, 7,* 1.

Puente, A. (1987). Psychological determination of Social Security Disability. In M. Glancy (Ed). *Medical aspects of disability* (Vol. 4). New York: Matthew Bender.

Resnick, P. (1984). The detection of malingered mental illness. *Behavioral Sciences and the Law, 2,* 21-38.

Rosenberg, N.S. (1986). A two-class mental health system. *The Mental Health Law Project's Update, 5,* 1-2.

Social Security Administration. (1985). *Operational report of the Office of Hearings and Appeals.* Washington, DC: U.S. Government Printing Office.

Social Security Administration. (1986). *Disability evaluation under Social Security: A handbook for physicians.* Washington, DC: U.S. Government Printing Office.

United States Bureau of the Census. (1983). Labor force status and other characteristics of persons with a work disability: 1982 (Current Population Reports, Series P-23, No. 127). Washington, DC: U.S. Government Printing Office.

United States Senate. (1982). *Social Security review of the mentally disabled.* Washington, DC: U.S. Government Printing Office.

The Clinical Neuropsychologist
1989, Vol. 3, No. 2, pp. 97-115

The TCN Salary Survey:
A Salary Survey of Neuropsychologists

Steven H. Putnam
University of Michigan and Ann Arbor VAMC

ABSTRACT

This paper reports the results of a national survey covering principal features of the compensation of neuropsychologists. Some 646 members from the Division of Clinical Neuropsychology of the American Psychological Association responded. They averaged nine years in post-doctoral experience, practiced principally in salaried positions as primary employment, worked at neuropsychological tasks 70% of their time, and earned a median salary of $ 59,500 (U.S.). A number of other parameters of work, experience, and satisfaction were analyzed in a correlational fashion. The results appear to reflect the unique role of neuropsychology service-providers in a number of environments.

Despite the emergence in recent years of many academic and clinical training programs for preparing neuropsychologists, and the establishment of a separate APA division in 1980 (currently the 9th largest Division of APA by numerical membership), there have been no published reports that address total income levels for those in this rapidly expanding field. People currently interested in entering the profession have been limited to indirect inference from the recent

The author would like to express his gratitude to the editors of TCN for their support in initiating and endorsing this project. Also, rich thanks are extended to APA and the members of Division 40 who participated in this study, and the many who took the time to thoughtfully share their opinions on the important issues addressed in this survey. This applied project in survey research is in fullfillment of the Research Methodology requirement (RMAC) for Graduate Programs at the University of Illinois at Urbana-Champaign.

surveys conducted by the Office of Demographic, Employment, and Educational Research of the American Psychological Association (Kohout, Pion, & Wicherski, 1988; Pion and Bramblett, 1985) for published data on salary levels. While these surveys were well conceived and provide valuable salary data for psychologists in various settings, one could only infer in the most general terms what the expected salary might be for those in neuropsychological practice. Furthermore, these surveys provide information regarding salaried positions and/or net salaried income and do not address the important issue of supplemental sources of income, i.e. gross professional income from all combined sources.

The need for empirical data regarding professional earnings is hardly limited to those considering neuropsychology as a career choice. Those currently in the field have no specific salary figures to refer to when negotiating salary, changing settings, or considering a move to another geographic location. This report provides data on selected professional and employment characteristics, gross income from combined sources, and supplemental income activities from the membership of Division 40 of the American Psychological Association.

METHOD

This survey was a single unrepeated mailing sent to 2,200 members of the APA's Division 40 (Division of Clinical Neuropsychology) in August 1988 (see Appendix). A total of 646 survey questionnaires were returned, for an overall response rate of approximately 30%. Thirty surveys were returned due to relocation and no forwarding address. The survey was anonymous and there was no follow-up communication to those failing to respond.

RESULTS

Characteristics of the Respondents
As shown in Table 1, 99% of those responding hold a doctoral degree, and more than 75% of these earned their degree subsequent to 1973 (Table 2), supporting Rourke and Brown's (1986) contention that clinical neuropsychology is a relatively new professional discipline.

Table 1. Number and Percentage of Respondents with Doctoral and Masters Degrees.

	Doctoral	Masters
N	623	9
%	99%	1%

Table 2. Quartile, Mean, and Standard Deviation Values by Year of Highest Degree.

N = 645
90% = 1984
75% = 1982
Median = 1979
25% = 1974
10% = 1967

Mean = 1977
SD = 7.1 years

Ninety-three respondents (15%) considered clinical psychology as their major field, while 190 (30%) reported clinical neuropsychology as their major field. However, 547 (86%) respondents considered either clinical psychology, clinical neuropsychology, or the combination of the two as their major field. While only 5 respondents ($<$ 1%) indicated developmental or school psychology as their major field, 41 (7%) indicated this area in combination with another area.

Table 3. Number and Percentage of Respondents Reporting Clinical Psychology (CP), Clinical Neuropsychology (CNP), the Combination of the Two (CP & CNP), Developmental or School Psychology (D/SP), or Developmental or School Psychology in Combination with another Area, as their Major Field.

	CP	CNP	CP & CNP	D/SP	D/SP & Other
N	93	190	547	5	41
%	15%	30%	86%	$<$ 1%	7%

Note: In tables 3, 15, 17, and 25 one respondent may be included in more than one category.

Table 4 presents the U.S. geographic location of respondents which was determined by stamped postal mark. The *North East* region includes Maine, New Hampshire, Vermont, Connecticut, Massachusetts, Rhode Island, New York, New Jersey, Delaware, Pennsylvania, Maryland, West Virginia, and the District of Columbia. The *North Central* region includes Ohio, Indiana, Illinois, Michigan, Wisconsin, Minnesota, Iowa, Missouri, North Dakota, South Dakota, Nebraska, and Kansas. The *South* region includes Virginia, North Carolina, South Carolina, Georgia, Florida, Kentucky, Tennessee, Alabama, Mississippi, Arkansas, Louisiana, Oklahoma, and Texas. The *West* region includes Montana, Idaho, Wyoming, Colorado, New Mexico, Arizona, Utah, Nevada, Washington, Oregon, California, Alaska, and Hawaii. The *Other* region includes Canada and cases where the geographic region could not be ascertained.

Table 4. Number and Percentage of Respondents from Each of 4 U.S. Geographic Regions and All Others.

North East	North Central	South	West	Other
175	128	142	163	38
(27%)	(20%)	(22%)	(25%)	(6%)

Employment Characteristics

The overwhelming majority of respondents (422) indicated that their *primary* employment capacity was in a salaried position. Another 169 (27%) are self-employed or in independent practice, and 32 (5%) are in group practice. Six respondents (< 1%) were currently in a postdoctoral training position (Table 5).

Table 5. Number and Percentage of Respondents by Primary Employment Capacity.

	Salaried	Group Practice	Self-employed	Training
N	422	32	169	6
%	67%	5%	27%	< 1%

Table 6 presents the percentage of professional work time (clinical, education, research, etc.) considered to be neuropsychological in nature. The median value for the percentage of neuropsychological work for the entire sample was 70% time.

Table 6. Quartile, Mean, and Standard Deviation Values for Percentage of Professional Work Time Considered to be Neuropsychological in Nature.

N = 645
90% = 99.5% time
75% = 90% time
Median% = 70% time
25% = 32% time
10% = 13% time

Mean = 63% time
SD = 32% time

These 645 respondents were grouped into four separate quarter categories based upon the total percentage of time involved in neuropsychological work. As can be seen from Table 7, for 67% of those responding, the majority of their professional work was neuropsychological in nature.

Table 7. Number and Percentage of Respondents Grouped According to Percentage of Work Considered to be Neuropsychological.

	< 25%	< 50%	< 75%	> 74%
N = 645	115	96	118	316
%	18%	15%	18%	49%

Table 8 presents the number of combined hours worked per week for all professional activities. The mean value was 50.5 hours, with a standard deviation of 10 hours.

Table 8. Quartile, Mean, and Standard Deviation Values for Number of Work Hours per Week.

N = 636
90% = 60 hours
75% = 58 hours
Median = 49.5 hours
25% = 44.5 hours
10% = 39.5 hours

Mean = 50.5 hours
SD = 10.0 hours

The mean number of total years work experience in neuropsychology is 9.8 years for those responding (Table 9). Three years, 5 years, 8 years, 12 years, and 18 years represent the 10th, 25th, 50th, 75th, and 90th centiles respectively.

Table 9. Quartile, Mean, and Standard Deviation Values for the Total Number of Years Work Experience in Neuropsychology.

N = 640
90% = 18 years
75% = 12 years
Median = 8 years
25% = 5 years
10% = 3 years

Mean = 9.8 years
SD = 6.3 years

154

Salary Characteristics

Gross professional yearly income from all combined sources was obtained for 604 respondents, all of whom were employed on a full-time professional basis. Although these figures will be analyzed in combination with other variables later, $38,000, $45,000, $59,500, $81,000, and $115,000 represent the 10th, 25th, 50th, 75th, and 90th centiles respectively (Table 10). Yearly gross salary figures ranged from a high of $500,000 to a low of $20,000. The mean salary figure was $71,078, with a standard deviation of $42,879. This mean value is positively skewed toward the more extreme salary values. For purposes of gross comparison, (averaged) salary data are presented in Table 10 from the most recent survey of the entire APA membership (Kohout et al., 1988). It should be emphasized that the Division 40 figures represent *gross* total earnings from all combined sources, while the APA figures represent only full-time salary or *net* income for licensed psychologists (i.e., total income after deducting office expenses *if self-employed*).

Table 10. Quantile, Mean, and Standard Deviation Values for Gross Income (Division 40), and Full-time Salary/Net Income (APA Membership).

Division 40		APA *membership**	
N	604	N	3,064
90%	$ 115,000	90%	$ 83,000
75%	$ 81,000	75%	$ 61,000
Median	$ 59,500	Median	$ 47,000
25%	$ 45,000	25%	$ 37,000
10%	$ 38,000	10%	$ 30,000
Mean	$ 71,078	Mean	$ 52,201
SD	$ 42,879	SD	$ 24,935

* Reprinted with permission from the Office of Demographic, Employment & Educational Research of the APA.

Primary Employment Setting

The primary employment setting of respondents was divided into the following categories (Table 11): Hospital System: 234 (39%), University or College: 51 (8%), Medical School: 96 (16%), Private Clinic: 34 (6%), and other: 189 (31%). Approximately 90% of the "other" category was comprised of respondents in private practice. While the income of this latter group appears to be substantially higher than the other groups, it should again be emphasized that these figures represent gross total income prior to deducting office expenses and other overhead costs. This may or may not change the interpretation of the results, but most employment contracts tend to be negotiated on the basis of gross income.

Table 11. Number, Percentage, Mean and Standard Deviation Salary Values by Primary Employment Setting.

	Hospital	Univ	Med School	Private Clinic	Other
N	234	51	96	34	189
%	39%	8%	16%	6%	31%
Mean salary	$ 59,000	$ 61,000	$ 58,000	$ 74,000	$ 90,000
SD	$ 23,000	$ 25,000	$ 21,000	$ 30,000	$ 63,000

Of 612 respondents providing codeable responses, 433 (67%) indicated they maintained a private practice, while the remaining 179 (28%) reported they did not (Table 12). No response was ascertained by the remaining respondents.

Table 12. Number and Percentage of Respondents Maintaining a Private Practice.

	Private Practice	No Private Practice	Not Ascertained
N	433	179	32
%	67%	28%	5%

Two hundred and fifty-three of those reporting that they maintained a private practice indicated that it was *in addition to* their salaried or regular employment, while 136 indicated it was not (Table 13). For the remaining respondents no response was ascertained.

Table 13. The Number and Percentage of Respondents Whose Private Practice is in Addition to Salaried or Regular Employment.

	Additional	Not Additional	Not Ascertained
N	253	136	44
%	59%	31%	10%

Billing

Codeable responses were ascertained for 640 respondents regarding direct involvement in the billing of patients. Four hundred and forty seven respondents (69%) indicated that they are involved in the billing of patients, while 193 (30%) indicated that they are not. However, 191 (42%) of those who are involved in the billing process reported that it was a burden or was excessive to their professional effort. Two hundred and twenty-nine (51%) did not feel that billing was such a problem, and another 27 (7%) were not sure (Table 14). The remaining cases were not ascertained.

Table 14. The Number and Percentage of Respondents Indicating that Involvement in the Billing of Patients is a Burden.

	A burden	Not a burden	Not Sure
N	191	229	27
%	42%	51%	7%

Supplemental Income

Regarding sources of supplemental income, 194 (32%) of the respondents reported having no such income. Ninety-two (15%) of the respondents indicated they were involved in three or more supplemental activities. This group was not coded further with respect to specific supplemental income activities and is *not* represented in the following individual activity break down.

As presented in Table 15, 38 of the respondents (6%) indicated additional income from publication royalties (PR), either alone, or in concert with another activity. Two hundred and three (33%) respondents indicated they earned additional income from consulting work (CW), either alone or combined with another activity. Seventy-two (12%) reported doing extra teaching (ET), either alone or in combination with another activity. One hundred and nineteen (20%) indicated forensic practice (FP), either alone or with another activity. Only 11 (2%) indicated that research activities (R) alone, or with another activity were a source of supplemental income. It should be emphasized that this particular question inquired about research as an income generating activity, and does not reflect the extent to which respondents are actually involved in ongoing research. The remaining respondents reported "other" (O) as an additional income source. The most commonly reported *pair* of supplemental income activities was consulting work and forensic practice. One hundred and ninety-nine (32%) of the respondents were involved in these activities alone or in combination.

Table 15. Number and Percentage of Respondents Reporting Various Supplemental Income Activities.

	PR	CW	ET	FP	R	O	> 3	None
N	38	203	72	119	11	17	92	194
%	6%	33%	12%	20%	2%	3%	15%	32%

Geographic Region and Salary

Six hundred and one questionnaires from those respondents in full-time employment were grouped according to four major geographic regions in the United States; North East: 173 (29%), North Central: 128 (21%), South: 139 (23%), and West: 161 (27%) (Table 16). The remaining respondents were either from Canada in insufficient numbers for a stable distribution or a geographic region could not be ascertained.

Table 16. Quartile, Mean, and Standard Deviation Values for Gross Professional Income Grouped by U.S. Geographic Region and Total.

North East	North Central	South	West	Total
n = 173	N = 128	N = 139	N = 161	N = 604
90% = $ 105,000	90% = $ 91,000	90% = $ 126,000	90% = $ 120,000	90% = $ 115,000
75% = $ 77,500	75% = $ 73,000	75% = $ 90,000	75% = $ 95,000	75% = $ 81,000
MDN = $ 59,500	MDN = $ 57,500	MDN = $ 58,500	MDN = $ 64,500	MDN = $ 59,500
25th = $ 44,500	25% = $ 44,500	25% = $ 44,500	25% = $ 47,500	25% = $ 45,000
10th = $ 34,500	10% = $ 35,500	10% = $ 35,000	10% = $ 39,000	10% = $ 38,000
Mean = $ 65,526	Mean = $ 64,328	Mean = $ 73,612	Mean = $ 77,913	Mean = $ 71,078
SD = $ 30,338	SD = $ 46,562	SD = $ 49,638	SD = $ 45,110	SD = $ 42,879

Gross Income in Relation to Other Variables

The questionnaires of those respondents earning $\geq$ $ 80,000 (U.S.) ($\geq$ 75th centile) were cross-examined to determine which professional activities they most frequently reported as sources of supplemental income. This is shown in Table 17. Of the 175 respondents satisfying this criterion, forty-eight (27%) indicated that they had no supplemental source of income (None), while another

158

42 (24%) reported having three or more sources of supplemental income (≥ 3). Another 56 (32%) reported consulting work alone, forensic practice alone, or the combination of the two (CW + FP).

Table 17. The Supplemental Income Activities of Respondents Earning ≥ $ 80,000.

	None	≥ 3	CW + FP
N	48	42	56
%	27%	24%	32%

Of 175 respondents meeting the criterion of ≥ $ 80,000 gross professional income, 89 were self-employed (SELF-EMPL), 67 were employed in a salaried position (SAL), 11 in group practice (GP PRACT), and the employment of the remaining respondents was coded "other" or was not ascertained (O/NA). This is shown in Table 18.

Table 18. Number and Percentage of Respondents Whose Gross Professional Income is ≥ $ 80K Grouped by Primary Employment Capacity.

	SAL	GP PRACT	SELF-EMPL	O/NA
N	67	11	89	8
%	(38%)	(6%)	(51%)	(5%)

Hours per Week in Relation to Gross Salary

One hundred and seventy-five respondents reported a salary level ≥ $ 80 K, ($ 80,000 US = $ 80 K) while 448 respondents reported an income level below $ 80 K. The mean number of hours for the former group was 54.9 with an SD of 9.8. The Pearson correlation between gross income and hours worked was .07 for this group ($t = .914$; NS). For the group with a gross yearly income level below $ 80 K, the mean number of hours worked per week was 48.9 with an SD of 9.6. The correlation between gross salary and weekly hours was .32 ($t =$ '7.-12; p <.0001).

Table 19. Correlations Between Gross Professional Income and Hours Worked Weekly for Income Categories Above and Below $ 80,000.

Gross yearly income > $ 80 K	Gross yearly income < $ 80 K
N = 175	N = 448
Mean salary = $ 117,550	Mean salary = $ 51,382
SD = $ 53,182	SD = $ 13,331
Mean hours per week = 54.9	Mean hours per week = 48.9
SD = 9.8	SD = 9.6
Correlation coefficient = .07	Correlation coefficient = .32
t = .914	t = 7.012
Significance = NS	Significance = $p < .0001$

For the entire sample of 627 respondents providing codeable responses, a correlation coefficient of .28 was obtained between weekly hours worked and gross salary. ($t = 7.34$; $p < .0001$).

Not suprisingly the correlation between weekly hours worked and gross salary increased to .33 for those respondents reporting self-employment (private practice) as their primary employment setting ($t = 4.36$; $p < .0001$).

As presented in Table 20, the correlation between the number of hours worked each week and gross income declines as the number of years of experience in the field increases. This is of course related to the fact that in the majority of cases earnings typically increase with years of experience, and become less dependent on the number of hours worked.

Table 20. Correlation Coefficients for Number of Hours Worked per Week and Gross Professional Income by Years of Experience in Neuropsychology.

Years of Experience	1-10 years	11-20 years	21-35 years
Correlation coefficient	.29	.28	.05
t	6.17	3.75	.309
Significance	$p < .0001$	$p < .0001$	NS
N	417	169	30

Years of Work Experience in Relation to Gross Yearly Salary

Salary data were grouped according to years of professional work experience for both a sample of Division 40 members (Table 21) and APA members employed in direct human service positions (Table 22). These are presented for comparison purposes in a fashion similar to the APA's Salaries in Psychology (Kohout et al.,

1988). As stated earlier, the APA figures represent only full-time salary or net income for licensed psychologists (i.e., total income after deducting office expenses if self-employed).

Table 21. Quartile Values for Gross Salary by Years of Professional Experience in Neuropsychology.

Years	0-4	5-9	10-14	15-19	20-24	25+
N = (631)	98	245	180	54	26	28
90%	105K	110K	120K	120K	125K	133K
75%	68K	75K	85K	85K	100K	93K
50%	43K	58K	65K	65K	63K	70K
25%	35K	44K	50K	58K	50K	62K
10%	30K	35K	40K	42K	40K	40K

Table 22. Quartile Values for Full-time Salary/Net Income by Years of Professional Experience for Licensed Psychologists Working in Direct Human Services Positions. Based on the Responses of 3,064 Members of APA (Kohout et al., 1988).*

Years	0-1	2-4	5-9	10-14	15-19	20-24	25-29	30+
N = (3,064)	33	309	745	865	539	264	170	139
90%	40K	54K	76K	91K	100K	100K	100K	100K
75%	36K	42K	58K	65K	73K	72K	70K	76K
50%	31K	33K	42K	47K	50K	52K	50K	59K
25%	27K	29K	34K	39K	40K	41K	43K	43K
10%	22K	25K	29K	32K	33K	30K	35K	35K

* Reprinted with permission from the Office of Demographic, Employment & Educational Research of the APA.

A number of those who responded to the survey indicated that the majority of their professional work was not neuropsychological in nature. Six hundred and thirty-six questionnaires were analyzed based on four categories of percentage time doing neuropsychological work (Table 23). The overall trend appears to suggest that at the upper income level the greater percentage of time involved in neuropsychological work, the less one's total income.

Table 23. Quartile Values for Salary Data Grouped by % of Time Doing Neuropsychological Work.

% NP work	< 25%	< 50%	< 75%	> 74%
N	113	96	117	310
90%	120K	115K	120K	102K
75%	90K	80K	80K	80K
50%	60K	65K	60K	59K
25%	45K	49K	45K	44K
10%	35K	37K	36K	37K
Mean	71K	77K	70K	67K
SD	40K	59K	40K	38K

Career Change

Five hundred and fifty-eight respondents (88%) indicated that they were *not* considering a career change out of neuropsychology. Thirty-nine respondents (6%) indicated that they were considering a career change out of neuropsychology, with the remaining 35 (6%) reporting they were uncertain.

Three hundred and twelve respondents (49%) indicated that they considered their economic reward to be appropriate, while 253 (39%) felt it was not satisfactory. Seventy-eight respondents (12%) were uncertain. This is shown in Table 24.

Table 24. Number, Percentage, Mean and Standard Deviation Salary Values for Respondents Indicating if the Economic Reward They Received Was Appropriate.

	Yes	No	Uncertain
N	312	253	78
%	49%	39%	12%
Mean salary	82K	56K	63K
SD	46K	37K	26K

Services Provided

Table 25 shows that the majority of respondents (365) reported that they provided three or more neuropsychological services, reflecting the expanding role of the neuropsychological practitioner. This group was not coded by individual services provided, and is not represented in the following break-down. Two hundred and sixty-one respondents (41%) provide assessment (ASMT), either alone or in combination with another activity. One hundred and nine respondents (17%) provide treatment (TRMT) alone or with another service. Sixty-three respondents (10%) were involved in providing educational services (EDUC), either alone or with another professional service. While only 22 respondents (3%) indicated that they provided rehabilitation services (REHAB), there may have been some definitional difficulty with this category and the "treatment" category.

Table 25. The Number and Percentage of Respondents Providing a Particular Neuropsychological Service in Combination with Another Unspecified Service.

	ASMT+1	TRMT+1	REHAB+1	EDUC+1	≥ 3	OTHER
N	261	109	22	63	365	9
%	41%	17%	3%	10%	57%	1%

A SYNOPSIS OF COMMENTS

Many of the respondents elaborated on their responses or expressed a variety of concerns pertaining to the practice of clinical neuropsychology. The majority of comments were generally very positive about the financial, personal, and professional rewards of neuropsychological practice. Most of the concerns expressed by respondents fell into several specific areas.

Clearly the most frequently reported concern, and the most inspired responses involved the issue of reimbursement for services. The tremendous variability and inconsistency between, and within, insurance companies in response to neuropsychological services often necessitates much additional time and effort to assure appropriate reimbursement. This also leaves one uncertain as to how to advise patients regarding the extent of coverage they can expect. Moreover, the delays, seeming "run-arounds", and resistances are a particularly frustrating exercise for a professional with 22+ years of education and specialized training who is attempting to provide a needed service to consumers. A number of respondents indicated that they have recently adopted a "cash only" policy due to the increasing demand from insurance companies for pre-authorization, the need to negotiate with carriers, and the demand to write additional justifications for the services provided. This of course requires additional clerical help and creates added expense which is not reimbursed. Also, the figures used to determine "reasonable fees" are obsolete in many cases, and in need of revision. The lag time between service delivery and actual payment is often very lengthy, and annoying, in the view of many respondents.

A variety of ideas were expressed addressing the cause and maintenance of these widespread irritations. Some health plans are reluctant to cover neuropsychological assessment without a physician referral. However, this referral need extends to most consultants and procedures required beyond basic general practice care. Some prepaid health plans do not provide any specific coverage for neuropsychological services, but must have arrangements in place for such needs on an *ad hoc* basis. Some respondents suggested that neuropsychological services are often associated with mental health services, and therefore are subjected to the limitations and restrictions of such policies. This linkage may reduce needed benefits for neurobehavioral conditions actually having no mental health complications.

The diagnostic categories included in DSM-III-R are also inadequate for many of the activities of a clinical neuropsychologist, thus interfering with the formation of procedure codes and uniform policies which would allow insurance carriers to process claims properly.

More generally, the insurance industry is not at present well educated with respect to the services provided by neuropsychologists, and has no prior base of experience by which they can understand the requirement of a full day of test administration, scoring, review of existing documents, report writing, and feedback session. The need and costs for a technician is another often overlooked consideration. Several respondents indicated that because of the time and frustration with billing they no longer bill patients or insurance companies directly. Rather, they have made contractual arrangements with hospitals to provide office space, equipment, secretarial assistance, and to carry out all of the billing.

Many respondents suggested that the first step toward resolving some of the obstacles in receiving 3rd party reimbursement is to establish a special licensing procedure for defining a neuropsychologist, or to insist that those in practice pursue the ABPP Diplomate. As Puente (1987) has pointed out, the neuropsychological evaluation is sometimes defined by the tests considered acceptable (e.g., Social Security Administration), without addressing the more pivotal issue of what constitutes a neuropsychologist. This lack of uniformity in training, practice, and demonstrated competence, encourages insurers to develop arbitrary reimbursement criteria, and often to look with uncertainty upon the field.

Some respondents complained of a "bandwagon of dabblers" who are improperly trained, charge excessive fees, generally promise more than they can deliver, and who complicate quality assurance for the insurance industry and consuming public. Particular mention was made of those calling themselves "neuropsychologists" while relying largely upon a computer-generated report, and those trained with adult patients offering services to children. Fortunately, many of these concerns are currently being addressed (Bornstein, 1988) and guidelines for self-monitoring have been developed by the Division 40/INS Joint Task Force (1987; 1988).

The need for a reliable and realistic payment and fee schedule for insurance companies would be a very practical help in the bookkeeping portion of practice, and may be welcomed by most insurers, in the view of many respondents. There were suggestions that the field make efforts to align itself more with neurology and move away from identification with mental health, in that medical coverage generally has superior reimbursement rates.

The matter of providing services to Medicare and Medicaid patients appears to be a particularly troublesome one for many respondents. A number suggested that the customary "reasonable rate" was so low that they were forced to do inferior work, see such patients as "charity cases" or as a "contribution to society", or more typically, to no longer serve such patients. Some respondents also indicated that they have encountered difficulty receiving reimbursement for services provided to the learning disabled. It was suggested that many HMO's and PPO's maintain a discriminatory practice towards neuropsychology, thus making it difficult to do comprehensive, yet cost-effective assessment. It was reported by some that receiving reimbursement from attorneys and workman's compensation cases was generally the most dependable and least conflictual of all referral sources, but impose unique burdens.

In terms of salary more generally, many expressed irritation with the earnings of psychologists *vis-à-vis* physicians. This was especially true with those working in government agencies. A large number puzzled about how a neuropsychologist in a medical center with a full-time technician could generate in excess of $ 250,000 a year and yet only be paid $ 50,000. The existence of "salary surveys" by management of these centers was directly questioned by respondents who doubted that such data could be either valid or generalizable to the neuropsychologist in such settings.

Many respondents expressed an interest in knowing what other practitioners were charging for their services, suggesting that a data collection effort in this regard could be especially helpful in ameliorating some of the difficulties with insurance companies. Such a study is already in process by this author.

Comment

No survey is perfect and captures every situation. Inferring the probable response of those individuals who did not respond to a mailed survey is always difficult, and a diversity of opinions exists regarding acceptable rates of response. The membership of Division 40 *responding* appears to be prototypic of the whole division, in as much as we can tell. While the current results are believed to be generalizable, the confirmation of the true representativeness of these data will necessarily be a next methodological step. This survey tool will be repeated and further refined and developed. Perhaps the more immediate matter is the fact that these 646 questionnaires are the only currently available data from which any judgment regarding gross total earnings can be made for those in the field of neuropsychology and those considering a career in the field.

While this initial effort does not permit one to offer firm and unequivocal conclusions, there appear to be some general trends clearly worthy of reiteration. The overwhelming majority of those responding to this survey are doctoral level psychologists trained in the areas of clinical psychology or clinical neuropsychology, having received their degree during the last 16 years. Most are currently employed in a salaried position or private practice working between 40 and 60 hours per week. The relationship between the number of hours worked and gross income tends to be stronger for those more recent to the field and in the lower income levels. With increased years of experience, and at the higher income levels, the number of hours worked appears to have a negligible effect on gross income, although in part this may be artifactual.

The amount of time spent in neuropsychological work was generally quite variable. However, for almost 70% of the group, the majority of their work was neuropsychological in nature. Interestingly, there is a slight tendency for salaries at the upper income levels to be lower for those doing exclusively neuropsychological work. For generalist clinicians in private practice this could be associated with more time spent doing psychotherapy, with neuropsychological practice serving largely as an enhancement to their clinical practice. Also, more than half of the respondents were employed in a salaried position in settings such as a hospital, university, or medical school doing exclusively neuropsychological practice. Average earnings in these settings appears to be well below those earned in private clinics and private practice offices.

Clinical neuropsychology is a distinct and legitimate area of professional practice, and it does seem reasonable to infer that the current earning potential of those in neuropsychological practice is slightly above that of the general practitioner of psychology. It appears that regional differences in income do exist within the field, which presumably are associated with regional differences in the cost of living. Regarding the important issue of supplemental income, those at the upper income levels are bimodal, either reporting having no supplemental income activities, or conversely, engaging in three or more such activities to enhance their income. Without question the two most commonly reported supplemental income activities at all levels of income are consulting work and forensic practice. Very few respondents report research as a supplemental income activity, although many indicated it to be something they engage in without direct monetary compensation. No specific inquiry was made about contributions of professional time to community organizations or actual *pro-bono* work, strongly advocated by Ethical Principles.

166

REFERENCES

Bornstein, R.A. (1988). Entry into clinical neuropsychology: Graduate, undergraduate, and beyond. *The Clinical Neuropsychologist, 2,* 213-220.

Division 40-International Neuropsychological Society (INS) Task Force on Education, Accreditation, and Credentialing (1987). Guidelines for doctoral training programs in clinical neuropsychology. *The Clinical Neuropsychologist, 1,* 29-34.

Division 40-International Neuropsychological Society (INS) Task Force (1988). Report of the INS-Division 40 Task Force on Education, Accreditation and Credentialing: Subcommittee on Continuing Education. *The Clinical Neuropsychologist, 2,* 22-29.

Kohout, J.L., Pion, G.M., & Wicherski, M.M. (1988). *Salaries in psychology 1987.* Washington, DC: American Psychological Association.

Pion, G.M., & Bramblett, P. (1985). *Salaries in psychology 1985.* Washington, DC: American Psychological Association.

Puente, A.E. (1987). Social security disability and clinical neuropsychological assessment. *The Clinical Neuropsychologist, 1,* 353-363.

Rourke, B.P., & Brown, G.G. (1986). Clinical neuropsychology and behavioral neurology: Similarities and differences. In S.B. Filskov & T.J. Boll (Eds.), *Handbook of clinical neuropsychology* (Vol. 2, pp. 3-18). New York: John Wiley and Sons.

APPENDIX

1. Is your present *primary* employment in a (salaried position, group practice, self-employment or independent, training status, or other) capacity. *PLEASE UNDERLINE ONE.*
2. Would you consider your major field to be (clinical psychology, adult or child clinical neuropsychology, developmental or school psychology, other psychology, or non-psychology) *PLEASE UNDERLINE NO MORE THAN TWO.*
3. Is your highest degree (doctoral, masters, baccalaureate, or other (i.e., medicine, law, etc). *PLEASE UNDERLINE ONE.*
4. Year of highest degree 19...... In What Country Do You Live? ......
5. Total years work experience in neuropsychology......
6. Total percentage of your work that you would consider to be neuropsychological (clinical, education, research, etc.)
   ...... %
7. Your *primary* employment setting is a (hospital system, college or university, medical school, private clinic, other) *PLEASE UNDERLINE ONE.*
8. Please indicate your gross professional income from *all combined* sources: $US ......
9. Do you gain *supplemental* income from (publication royalties, consulting work, extra teaching, inventions, forensic practice, research, or other) activities. *PLEASE UNDERLINE AS MANY AS APPLY.*
10. Do you maintain a private practice? YES or NO. *PLEASE UNDERLINE ONE.*
11. Is this practice in addition to your salaried or regular employment? YES, NO, DOES NOT APPLY. *PLEASE UNDERLINE ONE.*
12. Does your salaried or regular employer (control or regulate, operate or assist, monitor or audit, proscribe or forbid, ignore or disregard) your private practice. *PLEASE UNDERLINE AS MANY AS APPLY.*

13. Do you involve yourself in the billing of patients for services? YES or NO.
14. If the answer to (13) is YES, do you consider the time spent in billing issues to be excessive or a burden to your professional effort? YES, NO, NOT SURE. *PLEASE UNDERLINE ONE.*
15. Do you provide (assessment, treatment, rehabilitation, educational, other) services? *PLEASE UNDERLINE AS MANY AS APPLY.*
16. How many hours per week do you work at all professional activities combined?
17. Given the work you do, do you consider your economic reward to be appropriate? YES, NO, NOT SURE. *PLEASE UNDERLINE ONE.*
18. Are you considering a career change out of neuropsychology? YES, NO, NOT SURE. *PLEASE UNDERLINE ONE.*

Finally, please feel free to add any comments you would like to make:

The Clinical Neuropsychologist
1990, Vol. 4, No. 3, pp. 199-243

The *TCN* Professional Practice Survey:
Part I: General Practices of Neuropsychologists in Primary Employment and Private Practice Settings

Steven H. Putnam   John W. DeLuca
Neuropsychology Program   Psychology Department
University of Michigan   Lafayette Clinic
Ann Arbor VAMC

ABSTRACT

The paper presents data obtained from 872 members of the Division of Clinical Neuro-psychology (Division 40) of the American Psychological Association. Issues covered a range of professional and clinical practices in primary employment and private practice positions. A hospital-medical center was the primary employment setting of over one-third of the respondents. Another one-third was employed exclusively in a private practice office. Twenty-nine percent reported being in private practice in addition to primary institutional employment. On the whole, Division 40 members spent approximately one-half of their clinical time doing neuropsychological assessment, saw an average of nine patients per month for assessment, the majority of whom were adults. The average hourly charge for assessment was $100, average fixed rate for a neuropsychological evaluation was between $700 and $750, with an average time of approximately 6.5 hours per assessment. In personal injury referrals the plaintiff was represented approximately 60% of the time, and attorneys were charged an average of $150 per hour. Those respondents providing neuropsychological treatment charged an average of $92 per hour, and psychotherapy and cognitive rehabilitation were reported as the most frequently practiced treatments. Technicians were utilized far more in primary employment settings and were paid an average hourly rate of between $13 and $21, with an average annual salary of $23,000. A variety of other issues related to clinical practices, patient characteristics, and fee setting were reported and discussed.

The authors would like to communicate their gratitude to the many Division 40 members who took time from very busy schedules to complete and return this questionnaire. To our knowledge this represents the largest number of respondents to a mailed survey in the field of neuropsychology.
We would also like to acknowledge the helpful comments of Stanley Berent, Ph.D. and Linas A. Bieliauskas, Ph.D. in the preparation of this manuscript as well as the tireless assistance of Mary Beth Putnam in all phases of this project.

In 1981 the Journal of Consulting and Clinical Psychology devoted a special section of volume 49 exclusively to the field of clinical neuropsychology. In that volume Chelune and Edwards (1981) declared that clinical neuropsychology has "come of age and has formally joined the ranks of the other neurosciences" (p. 777). The growth within the field of clinical neuropsychology during the middle and latter parts of the 1980's continues to be reflected today in burgeoning employment opportunities and clinical activities of practitioners in a wide variety of settings.

At the time of the Chelune and Edwards' (1981) overview diagnostic inference had long been the predominant role of the clinical neuropsychologist. However, the evolution into applied and prescriptive areas, viz., treatment, rehabilitation, consultation, and forensics, seems to be at least one natural manifestation of what Rourke (1982) has designated as the "dynamic" phase of neuropsychology. Different facets of this broadening role have been reviewed by a number of authors during the last decade (Bornstein, Costa, & Matarazzo, 1986; Diller & Gordon, 1981; Grimm & Bleiberg, 1986; McMahon, 1983; Tarter, Van Thiel, & Edwards, 1988).

In response to this unparalleled expansion with its concomitant influx of neuropsychological practitioners, Division 40 (Clinical Neuropsychology) of the American Psychological Association has established various guidelines addressing such issues as education, training, credentialing, practice, and the use of technicians (Reports of the Division 40/INS Task Force on Education, Accreditation, and Credentialing, 1987; 1988; 1989). The purpose of such self-monitoring guidelines is to facilitate the further development of and adherence to professional standards and, ultimately, to ensure and expedite quality services to consumers. Furthermore, since 1984 the American Board of Professional Psychology (ABPP) in affiliation with the American Board of Clinical Neuropsychology (ABCN) has made possible "*de jure* specialization" (p. 658) (Costa, Matarazzo, & Bornstein, 1986) through achievement of Diplomate status in the practice area of clinical neuropsychology (Bieliauskas & Matthews, 1987). Attainment of this credential has been defined as "the clearest evidence of competence as a clinical neuropsychologist" (p. 22) (Reports of the Division 40 Task Force on Education, Accreditation, and Credentialing, 1989).

In recent years there has been an increasing number of attempts to enumerate, analyze, and characterize the tremendous expansion which has occurred within the field of clinical neuropsychology. The mailed survey method has been the most popular approach as it clearly offers cost, time, and logistical advantages over face-to-face and telephone interview approaches (Kanuk & Berenson, 1975). This is particularly true when the targeted group is a large voluntary professional or interest-based organization. Most professionals within the field of clinical neuropsychology holding membership in a professional group (e.g., APA Division 40, INS, NAN) have presumably been solicited to participate in such surveys during the last several years.

A number of these surveys have had specific foci such as training and education parameters for neuropsychologists (McCaffery & Isaac, 1984), graduate training programs in neuropsychology (McCaffery, Malloy, & Brief, 1985), professional self-designation and putative professional characteristics (Slay & Valdivia, 1988), opinions regarding posttraumatic syndrome (McMordie, 1988), salary levels (Putnam, 1989), the use of neuropsychology technicians (DeLuca, 1989), and practices and beliefs among ABPP and non-ABPP neuropsychologists (Sweet & Moberg, 1990). Only a few studies have attempted a broad focus (Hartlage & Telzrow, 1980; Seretny, Dean, Gray, & Hartlage, 1986). Given the remarkable growth in the field in the last several years the findings from these pioneer surveys are dated, which diminishes their relevance to the contemporary practitioner of neuropsychology. Although Guilmette, Faust, Hart, and Arkes (in press) recently published the results of a survey of a randomly selected group of neuropsychologists, the data collection took place in early 1986. Thus, the data they present may not be representative of *current* practices. To underscore this point, Fowler and VandenBos (1989) very recently reported a 502% increase in Division 40 membership between 1980 and 1989. Considering such growth there is obviously a need for continually updated and current information which the practitioner of neuropsychology can reference when making decisions regarding business and professional matters. Moreover, as with all data collected via the mailed survey method, recency as well as breadth of sample size can significantly improve the quality and applicability of the information obtained.

Purpose of the Study
The present study was conducted with the intention of fulfilling a two-fold purpose: (1) to delineate current clinical practices among those in Division 40 which can be utilized as a general reference source for neuropsychological practitioners; and (2) to examine and discuss critical issues related to the continuing growth occurring within the field. The topics addressed included fees, billing procedures, patient types, referral sources, assessment approaches, job satisfaction, scope of practice, and other issues of pragmatic importance to the practitioner of neuropsychology. The results of this survey study will be presented in two separate parts. The present report (Part I) will present data for respondents in primary employment with those in private practice. When applicable the findings of Seretny et al. (1986) and/or Sweet and Moberg (1990) will be presented for comparison study. However, regarding the former, it is uncertain how directly comparable Seretny et al.'s (1986) data are with the current data. The specific questions asked by these investigators were not reported, except by implication. Moreover, the only measure of central tendency specified was the mean and no measures of variability were provided. Sweet and Moberg's (1990) data may be more directly comparable except in cases where respondents who do not appear to be involved in an activity (e.g. neuropsychological treatment) are not identified, artificially lowering the reported percentages in some cases. Furthermore, much of Sweet and Moberg's (1990) data is presented in class inter-

vals which does not facilitate simple comparison with the present data in many instances.

The next report (Part II) will be presented in volume 4, number 4 of *TCN* and will delineate more detailed findings associated with selected characteristics and practices of the respondent groups (e.g., area of clinical practice, geographic region, neuropsychological assessment methodology, etc.) Finally, a synopsis of the myriad of comments and concerns expressed by respondents will be presented.

METHOD

A four page (double-sided) anonymous questionnaire was sent to 2,402 U.S. members of Division 40 (Clinical Neuropsychology) of the American Psychological Association in November 1989 (See Appendix A). A cover letter was included which explained the intention, design, and purpose of the survey as well as instructions for completion. The questionnaire was divided into two separate sections, one addressing Primary Employment and the other addressing Private Practice. Colored stationary and bold faced headings differentiated the two sections from one another; however, the item content covered in each section was virtually identical. A franked and addressed envelope was included for return convenience. There was no follow-up communication with those members failing to respond.

A total of 936 surveys were returned which resulted in an overall return rate of 40%. However, 64 questionnaires were carefully evaluated, but eliminated from the data analysis due to factors such as retirement, being clinically inactive, or similarly, being identified with Division 40 on a personal interest basis only. Thirty-eight questionnaires were returned due to relocation and/or no forwarding address. The following parametric data analysis was performed on the usable questionnaires of 872 individuals.

RESULTS

Due to the scope of the data the format for presentation will begin with general respondent parameters of the *entire* sample and move toward more specific practice characteristics. It should be noted that 256 of the 872 respondents in this study were active in *both* a primary employment position *and* a private practice. These 256 respondents returned *both* sections of the questionnaire, resulting in a total of 1,128 usable observations (questionnaires) upon which the combined analyses are based. However, not all items were uniformly completed by all respondents. This resulted in some variability in the number of observations across variables.

In the interest of parsimony no attempt was made in this study to critically evaluate the neuropsychological competence or credentials of respondents. The interested reader is referred to Adams (1988) and Slay and Valdivia (1988) for recent discussions of this issue. In short, membership in Division 40 is elective and open to any member of APA willing to pay annual dues. No doubt, some respondents to this survey may possess minimal qualifications to practice neuro-

172

psychology or perhaps not satisfy the recently adopted operational definition of a clinical neuropsychologist (Reports of the Division 40 Task Force on Education, Accreditation, and Credentialing, 1989). Nevertheless, all of the respondents whose questionnaires were included in the following data analyses were involved in the clinical practice of neuropsychology, in either an institutional or private practice office setting, or both. Therefore, they form a sizeable sample of the profession of clinical neuropsychology in the United States, circa 1989-90.

General Characteristics of the Respondents

Data regarding current clinical practice were obtained for 828 respondents. As seen in Figure 1, the overwhelming majority of those responding indicated that their current practice was in clinical neuropsychology. Respondents identifying other areas of clinical practice were nonetheless engaged in neuropsychological activities on a regular basis. Forty-four respondents did not specify their area of clinical practice. The overall distribution by area was similar to that of the *TCN* salary survey (Putnam, 1989), with the exception that 6% of the current group indicated that rehabilitation psychology best described their area of clinical practice. The latter may reflect an emerging trend within the field as more emphasis is placed on the issue of treatment and as the rehabilitation industry continues to expand and prosper. In this context it may of some interest that a recent survey of randomly selected Division 22 (Rehabilitation Psychology) members reported a median salary of $60,000 (mean salary of $68,860) for this group (Kelly, 1990). While this figure is based on a relatively small sample (80 respondents), it is comparable to the median salary value of $59,500 (mean salary $71,078) reported for Division 40 members (Putnam, 1989).

Considering what appears to be an overlapping relationship between clinical psychology and clinical neuropsychology among contemporary practitioners, a brief review may be instructive. Stapp, Tucker, and VandenBos (1985) reported in their landmark 1983 census of psychological personnel that 48.9% of the doctoral level members of APA indicated that clinical psychology was their major field. The most recent report of divisional memberships within the APA (Fowler & VandenBos, 1989) reveals that Division 12 (Clinical Psychology) continues to be the largest division by numerical membership, followed closely by Division 42 (Psychologists in Independent Practice). Undoubtedly there are many more clinical psychologists represented in other divisional memberships with the APA. While it is not known what percentage of these members identify with or practice clinical neuropsychology, Putnam (1989) found that 86% of the Division 40 members returning the *TCN* salary survey identified clinical psychology as either their primary or secondary major field. In the present study 30% of those responding reported clinical psychology as exemplifying their current clinical practice. Given the growing number of graduate training programs in neuropsychology (Cripe, 1989) and the continuing attention to the issue from the INS/Division 40 Task Force on Education, Training, and Credentialing (1987;1988) as well as by leaders in the field (Costa et al., 1986; Meier, 1981), it

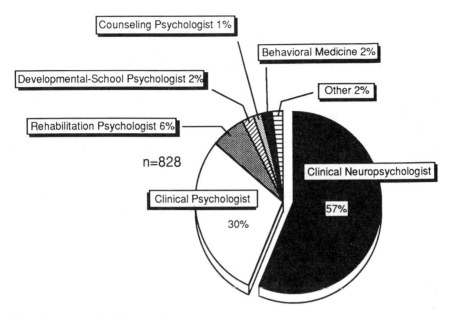

Fig. 1. Response distribution of respondents by area of clinical practice.

seems reasonable to expect a decrease in this figure over time. That is, new Division 40 members may increasingly identify neuropsychology, as opposed to clinical psychology, as their primary field and area of clinical practice.

Several surveys have inquired about the academic degree area of practicing neuropsychologists. Guilmette et al. (in press) report that 76% of a combined group of 449 individuals involved with neuropsychology received their doctoral degrees in either clinical or counseling psychology. Another 8% earned their degree in educational/school psychology, 3% in experimental psychology, and 3% in developmental psychology. Only 3% of this group earned their degree in neuropsychology. Sweet and Moberg (1990) report that 64% of 102 ABPPs responding to their survey received their degree in clinical psychology, 13% in counseling psychology, and only 6% in neuropsychology. The distribution was similar for non-ABPP Division 40 members with the exception that fewer non-ABPP psychologists had received their degree in clinical psychology (55%). While the current survey did not inquire specifically about degree area, respondents' area of current clinical practice and employment setting were identified.

Representation by State
Questionnaires were received from all states within the U.S. (including the District of Columbia) except for Wyoming and Alaska. It may be pertinent that Stapp et al. (1985) estimated that only South Dakota had fewer psychological

174

personnel than Wyoming and Alaska in their 1983 census. At the other extreme, California and New York comprised 11.8% and 10.4% respectively of the total percentage of respondents to the Stapp et al. (1985) census. As can be seen in Table 1, these figures are very comparable to the geographic distribution represented in the current study. The ordinal rank for the states representing at least 5% of the total number of respondents is also presented in Table 1. The seven states identified comprise almost one-half of the total sample of respondents.

The entire sample of respondents was divided into the four U.S. geographic regions designated in the 1982 Rand McNally Commercial Atlas and Marketing Guide and employed in the *TCN* salary survey (Putnam, 1989). The total number of returned questionnaires from each state within each of these four regions is graphically presented in Figure 2. As noted earlier, 256 respondents returned questionnaires for both primary employment and private practice (i.e., two observations).

The rank ordering of U.S. regions by highest to lowest number of respondents is identical to the results from the *TCN* salary survey of Division 40 members (Putnam, 1989). The North East region, led by New York, Massachusetts, and Pennsylvania, comprised 27% of the total number of responses to the salary survey and 28% to the present survey.

Employment Setting
As noted earlier, the questionnaire was divided into two independent sections addressing practices and fees in primary employment *and* private practice employment. As presented in Figure 3 the distribution of employment settings was fairly equally divided among those *exclusively* in private practice (34%), *exclusively* in primary employment (37%), and those both in private practice *and* primary employment (29%). Generally speaking, these figures correspond to what Dorken, Stapp, and VandenBos (1986) found in a national count of licensed/certified doctoral psychologists. These investigators reported that 27%

Table 1. Ordinal Rank, Number, and Percentage of Returned Questionnaires from States Representing at least 5% of the Total Sample.

State	Ordinal Rank	Number	Percentage
California	1	144	13%
New York	2	85	8%
Texas	3	64	6%
Massachusetts	4	59	5%
Pennsylvania	5	57	5%
Michigan	6	55	5%
Florida	7	52	5%

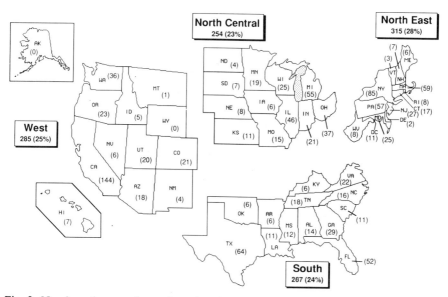

Fig. 2. Number of returned questionnaires from each state and U.S. geographic region.

indicated private practice was their primary employment. Moreover, 45% of the psychologists declaring secondary employment were in a private practice.

The primary employment setting of respondents is presented in Figure 4. Of the 578 subjects whose primary employment was in an institutional or nonprivate practice office, the majority indicated that they were employed in a hospital or medical center setting. In most cases the latter involved association with a university hospital or medical center. However, these figures do not include respondents employed in a Veterans Affairs Medical Center (VAMC) due to the public funding structure in these government facilities. VAMC employees were classified under Government agency/facility, and hence make up the overwhelming majority of respondents within this designation in Figure 4.

Stapp et al. (1985) reported that 9.8% of the APA members holding a doctorate degree who responded to their census were employed in a hospital setting in 1983. Twenty percent of these respondents indicated that their primary employment was individual private practice. While Stapp et al. (1985) found that these two groups combined comprised less than one-third of the APA memberships' employment standing, they comprise more than two-thirds in the current groups of Division 40 respondents. Thus, there appears to be a disproportionate number of hospital based personnel and private practitioners in Division 40 relative to the APA membership more generally.

However, there does not appear to be any appreciable change in the percentage of Division 40 members currently reporting private practice as their primary

176

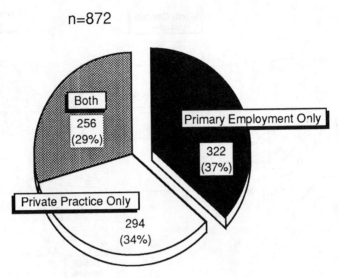

n=872

Both
256
(29%)

Primary Employment Only
322
(37%)

Private Practice Only
294
(34%)

Fig. 3. Employment status of respondents.

employment when compared with the findings of Seretny et al. (1986). These investigators found that 34% of the Division 40 members responding to their 1984-85 survey reported private practice as their primary employment. There does, however, appear to be a far greater percentage of Division 40 members presently employed in a hospital setting; 25% reported by Seretny et al. (1986) compared to 36% in the present study. When VAMC employees are included the total percentage of respondents working in a hospital based setting this figure increases to approximately 43. While only 8% of the current sample indicated that their primary employment was in a rehabilitation setting, the questionnaire specified *independent* or *free-standing* rehabilitation facility. A relatively small number of respondents indicated that they were employed in a hospital or university based rehabilitation facility.

Fees for Neuropsychological Assessment Services
Approximately one-half (51%) of those in a (nonprivate practice) primary employment setting specified that they were personally involved in the setting of fees for neuropsychological services. The remaining 49% were not involved in such fee setting activities. This question was not addressed to respondents in private practice.

As can be seen in Table 2 an hourly fee charge for neuropsychological assessment is unquestionably the most common billing method for the entire sample. Of the 548 respondents in primary employment and 544 in private practice, 689 (63%) indicated that billing was done on an *hourly* basis. A "no charge" arrange-

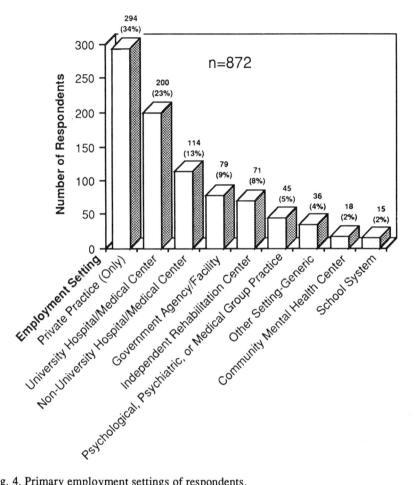

Fig. 4. Primary employment settings of respondents.

ment was in place for 117 respondents (21%) in an institutional primary employment setting. The majority of these respondents were employed in either a government-based facility (e.g., VAMC), a prepaid health care organization, or examined patients without charge for research purposes.

Table 3 shows the average *hourly* fee charged for neuropsychological assessment of adults and children. Several outliers were removed based on logical breaks in the extremes of the frequency distribution. There appears to be a great deal of similarity in the fees charged for neuropsychological assessment despite the broad range of work settings represented. Hourly fees between $75 and $125 are charged by the vast majority of respondents to this survey. Both Division 40 and NAN members charged an hourly rate of $76 for neuropsychological serv-

Table 2. Billing Procedure for Neuropsychological Assessment in Primary Employment and Private Practice.

	Primary Employment	Private Practice
N	548	544
Hourly Rate	294(54%)	395(73%)
Fixed Rate Per Patient	98(18%)	114(21%)
Protocol or Referral Question	27(5%)	17(3%)
Per Test Basis	12(2%)	16(3%)
No Charge	117(21%)	2(<1%)

Table 3. Hourly Rates Charged for Neuropsychological Assessment.

	Primary Employment		Private Practice		Adult Combined	Child Combined
	Adult Rate	Child Rate	Adult Rate	Child Rate		
N	275	176	386	261	661	437
Mean	$105	$103	$100	$100	$102	$101
SD	($32)	($29)	($25)	($25)	($28)	($27)
Mode	$100	$100	$100	$100	$100	$100
99%	$200	$200	$175	$165	$182	$178
95%	$155	$150	$150	$150	$150	$150
90%	$150	$150	$135	$130	$150	$142
75%	$125	$120	$110	$115	$120	$120
Median	$100	$100	$95	$95	$100	$100
25%	$85	$85	$80	$80	$85	$84
10%	$75	$75	$75	$75	$75	$75
5%	$60	$65	$70	$65	$65	$66
1%	$20	$25	$50	$40	$26	$27

ices according to Seretny et al.'s (1986) findings. This figure is based on information obtained during 1984-85 and would rank at approximately the 10th centile in the present data base.

As shown in Table 4 the average number of hours to complete a neuropsychological assessment tends to be slightly greater among the private practitioners, and more so for the examination of adults (i.e., 7 hours). This may reflect the absence of institutional time and space constraints on some private practitioners, which could permit a more comprehensive examination. The fact that the majority of those in private practice perform their own testing (only 31% employ technicians) and evaluate, on the average, fewer patients (cf. Figure 9), may also contribute to a longer examination. This particular questionnaire item was intended to address the number of hours required to clinically assess the patient *not* including subsequent activities such as test scoring and report generating. There were only several extreme values (>12 hours) reported. The overwhelming majority of responses seemed reasonable considering the variety of settings, patients served, and methodological and philosophical approaches to neuropsychological assessment represented by the Division 40 membership. Other published reports addressing hours per neuropsychological assessment are those of Seretny et al. (1986) and DeLuca (1989). Seretny et al. (1986) found that Division 40 members required an average of 7.18 hours to complete an assessment while members of the NAN required 7.48 hours. More recently, DeLuca (1989) reported an average time of 5.77 hours per neuropsychological assessment, with a range from 2 to 8 hours. Approximately one-half of Seretny et al.'s (1986) respondents utilized technicians, though 100% of DeLuca's (1989) respondents utilized technicians. Apparently, neither of these investigators addressed possible time differences in the assessment of adults versus children.

Ninety-eight respondents (18%) indicated that they utilized a *fixed* rate per patient for the billing of neuropsychological assessment. The figures presented in Table 5 are comparable to the averaged values obtained when the mean number of hours (Table 4) is multiplied by the mean hourly charge (Table 3). This results in total average charges between $630 and $700 for adult assessments and $600 and $660 for child assessments. However, these values do not allow for

Table 4. Average Number of Hours per Neuropsychological Assessment.

	Primary Employment		Private Practice		Adult Combined	Child Combined
	Adult Rate	Child Rate	Adult Rate	Child Rate		
N	232	155	324	219	556	374
Mean	6 hours	5.8 hours	7.0 hours	6.6 hours	6.6	6.3
SD	(2.1 hours)	(2.0 hours)	(2.4 hours)	(2.4 hours)	(2.3)	(2.3)
Mode	4 hours	6 hours	6 hours	6 hours	6	6
99%	12 hrs.	11 hrs.	14 hrs.	15 hrs.	12	13
95%	10 hrs.	10 hrs.	12 hrs.	10 hrs.	11	10
90%	9 hrs.	9 hrs.	10 hrs.	10 hrs.	10	10
75%	7 hrs.	7 hrs.	8 hrs.	8 hrs.	8	8
Median	6 hrs.	6 hrs.	7 hrs.	6 hrs.	6	6
25%	4 hrs.	4 hrs.	5 hrs.	5 hrs.	5	3
10%	4 hrs.	3 hrs.	4 hrs.	4 hrs.	4	4
5%	3 hrs.	3 hrs.	3 hrs.	3 hrs.	3	3
1%	2 hrs.	2 hrs.	3 hrs.	2 hrs.	3	2

Table 5. Fixed Rate per Patient for Neuropsychological Assessment.

	Primary Employment		Private Practice		Adult	Child
	Adult Rate	Child Rate	Adult Rate	Child Rate	Combined	Combined
N	88	73	126	91	214	164
Mean	$680	$685	$805	$815	$753	$758
SD	($215)	($245)	($330)	($330)	($294)	($301)
Mode	$500	$500	$800	$600	$800	$600
99%	$1200	$1500	$1800	$1800	$1800	$1768
95%	$1045	$1115	$1500	$1500	$1313	$1350
90%	$950	$1000	$1230	$1200	$1097	$1200
75%	$800	$825	$950	$1000	$900	$940
Median	$700	$700	$755	$750	$728	$723
25%	$535	$490	$600	$600	$563	$550
10%	$350	$350	$450	$450	$425	$413
5%	$270	$315	$325	$380	$315	$350
1%	$225	$225	$195	$300	$229	$242

Table 6. Charges for Diagnostic and Screening Neuropsychological Test Batteries.

	Primary Employment		Private Practice		Diagnostic	Screening
	Diagnostic	Screening	Diagnostic	Screening	Combined	Combined
N	12	19	13	9	25	28
Mean	$620	$340	$710	$320	$665	$334
SD	$220	$135	$215	$140	$219	$135
Mode	$700	$150	$500	$250	$700	$150
Minimum	$300	$150	$300	$145	$300	$145
Maximum	$1200	$600	$1000	$600	$1200	$600

billing over and beyond the actual clinical time to complete the assessment (e.g., scoring, interpretation, report generation). Seretny et al. (1986) reported figures of $501 for APA Division 40 members and $449 for NAN members for "a complete neuropsychological evaluation" (p. 9) .

A relatively small percentage of respondents indicated that they typically charged by the type of referral question or testing protocol employed. In the interest of parsimony, no attempt was made to specifically define what constitutes a diagnostic or screening protocol. However, in a gross sense, it was clear that a diagnostic battery was more comprehensive, while the screening battery was limited in scope. These data are presented in Table 6 for general reference purposes only. Seretny et al. (1986) report an average fee of $288 for "an un-specified abbreviated evaluation" for Division 40 and NAN members participating in their study.

Distribution of Clinical Time
In recent years it has become apparent that the role and responsibilities of the clinical neuropsychologist have expanded into a number of new areas of endeavor and challenge (Bornstein et al., 1986; Chelune & Moehle, 1986). While those practicing neuropsychology may no longer practice exclusively as diagnosticians or evaluators, it does appear from the data presented in Table 7 that more time is allocated to neuropsychological assessment than other clinical activities. This of course has long-standing historic precedent. However, as Bornstein et al. (1986) have suggested, while our methodological approaches may not significantly change, the questions which are raised have indeed changed in response to continuing advances within the field and allied disciplines.

It is apparent from the data presented in Table 7 and Figure 5 that the trichotomy of neuropsychological activities (i.e., assessment, treatment, and consultation) employed in this study is inadequate for completely capturing the diversified activities of many neuropsychological practitioners. The generic "other neuropsychological activities" category resulted in higher mean values than either the treatment or consultation categories. Presumably this reflects predominantly research and teaching responsibilities for many of the respondents. However, a number of respondent comments associated with this particular item could be regarded as ventures directly related to illness prevention as well.

Neuropsychological Treatment Services and Fees
With respect to the treatment of neuropsychological impairments, Barth and Boll (1981) have referred to the psychologist as "the new kid on the block" (p. 257) compared to other behavioral scientists. In fact, Satz and Fletcher concluded in their 1981 overview which addressed emergent trends in the field of neuropsychology that, "The therapeutic role of the neuropsychologist is only beginning to be defined" (p. 860). This maturational process will no doubt continue as increasing attention is cast towards issues of neuropsychologically oriented treatment. Lezak (1983) has pointed out that this is the natural and expected evolution of a discipline as it grows in knowledge and sophistication; "assessment tends to play a predominant role while these (clinical) sciences are relatively young. Treatment techniques develop as diagnostic categories and etiological relationships are defined and clarified (p. 7)." Noting the increased diagnostic precision in the field, Costa (1983) forecasted in his 1982 Presidential Address to the Division 40 membership that "More concern will be given to the behavioral consequences of neurologically related disorders and to intervention techniques aimed at remediation" (p. 3).

During the last decade the treatment emphases within neuropsychology have

Table 7. Percentage of Clinical Time in Various Neuropsychological Activities.

	Primary Employment	Private Practice	Combined
N	547	511	1,058
Neuropsychological Assessment			
Mean	44%	48%	46%
SD	(29%)	(30%)	(30%)
MDN	40%	50%	48%
% of respondents reporting <1%	6%	2%	4%
% of respondents reporting ≥25%	68%	71%	70%
Neuropsychological Treatment			
Mean	13%	13%	13%
SD	(19%)	(19%)	(19%)
MDN	0%	5%	2%
% of respondents reporting <1%	51%	48%	50%
% of respondents reporting ≥25%	21%	20%	20%
Neuropsychological Consultation			
Mean	13%	13%	13%
SD	(15%)	(17%)	(16%)
MDN	10%	10%	10%
% of respondents reporting <1%	29%	25%	27%
% of respondents reporting ≥25%	17%	15%	16%
Other Neuropsychological Activities			
Mean	30%	26%	29%
SD	(36%)	(34%)	(35%)
MDN	10%	0%	3%
% of respondents reporting <1%	46%	53%	50%
% of respondents reporting ≥25%	45%	38%	42%

appeared to progress beyond the traditional adjustment to loss paradigm and increasingly towards *active* remediation of neuropsychological deficits. Much of this development falls under the general rubric of cognitive rehabilitation. The Task Force on Head Injury of the American Congress of Rehabilitation Medicine (1986) put forth the first guidelines in 1986 defining the nature, purpose, and objectives of cognitive rehabilitation treatments, along with proposed admission criteria for patients entering such treatment programs. However, while such

n=1,058

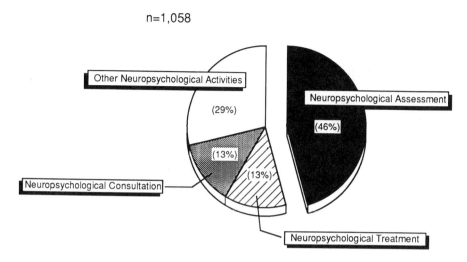

Fig. 5. Distribution of clinical time in various neuropsychological activities for entire sample of respondents.

advances continue, the *industry* of some neuropsychological treatment approaches appear to have preceded the scientific foundations of such endeavors (Adams & Putnam, 1989).

Figure 6 displays the percentage of respondents who report presently being involved in the delivery of neuropsychological treatment services. Percentages are similar, but the trend is for more private practitioners to provide treatment services. Table 8 presents how much time is spent in the following treatment activities; cognitive rehabilitation, vocational counseling, remedial educational services, psychotherapy, health care consultation, and "other" neuropsychologically oriented treatments. In the interest of parsimony, no attempt was made to precisely define the categories utilized, although explicit definitions have been proposed by certain innovators in the field (Diller & Gordon, 1981). Psychotherapy with patients suffering neurological deficit is of course multidimensional and multifaceted (see Butler & Satz, 1988) and may not be amenable to a succinct definition.

Nevertheless, it is very apparent from examining Table 8 that psychotherapy in some form is practiced by all but a small percentage of respondents who provide neuropsychological treatment. Psychotherapy comprises more than one-quarter of the treatment time for 68% of those in primary employment and 78% for those in private practice. Cognitive rehabilitation is the second most implemented treatment service. However, approximately one-third of the respondents indicated that they were not involved in this form of treatment. Various degrees of consulting activity were reported by more than one-half of those offering

184

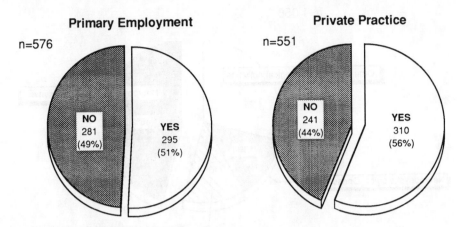

Fig. 6. Number and percentage of respondents in primary employment and private practice providing neuropsychological treatment services.

treatment, and less than one-quarter indicated involvement in remedial educational services.

The average hourly rates charged for various neuropsychological treatment
services were generally between $75 and $115 (Table 9), figures which are
comparable, but slightly lower than the average hourly rates for neuropsychological assessment presented earlier in Table 3.

On the whole, those in a primary employment setting tend to treat more
patients than those in private practice. However, on the average the latter group
may see more children (Table 10). In both groups far fewer children are seen for
both neuropsychological treatment and assessment (Figure 9) than adult patients.
Indeed, there is a marked degree of variability in the figures presented in Table
10 which would appear to defy a recognizable pattern to account for these data.
However, these findings appear to differ with those of Sweet and Moberg (1990)
who reported that 77% of the ABPP's and 57% of the non-ABPP's returning
their questionnaire saw less than 5 patients per month, on the average, for neuropsychological treatment. As mentioned earlier, this figure may be the result of
including respondents in their analysis who did not engage in treatment activities
at all.

The question addressing satisfaction with monetary compensation for treatment and assessment (Tables 11 and 12) produced results in the expected direction when considered in the context of the *TCN* salary survey (Putnam,1989)
findings. While overhead and allied office expenses were not deducted, and there
was much variability in reported earnings, the private practitioners earned, on
the average, approximately $30,000 more annually than those employed in an
institutional setting (Putnam, 1989). In the current study, respondents in private

Table 8. Mean Percentage of Treatment Time in Various Activities.

	Primary Employment	Private Practice	Combined
N	284	309	593
Cognitive Rehabilitation	21%	18%	20%
SD	(24%)	(22%)	(23%)
Median	14%	10%	10%
Mode	0%	0%	0%
% of respondents reporting <1%	31%	37%	34%
% of respondents reporting ≥25%	33%	30%	32%
Vocational Counseling	6%	7%	7%
SD	(10%)	(11%)	(10%)
Median	0%	0%	0%
Mode	0%	0%	0%
% of respondents reporting <1%	56%	52%	54%
% of respondents reporting ≥25%	9%	10%	9%
Remedial Educational Services	5%	4%	5%
SD	(15%)	(11%)	(14%)
Median	0%	0%	0%
Mode	0%	0%	0%
% of respondents reporting <1%	81%	78%	79%
% of respondents reporting ≥25%	7%	5%	6%
Psychotherapy	42%	52%	47%
SD	(31%)	(31%)	(31%)
Median	40%	50%	50%
Mode	50%	50%	50%
% of respondents reporting <1%	13%	8%	10%
% of respondents reporting ≥25%	68%	78%	73%
Consulting - Health Care	14%	11%	12%
SD	(22%)	(20%)	(21%)
Median	0%	0%	0%
Mode	0%	0%	0%
% of respondents reporting <1%	54%	56%	55%
% of respondents reporting ≥25%	21%	16%	19%
Other Neuropsych Treatment	11%	7%	9%
SD	(24%)	(20%)	(22%)
Median	0%	0%	0%
Mode	0%	0%	0%
% of respondents reporting <1%	74%	82%	78%
% of respondents reporting ≥25%	18%	10%	14%

practice indicated far higher levels of satisfaction with the financial rewards for both neuropsychological treatment and assessment than those in institutional primary employment.

Table 9. Hourly Rates Charged for Treatment Services.

	Primary Employment	Private Practice	Combined
N	234	306	540
Mean	$97	$92	$94
SD	($24)	($18)	($21)
Mode	$100	$90	$100
99%	$185	$150	$156
95%	$140	$125	$137
90%	$129	$129	$125
75%	$110,	$100	$100
Median	$95	$90	$90
25%	$80	$80	$80
10%	$70	$75	$75
5%	$60	$70	$70
1%	$50	$60	$50

Table 10. Number of Patients Seen Monthly for Neuropsychological Treatment

	Primary Employment	Private Practice
N	259	290
$\overline{X}$ Total patients per month	14	11
SD	(17)	(15)
MDN	10	5
$\overline{X}$ Adult patients per month	12	9
SD	(15)	(13)
MDN	7	4
$\overline{X}$ Children patients per month	2	4
SD	(7)	(10)
MDN	0	0

Table 11. Responses to the Statement, "The Monetary Compensation I Receive for Neuropsychological Treatment Services is Satisfactory".

	Primary Employment	Private Practice
	248	300
1. Strongly Agree	19 (8%)	35 (12%)
2. Agree	118 (48%)	205 (68%)
3. Uncertain	26 (11%)	26 (9%)
4. Disagree	51 (21%)	26 (9%)
5. Strongly Disagree	34 (14%)	8 (3%)
Mean	2.8	2.2
SD	(1.2)	(0.86)
Mode	2	2

Table 12. Responses to the Statement, "The Monetary Compensation I Receive for Neuropsychological Assessment Services is Satisfactory".

	Primary Employment	Private Practice
N	447	500
1. Strongly Agree	37 (8%)	69 (14%)
2. Agree	196 (44%)	325 (65%)
3. Uncertain	37 (8%)	47 (9%)
4. Disagree	110 (25%)	46 (9%)
5. Strongly Disagree	67 (15%)	13 (3%)
Mean	2.9	2.2
SD	(1.2)	(0.88)

Direct Patient Contact

The majority of respondents in both primary and private practice settings indicated that they engaged in direct patient contact through clinical interviews or test administration; 78% and 95% respectively (Table 13). Less than 1% from each group reported *never* having direct contact with the patient being examined.

The issue of patient contact is a multifaceted one. For instance, the work of neuropsychologists employing technical personnel to administer neuro-psychological tests has been questioned in legal arenas as well as by 3rd party health care providers. In one instance (*Indianapolis Union Railway vs. Walker*, 1974) the testimony of Ralph M. Reitan, on behalf of the plaintiff, was contested on the grounds that it was hearsay evidence since Dr. Reitan did not actually assess the patient in question. However, the trial court ruled decisively in favor of the professional/technical model utilized in Dr. Reitan's laboratory (DeLuca, 1989).

In other cases this professional practice option has been upheld. In another venue, some health care providers have eliminated reimbursements to neuro-psychologists utilizing technical personnel. In fact, a California psychologist was charged with Med-Cal fraud on behalf of the referring insurers for payments made to the psychologist for services rendered by his registered psychological assistant (T. R. Hardey, personal communication, December 6, 1989 and February 8, 1990). These charges notwithstanding, the psychologist was found to be practicing in full accordance with California rules and regulations for psychologists and the charges were dismissed. Moreover, the presiding judge ruled that there was no California Statute or regulation that prohibited the reimbursement for services rendered by a registered psychological assistant. The prosecuting attorney was censured since, in effect, no laws were violated by the principal involved. This case had precedent setting merit with regard to Med-Cal reimbursement for services delivered by registered psychological assistants. Of course, no such rulings in any state prohibit the use of technicians (e.g., EEG technicians, physicians assistants) by neurologists and other physicians.

Table 13. Percent of Respondents Having Direct Patient Contact Through Interview or Test Administration.

	Primary Employment	Private Practice
N	553	543
1. Always	78%	95%
2. Usually	15%	4%
3. Half The Time	3%	<1%
4. Seldom	4%	<1%
5. Never	<1%	<1%
Mean	1.3	1.1
SD	(0.7)	(0.3)

As shown in Table 14 a follow-up session with the patient or a significant other to review test results appears to be quite characteristic of both groups, but more so with the private practitioners. The number of respondents conducting such sessions does indeed seem inflated from strictly an intuitive-experiential perspective. However, no published reports regarding the prevalence of this practice could be located, and in fact, would appear not to exist at this time. It may be the case that as increasing emphasis is placed on prescriptive treatment and intervention by neuropsychological practitioners, follow-up sessions have become more customary and integral to shaping treatment plans for patients.

Neuropsychology Technicians

As elaborated by DeLuca (1989), while the practice of employing technical personnel to administer psychological tests dates back to the World War II era, it is not without controversy. This issue is often near the epicenter of the "tiresome food-fight debate" (Adams, 1985) over flexible versus fixed neuropsychological test batteries. While the practice unquestionably reduces patient contact for the neuropsychologist, it does allow service to a greater number of patients. Those adhering to a more quantitative assessment methodology have argued that the practice actually offers a more objective and unbiased data collection effort than when the neuropsychologist conducts the testing. Moreover, it is cost effective as well (DeLuca, 1989).

Recently, the Division 40 Task Force on Education, Accreditation, and Credentialing concluded that "the use of . . . technicians is a common and accepted practice when the supervising psychologist maintains and monitors high standards of quality assurance" (p. 25) (Task Force, 1989). Of course, this practice

Table 14. Percent of Respondents Having Follow-Up Session to Discuss Neuro-psychological Test Results

	Primary Employment	Private Practice
N	547	541
1. Always	33%	47%
2. Usually	35%	32%
3. Half The Time	14%	11%
4. Seldom	15%	9%
5. Never	2%	1%
Mean	2.1	1.9
SD	(1.1)	(1.0)

has its detractors as well as supporters, both inside and outside the profession of psychology, a discussion of which is beyond the scope of this paper. Be this as it may, the use of technicians appears to be a common practice in contemporary neuropsychological practice. As shown in Figure 7 approximately 53% of the respondents in primary employment settings reported that they utilized technicians, psychometrists, or psychological assistants to administer neuropsychological tests. Only 31% of those in private practice office indicated such a practice. Seretny et al. (1986) reported that "approximately half of the respondents [614 APA and NAN members] do not employ technicians, a figure which has been consistent over the last 5 years" (p. 8). While this figure is proximal to the present findings for those in primary employment, apparently no distinction was made by these investigators between the use of technicians in primary employment versus a private practice setting. Guilmette et al. (in press) report that only 19% of the respondents to their 1986 survey employed technicians, a finding at odds with the other published studies reviewed here. However, when they compared groups of respondents differentiated on the basis of amount of time actually spent practicing neuropsychology (i.e., those reporting less than 10% with those reporting greater than 30%), it was determined that the latter, more neuropsychologically active group actually made *greater* use of technicians. Unfortunately, Guilmette et al. (in press) failed to report the actual frequencies/percentages associated with these conclusions in their paper.

A recent survey conducted by Sweet and Moberg (1990) found that 77.2% and 58.5% of ABPP and non-ABPP neuropsychologists, respectively, employed technicians to perform neuropsychological testing. Furthermore, they state that this figure was generally stable across theoretical approaches to assessment. Interestingly, 68.9% of Sweet and Moberg's (1990) respondents who did not utilize a standardized neuropsychological test battery indicated that they employed technicians. This is reminiscent of Adam's (1985) criticism of simplistic dichotomies and stereotypes.

Further analysis of the current technician data will be presented in Part II; comparisons of respondents by clinical practice as well as assessment methodology will be delineated. No attempt was made to evaluate the training background of technical personnel. The reader is referred to DeLuca (1989) for a thorough discussion of the training and deployment patterns of neuropsychological technicians and to Miller and Auvenshine (1988) for discussion of a state board of psychology's reaction in a recent case involving the supervision of technicians.

The ratio of technicians to neuropsychologists was 2.4/2.1 for respondents in primary employment, and 1.8/1.3 for those in a private practice setting (Table 15). These figures approximate the 1 to 1 ratio of technicians to neuropsychologists found by DeLuca (1989). Similarly, they closely correspond with Seretny et al.'s (1986) report of 1.1 technicians per Division 40 respondent.

As presented in Table 16, technicians were most often compensated by either an hourly pay rate (45%) or an annual salary (40%). In contrast to this, technicians employed by private practitioners were far more likely to be compensated

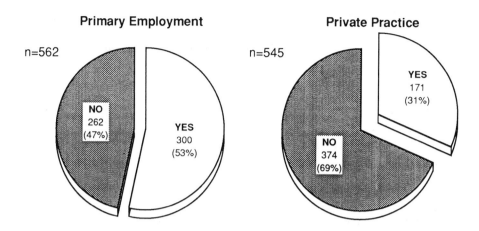

Fig. 7. The number and percentage of respondents employing technicians to administer neuropsychological tests.

Table 15. Number of Technicians and Neuropsychologists in Settings Employing Technicians.

	Primary Employment	Private Practice
Mean Number of Technicians	2.4	1.8
SD	(1.8)	(1.1)
Median	2	1
Mode	1	1
Minimum	1	1
Maximum	13	8
Mean Number of Neuropsychologists	2.1	1.3
SD	(1.8)	(0.67)
Median	2	1
Mode	1	1
Minimum	1	1
Maximum	14	4

Table 16. Methods for Compensating Technicians.

	Primary Employment	Private Practice
N	293	170
1. Hourly Rate	132 (45%)	125 (74%)
2. Per Patient Fee	6 (2%)	21 (12%)
3. Students for Supervision	37 (13%)	4 (2%)
4. Annual Salary	118 (40%)	20 (12%)

by an hourly pay rate (74%). There was a clear difference in hourly rates paid to technicians in a primary versus private practice setting; $13 and $21 per hour respectively (Table 17). However, health care and other benefits need to be considered in accounting for this lower hourly pay rate for technicians in an institutional setting. The fact that the average annual salaries between the two groups is virtually identical ($23,000) would seem to offer support for this explanation. These figures are very similar to those reported by DeLuca (1989): an average annual salary of approximately $20,100 (range between $13,500 and $31,000).

Referral Sources for Neuropsychological Services
It appears from the data presented in Table 18 that referrals from managed care systems comprise only a very small part of the clinical practice of most respondents. This is true for both those in primary employment as well as private practice. Approximately two-thirds receive no referrals from HMO's, PPO's, or other prepaid systems. Only 6-10% indicated that referrals from these organizations made up more than one-quarter of their total patient referrals. It is of some relevance that the Bush administration is expected to propose legislation to Congress which would be intended to include more lower-income and elderly patients (Medicaid and Medicare recipients) in such managed health care programs (Adler, 1990). Similar legislation has been rejected in the past under the Reagan administration.

The "other sources" category in Table 18 is largely made up of the more traditional referral sources, namely, neurologists, neurosurgeons, and psychiatrists, as well as other psychologists. The two largest referral sources for neuropsychological examinations in the Seretny et al. (1986) study were neurologists and psychiatrists. Referrals from these colleagues constituted 46% of the APA members' referrals, and 29% of the NAN members referrals. Sweet and Moberg (1990) reported that neurology and psychiatry were the two major sources of referrals for both ABPP and non-ABPP neuropsychologists responding to their survey.

Table 17. Average Hourly Rates, Fixed Rates Per Patient, and Annual Salaries Paid to Neuropsychological Technicians.

	Primary Employment	**Private Practice**
N	132	125
Average Hourly Rate	$13	$21
SD	($6)	($11)
Mode	$9	$15
99%	$48	$60
95%	$25	$50
90%	$21	$35
75%	$15	$25
Median	$12	$18
25%	$10	$13
10%	$9	$10
5%	$8	$10
1%	$7	$8
Adult Fee	$155	$175
SD	($70)	($95)
Child Fee	$145	$180
SD	($95)	($100)
Maximum	$250	$425
Minimum	$80	$75
Annual Salary	$23,000	$23,000
SD	($4000)	($7,000)
Mode	$19,000	$18,000
99%	$33,000	$35,000
95%	$32,000	$35,000
90%	$30,000	$30,000
75%	$25,000	$23,000
Median	$22,000	$18,000
25%	$20,000	$15,000
10%	$18,000	$15,000
5%	$17,000	$15,000
1%	$16,000	$15,000

The classic volume entitled *"The Late Effects of Head Injury,"* edited by Walker, Caveness, and Critchley (1969), devoted an entire section (9 chapters) to "medicolegal problems of the head-injured". The contributors to the impressive collection of papers in this section were all physicians and jurists. The work pre-dated the presence (and stature) of contemporary clinical neuropsychology in the medical and legal spheres. Thus, no references were made to neuropsychologists, and only several references were made to clinical psychologists, e.g. "quantitating mental impairment" (p. 492) (Beresford, 1969). However, the content of these chapters seemed to suggest a vacuum with respect to diagnosis, causal relationships, objective evidence, criteria for return to work, etc., and in effect portended the entry of clinical neuropsychology into the legal arena. Recently, Schwartz (1987) has eloquently noted that, "Neuropsychology is . . . rapidly establishing a presence in the forensic area" (p. 51). He goes on to discuss some of the principal reasons for this growing affinity between neuropsychology and law as due to several factors: (1) neuropsychological assessment is painless and non-life-threatening; (2) it is an acceptable method for determining the presence or absence of brain damage; (3) it is an acceptable method for making pre- and post-injury comparisons of changes in mental and emotional functioning; (4) it is an acceptable method for characterization of an individual in relation to normative groups in order to determine current level of ability and degree of deviation from the norm; (5) it is an acceptable method for anatomic comparison and contrast with neurodiagnostic measures, and finally, (6) via pattern analysis of neuropsychological data the type of brain damage can sometimes be ascertained.

A law publication (*Trial*) recently contained a chapter discussing the role of neuropsychology in mild brain injury claims which seemed to corroborate these contentions;

the neuropsychological evaluation can substantiate causality. . . . the neuropsychologist knows how certain injuries occur and may be able to explain troubling claims like reports of loss of memory for critical events. . . The neuropsychologist can also explain apparent discrepancies in the claim (e.g., when some brain functions appear normal in someone claiming serious brain impairment) (Lees-Haley, 1987, pp.84-85).

An extensive literature has begun to accumulate on the applications of clinical neuropsychology in the legal environment. Virtually every edited "handbook" in the field has devoted a chapter to this pertinent issue (Bigler, 1986; McMahon, 1983; McMahon & Satz, 1983) and at least one book has focused exclusively on the subject (Golden & Strider, 1986). The Journal of Head Trauma Rehabilitation has a regular section devoted to medicolegal issues and *TCN* publishes a "Courting the Clinician" series. Just this year Ralph M. Reitan (1990) has added a new advanced level offering to his training workshop series entitled "The Neuropsychologist As An Expert Witness" and the upcoming 1990 Annual Meeting of the National Academy of Neuropsychologists has no less than five

Table 18. Referral Sources for Neuropsychological Services.

	Primary Employment	Private Practice
N	492	498
Health Maintenance Organizations		
Mean %	7%	5%
SD	(15%)	(12%)
MDN	0%	0%
% of respondents reporting <1%	63%	70%
% of respondents reporting ≥25%	10%	6%
Preferred Provider Organizations		
Mean %	5%	5%
SD	(12%)	(12%)
MDN	0%	0%
% of respondents reporting <1%	70%	71%
% of respondents reporting ≥25%	8%	6%
Other Pre-Paid Groups		
Mean %	14%	13%
SD	(27%)	(25%)
MDN	0%	0%
% of respondents reporting <1%	67%	70%
% of respondents reporting ≥25%	19%	18%
Criminal Cases		
Mean %	4%	3%
SD	(16%)	(8%)
MDN	0%	0%
% of respondents reporting <1%	82%	70%
% of respondents reporting ≥25%	4%	3%
Personal Injury		
Mean %	11%	22%
SD	(21%)	(27%)
MDN	0%	10%
% of respondents reporting <1%	55%	25%
% of respondents reporting ≥25%	17%	33%
Other Civil		
Mean %	4%	5%
SD	(14%)	(12%)
MDN	0%	0%
% of respondents reporting <1%	82%	75%
% of respondents reporting ≥25%	4%	6%
Other Sources		
Mean %	52%	47%
SD	(42%)	(37%)
MDN	60%	50%
% of respondents reporting <1%	28%	26%
% of respondents reporting ≥25%	63%	66%

Table 19. Referral Source for Neuropsychological Services in Personal Injury Cases.

	Primary Employment	Private Practice
N	226	371
Referral Represents Plaintiff	56%	61%
SD	(31%)	(29%)
MDN	50%	60%
% of respondents reporting <1%	10%	7%
% of respondents reporting ≥25%	82%	86%
Referral Represents Defendant	30%	33%
SD	(26%)	(27%)
MDN	25%	30%
% of respondents reporting <1%	21%	19%
% of respondents reporting ≥25%	55%	59%
Referral Represents Neither	14%	6%
SD	(32%)	(20%)
MDN	0%	0%
% of respondents reporting <1%	76%	88%
% of respondents reporting ≥25%	15%	7%

scheduled presentations addressing forensic neuropsychology by different presenters. Bigler (1986) has forecasted "an ever-increasing role for specialization in forensic neuropsychology" (p. 545). This would seem to be a necessary outgrowth given the sometimes conflicting demands made on the neuropsychologist in the clinical *vis-a-vis* the legal circumstance (i.e., cooperative versus adversarial).

Personal injury litigation appears to be the area where neuropsychology and law most frequently interface (McMahon, 1983), primarily because of the requirement by triers of fact to provide an expert witness to the court (Schwartz, 1987). However, both Schwartz (1987) and Satz (1988) have expressed passionate concerns regarding the recent procession of psychologists into the courtroom claiming to have "expertise" in neuropsychology. Satz (1988) raised the issue of "potential restriction" being placed on expert neuropsychological testimony as the result of admissibility of incompetent "expert" witness testimony in several recent cases.

Table 19 presents the referral source (i.e., plaintiff or defendant) for respondents engaged in neuropsychological work in cases involving personal injury litigation. Quite clearly the majority of those involved in such civil proceedings indicated that they represented the plaintiff more than one-half of the time and represented the defendant approximately one-third of the time. Few definitive conclusions can be drawn from these data; however, the far greater proportion of private practitioners involved in such forensic activities (also see Table 21) is noteworthy. While 492 respondents in institutional primary employment indicated involvement in personal injury cases, only 226 (46%) of these reported participation in legal cases. In the private practice sector, however, 498 respondents indicated they were involved with personal injury cases and 371 (74%) of these accepted legal referrals. Schwartz (1987) as well as Satz (1988) have made reference to research qualifications and professional publications as indispensable in establishing "expert" witness status in the courtroom. For the practitioner who is exclusively in private practice and/or who has a limited research record, this may create considerable hardship. Moreover, it may be these individuals about whom Schwartz (1987) and Satz (1988) were directing their comments noted earlier.

This discussion should not obscure the fact that in this sample of Division 40 respondents, there are many who do *not* participate in such forensic proceedings. Of 492 respondents in primary employment, 269 (55%) do not do personal injury evaluations. Of 498 respondents in a private practice setting, 123 (25%) do not do personal injury evaluations. Indeed, private practitioners appear to be far more involved in this particular activity. This may be associated with the increased financial benefits of such work.

The average (mean and median) hourly fee charged for legal activities such as depositions or legal consulting was $150 (*SD* = $60) for 441 private practitioners. This figure is of course considerably higher than the hourly assessment rate of $100 and treatment rate of $92 reported earlier.

Characteristics of Patients

Age groups.

Perusal of Table 20 underscores the extent to which clinical neuropsychology appears to serve a disproportionate number of adults, *viz-a-viz* children and geriatric patients. One-half of the respondents indicated that clinical involvement with young adults and older adults comprised more than 25% of their time. In all, these data are generally equivalent with the findings reported by Sweet and Moberg (1990), with several exceptions. These investigators found that 33% and 26% of their group of ABPP and non-ABPP respondents had no clinical involvement with adolescent patients. As shown in Table 20, this was true of only 14% of the respondents to the present study. Furthermore, only 7% of the ABPP respondents specified that they did not see geriatric patients. However, over one-third of the respondents in the present study indicated the same. Finally, more than one-half of the Sweet and Moberg (1990) respondents did *not* serve children, a figure very similar to the present findings for those in institutional employment. Such results may underscore the unique training required in working with this population. However, 62% of those in private practice did include services to children (more if infants are included) (Table 20). This may be particularly noteworthy in the context of Slay and Valdivia's (1988) report that 61% of a group who listed neuropsychology as a specialization area in the

National Register, but who in fact did not identify themselves as neuro-psychologists indicated that they provided neuropsychological services to children.

Diagnostic groups.

The following questions addressed diagnostic groups of patients served. In general the data presented in Table 21 support the contention of Bornstein et al. (1986) of an increasing diversity with regard to the kinds of patients referred for neuropsychological services. However, it appears that head trauma and psychiatric patients are the "staple" of many respondents, comprising 10-15% (median

Table 20. Clinical Time Involved Serving Patients by Age Groups.

	Primary Employment	Private Practice	Combined
N	549	513	1,062
Infants-Mean%	1%	<1%	<1%
SD	(6%)	(2%)	(5%)
MDN	0%	0%	0%
% of respondents reporting <1%	90%	91%	90%
% of respondents reporting ≥25%	1%	<1%	1%
Children-Mean%	14%	14%	14%
SD	(24%)	(20%)	(22%)
MDN	0%	5%	5%
% of respondents reporting <1%	54%	38%	46%
% of respondents reporting ≥25%	23%	24%	23%
Adolescents-Mean%	13%	15%	14%
SD	(16%)	(12%)	(14)
MDN	10%	10%	10%
% of respondents reporting <1%	34%	18%	26%
% of respondents reporting ≥25%	19%	22%	21%
Young Adults-Mean%	30%	31%	31%
SD	(25%)	(20%)	(23%)
MDN	25%	30%	25%
% of respondents reporting <1%	13%	7%	10%
% of respondents reporting ≥25%	53%	62%	57%
Older Adults-Mean%	26%	29%	27%
SD	(22%)	(22%)	(22%)
MDN	20%	25%	25%
% of respondents reporting <1%	18%	11%	15%
% of respondents reporting ≥25%	48%	52%	50%
Geriatrics-Mean%	16%	10%	13%
SD	(20%)	(14%)	(18%)
MDN	10%	5%	5%
% of respondents reporting <1%	36%	40%	38%
% of respondents reporting ≥25%	26%	13%	20%

values) of the cases seen clinically. Just over one-third of the sample reported that head trauma patients made up more than a quarter of their patient caseload, and many of these case involved litigation. At the other extreme very few respondents see AIDS patients clinically, despite the recent increase in published research with this population. However, most patients seen clinically do not fall exclusively into one diagnostic category and in many cases several could apply equally. Given this problem of overlap and artifact the data in Table 21 should be viewed only as approximations of the respondents' actual clinical practice.

Figure 9 presents the average number of neuropsychological assessments completed per month. On the whole, respondents in primary employment settings appear to evaluate more patients. This may be due to several factors: (1) many private practitioners are not active in their practice on a full-time basis; (2) fewer private practitioners employ technicians to administer neuropsychological tests (see Figure 7); and (3) the average number of hours to complete a neuropsychological evaluation tends to be greater among private practitioners (see Table 4). Seretny et al. (1986) reported that Division 40 and NAN members performed an average of 11-12 neuropsychological evaluations per month during 1984-85. More recently, Sweet and Moberg (1990) indicate that approximately 24% of the ABPP respondents in their study saw between 5-10 patient monthly, and 20% saw between 11-19.

Indigent and underprivileged groups
One of the more emotion-laden issues addressed in this study concerned patient groups whom respondents were unable to offer their services to due to a low fee schedule. While the majority of respondents in both primary employment and

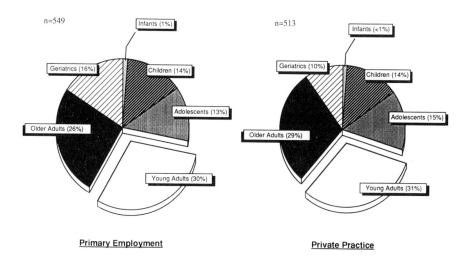

Fig. 8. Distribution of patients served by age categories.

Table 21. Clinical Time Involved Serving Patients by Diagnostic Categories.

	Primary Employment	Private Practice
N	546	496
Head Trauma Patients	22%	23%
SD	(26%)	(24%)
MDN	10%	15%
% of respondents reporting <1%	20%	16%
% of respondents reporting ≥25%	34%	36%
Seizure Patients	6%	3%
SD	(13%)	(7%)
MDN	0%	0%
% of respondents reporting <1%	51%	63%
% of respondents reporting ≥25%	6%	1%
Stroke Patients	9%	5%
SD	(13%)	(9%)
MDN	5%	0%
% of respondents reporting <1%	41%	54%
% of respondents reporting ≥25%	12%	3%
Pain Patients	2%	4%
SD	(7%)	(9%)
MDN	0%	0%
% of respondents reporting <1%	76%	64%
% of respondents reporting ≥25%	3%	4%
Psychiatric Patients	16%	19%
SD	(23%)	(24%)
MDN	5%	10%
% of respondents reporting <1%	39%	33%
% of respondents reporting ≥25%	23%	31%
Learning Disabled Patients	11%	12%
SD	(20%)	(19%)
MDN	0%	5%
% of respondents reporting <1%	55%	41%
% of respondents reporting ≥25%	17%	17%
Substance Abuse Patients	5%	4%
SD	(13%)	(10%)
MDN	0%	0%
% of respondents reporting <1%	64%	63%
% of respondents reporting ≥25%	6%	4%
AIDS Patients	2%	<1%
SD	(6%)	(2%)
MDN	0%	0%
% of respondents reporting <1%	80%	91%
% of respondents reporting ≥25%	2%	<1%

Table 21. Continued.

Table 21. Continued

	Primary Employment	Private Practice
Demyelinating Patients	2%	<1%
SD	(7%)	(3%)
MDN	0%	0%
% of respondents reporting <1%	73%	83%
% of respondents reporting ≥25%	<1%	<1%
Toxic Patients	2%	2%
SD	(7%)	(9%)
MDN	0%	0%
% of respondents reporting <1%	71%	75%
% of respondents reporting ≥25%	1%	1%
Tumor Patients	3%	1%
SD	(6%)	(4%)
MDN	0%	0%
% of respondents reporting <1%	62%	77%
% of respondents reporting ≥25%	2%	1%
Dementia Patients	11%	7%
SD	(17%)	(11%)
MDN	5%	3%
% of respondents reporting <1%	39%	44%
% of respondents reporting ≥25%	15%	6%
Other Generic Patients	5%	5%
SD	(14%)	(16%)
MDN	0%	0%
% of respondents reporting <1%	76%	79%
% of respondents reporting ≥25%	6%	8%
Forensic/Legal Patients	5%	11%
SD	(14%)	(18%)
MDN	0%	5%
% of respondents reporting <1%	67%	44%
% of respondents reporting ≥25%	5%	14%

private practice indicated that there were *no* patient groups they could not serve, the low fee schedule prevented many from serving Medicaid and Medicare patients (Table 22). However, a number of respondents indicated that they saw a limited number of such patients on a *pro bono* basis. Under the provisions of the new Medicare bill (passed by the U. S. Congress on November 22, 1989 and signed by President Bush on December 19, 1989) psychologists are no longer excluded from reimbursement by this government program. Beginning in July 1990 significant changes are likely to occur in the availability and delivery of psychological care to the elderly and disabled. In particular, the $1,100 yearly limit on payment for outpatient mental health services has been eliminated.

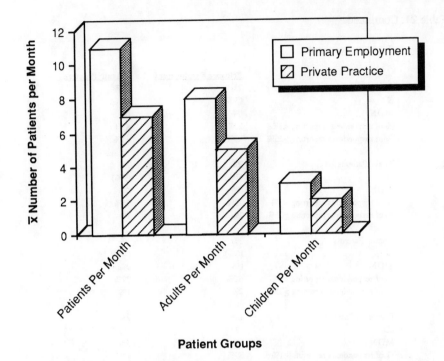

Patient Groups

Fig. 9. Average number of patients seen monthly for neuropsychological assessment.

However, one of the potentially most important aspects to this new legislation would be psychologists' inclusion in national health insurance, should this come to pass (Buie, 1990). The Health Care Financing Administration is still in the process of writing the regulations for the administration of the new law and it likely will be some time before direct impact is seen in the day to day practice of

Table 22. Patients Groups Whom Respondents Are Unable to Provide Services Due to Low Payment Schedule.

	Primary Employment	Private Practice
N	498	470
None	81%	49%
Medicaid/Medicare	13%	29%
Other State/Fed Supported	1%	7%
HMO's	<1%	2%
Non-insured patients	2%	4%
Others	2%	8%

psychologists. Moreover, it remains to be seen how many psychologists practicing neuropsychology will actually seek medicare reimbursement, in spite of the significance this landmark victory for the profession.

SUMMARY

The current response rate of 40% compares acceptably with the 46% (SD = 12.4%) reported by Heberlein and Baumgartner (1978) in their quantitative review of 107 surveys based on a single mailing (i.e., no follow-up contacts with non-respondents) (Also see Goyder, 1982). While these investigators found that the number of contacts with potential respondents was the best predictor of final response rate (accounting for approximately 42% of the variance in final response rate), budgetary constraints did not permit additional contact with those failing to respond to this questionnaire.

There is reason to believe that the exponential increase in the number of individuals practicing clinical neuropsychology during the 1980's will continue into the 1990's. As the number of academic and clinical training opportunities improve, in part as the result of identified deficiencies resulting from survey studies (McCaffrey & Isaac, 1984; McCaffrey et al., 1985) they will produce better prepared professionals. With training available which corresponds to the guidelines established by the INS-Division 40 Task Force, neuropsychological scientist-practitioners entering the field can contribute to as well as draw upon advances in the neuro and behavioral sciences. While the field of neuropsychology is influenced by the technological and scientific advances around it, so to will it be a forerunner and shaper of other disciplines.

However, the practitioner side of our development cannot be ignored or discounted. For many clinical neuropsychology is a business, as well as a scientific discipline. Like scientific endeavors, business decisions must be based on data, with recognition of standard practice, policy, and precedent taking place within the professional community. This occurs when practitioners are able to communicate in a centralized and public venue. Our rapid expansion makes the mailed survey method the most reasonable avenue for attaining these important goals, despite inevitable limitations on the reliability and validity of survey data. However, such endeavors cannot be done capriciously or without principle. Inappropriate methodology, improper generalizations, and spurious conclusions of survey data (see Bigler, 1990) could create an attitude of mistrust among those being surveyed. This, combined with an eventual saturation effect could create an attitude of apathy or even resistance among potential respondents, pushing down response rates and increasing nonresponse bias in the data generated. This could result in an uncertain, if not ominous future for such important data collection efforts.

In closing, the prevailing impression that emerges from these survey data is consistent with Costa's (1983) astute forecast nearly a decade ago that "the tendency of clinical neuropsychology to spread beyond the bounds of acute neurology service and outpatient neurology-related clinics will increase. Diagnostic horizons will be widened and intervention techniques will evolve" (p. 6). As we enter the final decade of the century, neuropsychology is becoming an unusually diverse and multifaceted professional discipline whose contributions and significance to the public welfare will continue to become more recognized.

REFERENCES

Adams, K. M. (1985). Will the real handbook of clinical neuropsychology please stand? *Journal of Clinical and Experimental Neuropsychology, 7*, 327-330.

Adams, K. M. (1988). Neuropsychology is not just in the eye of the provider. *Professional Psychology: Research and Practice, 19*, 448-449.

Adams, K. M., & Putnam, S. H. (1989). *The efficacy of multidisciplinary rehabilitation programs for the traumatically brain-injured: A case study retrospective pilot study*. Livonia, MI: The Michigan Catastrophic Claims Association.

Adler, T. (1990). HMO fever: Bush budget spotlights managed care. *The APA Monitor, 21* (4), 17-18.

American Congress of Rehabilitation Medicine, (1986). *Standards for cognitive rehabilitation*, unpublished manuscript.

Barth, J. T., & Boll, T. J. (1981). Rehabilitation and treatment of central nervous system dysfunction: A behavioral medicine perspective. In C. K. Prokop & L. A. Bradley (Eds.), *Medical psychology: Contributions to behavioral medicine* (pp. 241-266). New York: Academic Press.

Beresford, H. R. (1969). Proof of mental impairment in civil suits. In A. E. Walker, W. F. Caveness, & M. Critchley (Eds.), *The late effects of head injury* (pp. 491-493). Springfield: Charles C. Thomas Publisher.

Bieliauskas, L. A., & Matthews, C. G. (1987). American Board of Clinical Neuropsychology: Policies and procedures. *The Clinical Neuropsychologist, 1*, 21-28.

Bigler, E. D. (1986). Forensic issues in neuropsychology. In D. Wedding, A. M. Horton, Jr., & J. Webster (Eds.), *The neuropsychology handbook: Behavioral and clinical perspectives* (pp. 526-547). New York: Springer Publishing Company.

Bigler, E.D. (1990). Neuropsychology and Malingering: Comment on Faust, Hart, and Guilmette (1988). *Journal of Consulting and Clinical Psychology, 58*, 244-247.

Bornstein, R.A., Costa, L.D., & Matarazzo, J.D. (1986). Interfaces between neuropsychology and health psychology. In S.B. Filskov & T.J. Boll (Eds.), *Handbook of clinical neuropsychology* (Vol. 2, pp. 19-41). New York: John Wiley and Sons.

Buie, J. (1990). Medicare win's effects said to be wide-ranging. *The APA Monitor, 21*, 22.

Butler, R. W., & Satz, P. (1988). Individual psychotherapy with head-injured adults: Clinical notes for the practitioner. *Professional Psychology: Research and Practice, 19*, 536-541.

Chelune, G J., & Edwards, P. (1981). Early brain lesions: Ontogenetic-environmental considerations. *Journal of Consulting and Clinical Psychology, 49*, 777-790.

Chelune, G. J., & Moehle, K. A. (1986). Neuropsychological assessment and everyday functioning. In D. Wedding, A. M. Horton, Jr., & J. Webster (Eds.), *The neuropsychology handbook: Behavioral and clinical perspectives* (pp. 489-525). New York: Springer Publishing Company.

Costa, L. (1983). Clinical neuropsychology: A discipline in evolution. *Journal of Clinical Neuropsychology, 5*, 1-11.

Costa, L.D., & Matarazzo, J.D., & Bornstein, R.A. (1986). Issues in graduate and postgraduate training in clinical neuropsychology. In S.B. Filskov & T.J. Boll (Eds.),

205

Handbook of clinical neuropsychology (Vol. 2, pp. 652-668). New York: John Wiley and Sons.

Cripe, L.I. (1989). Listing of training programs in clinical neuropsychology-1988. The Clinical Neuropsychologist, 3, 116-128.

DeLuca, J. W. (1989). Neuropsychology technicians in clinical practice: Precedents, rationale, and current deployment. The Clinical Neuropsychologist, 3, 3-21.

Diller, L., & Gordon, W. A. (1981). Interventions for cognitive deficits in brain-injured adults. Journal of Consulting and Clinical Psychology, 49, 822-834.

Division 40-International Neuropsychological Society (INS) Task Force on Education, Accreditation, and Credentialing (1987). Guidelines for doctoral training programs in clinical neuropsychology. The Clinical Neuropsychologist, 1, 29-34.

Division 40-International Neuropsychological Society (INS) Task Force (1988). Report of the INS-Division 40 Task Force on Education, Accreditation, and Credentialing. Subcommittee on Continuing Education. The Clinical Neuropsychologist, 2, 22-29.

Dorken, H., Stapp, J., & VandenBos, G. (1986). Licensed psychologists: A decade of major growth. In H. Dorken (Ed.), Professional psychology in transition (pp. 3-20). San Francisco: Jossey-Bass.

Fowler, R. D., & VandenBos, G. R. (1989). Divisions reflect APA's diversity. The APA Monitor, 20, (10), 4-5.

Golden, C. J., & Strider, M. A. (Eds.) (1986). Forensic neuropsychology. New York: Plenum Press.

Goyder, J. C. (1982). Further evidence of factors affecting response rates to mailed questionnaires. American Sociological Review, 47, 550-553.

Grimm, B. H., & Bleiberg, J. (1986). Psychological rehabilitation in traumatic brain injury. In S.B. Filskov & T.J. Boll (Eds.), Handbook of clinical neuropsychology (Vol. 2, pp. 495-560). New York: John Wiley and Sons.

Guilmette, T. J., Faust, D., Hart, K., & Arkes, H. R. (in press). A national survey of psychologists who offer neuropsychological services. Archives of Clinical Neuropsychology.

Hartlage, L. C., & Telzrow, C. F. (1980). The practice of clinical neuropsychology in the U.S.. Clinical Neuropsychology, 2, 200-202.

Heberlein, T.A. & Baumgartner, R.M. (1978). Factors affecting response rates to mailed questionnaires: A quantitative analysis of the published literature. American Sociological Review, 43, 447-462.

Indianapolis Union Railway vs. Walker, 162 Ind. App. 166, 318 N. E. 2d. 578 (1974).

Kanuk, L., & Berenson, C. (1975). Mail surveys and response rates: A literature review. Journal of Marketing Research, 12, 440-453.

Kelley, D. G. (1990). An analysis of rehabilitation psychologists trained in clinical, counseling, and rehabilitation psychology doctoral programs. Unpublished doctoral dissertation, University of Illinois at Urbana-Champaign.

Lees-Haley, P. (November, 1987). Mild brain injury: Proving lost earnings. Trial, pp.83-86.

Lezak, M. D. (1983). Neuropsychological assessment (2nd ed.). New York: Oxford University Press.

McMahon, E. A. (1983). Forensic issues in clinical neuropsychology. In C. J. Golden & P. J. Vicente (Eds.) Foundations of clinical neuropsychology (pp. 401-427). New York: Plenum Press.

McCaffery, R. J., & Isaac, W. (1984). Survey of the educational backgrounds and specialty training of instructors of clinical neuropsychology in APA-approved graduate training programs. Professional Psychology: Research and Practice, 15, 26-33.

McCaffery, R. J., Malloy, P.F. & Brief, D. (1985). Internship opportunities in clinical

206

neuropsychology emphasizing recent INS training guidelines. *Professional Psychology: Research and Practice, 16,* 236-252.

McMordie, W. R. (1988). Twenty-year follow-up of the prevailing opinion on the posttraumatic or postconcussional syndrome. *The Clinical Neuropsychologist, 2,* 198-212.

Meier, M.J. (1981) Education for competency assurance in human neuropsychology: Antecedents, models, and directions. In S.B. Filskov & T.J. Boll (Eds.), *Handbook of clinical neuropsychology* (Vol. 1, pp. 754-781). New York: John Wiley and Sons.

Miller, T. W., & Auvenshine, D. (1988). Ethical issues in psychology: The case of who does the testing. *Professional Practice of Psychology: Legal, Regulatory, and Licensure Issues, 9,* 19-27.

Putnam, S.H. (1989) The TCN salary survey: A salary survey of neuropsychologists. *The Clinical Neuropsychologist, 3,* 97-115.

Reitan, R. M. (1990). Halstead-Reitan Neuropsychological Test Batteries: 1990 Catalog. Tucson: Reitan Neuropsychology Laboratory.

Reports of the INS-Division 40 Task Force on Education, Accreditation, and Credentialing. (1987). Guidelines for doctoral training programs in clinical neuropsychology. *The Clinical Neuropsychologist, 1,* 29-34.

Reports of the Division 40 Task Force on Education, Accreditation, and Credentialing (1988). Guidelines for continuing education in clinical neuropsychology. *The Clinical Neuropsychologist, 2,* 25-29.

Report of the Division 40 Task Force on Education, Accreditation, and Credentialing (1989). Guidelines regarding the use of nondoctoral personnel in clinical neuropsychological assessment. *The Clinical Neuropsychologist, 3,* 23-24.

Report of the Division 40 Task Force on Education, Accreditation, and Credentialing (1989). Professional Issues: Definition of a clinical neuropsychologist. *The Clinical Neuropsychologist, 3,* 22.

Rourke, B. P. (1982). Central processing deficiencies in children: Toward a developmental neuropsychological model. *Journal of Clinical Neuropsychology, 4,* 1-18.

Satz, P. (1988). Neuropsychological testimony: Some emerging concerns. *The Clinical Neuropsychologist, 2,* 89-100.

Satz, P., & Fletcher, J M. (1981). Emergent trends in neuropsychology: an overview. *Journal of Consulting and Clinical Psychology, 49,* 851-865.

Schwartz, M. L. (1987). Limitations on neuropsychological testimony by the Florida appellate decisions: Action, reaction, and counteraction. *The Clinical Neuropsychologist, 1,* 51-60.

Seretny, M. L., Dean, R. S., Gray, J. W., & Hartlage, L. C. (1986). The practice of clinical neuropsychology in the United States. *Archives of Clinical Neuropsychology, 1,* 5-12.

Slay, D. K., & Valdivia, L. (1988). Neuropsychology as a specialized health service listed in the National Register of Health Service Providers in Psychology. *Professional Psychology: Research and Practice, 19,* 323-329.

Stapp, J., Tucker, A. M., & VandenBos, G. R. (1985). Census of psychological personnel: 1983. *American Psychologist, 40,* 1317-1351.

Sweet, J. J., & Moberg, P. J. (1990). A survey of practices and beliefs among ABPP and Non-ABPP clinical neuropsychologists. *The Clinical Neuropsychologist, 4,* 101-120.

Tarter, R. E., Van Thiel, D. H., & Edwards, K. L. (1988). *Medical neuropsychology: The impact of disease on behavior.* New York: Plenum Press.

Walker, A. E., Caveness, W. F., & Critchley, M. (1969). *The late effects of head injury.* Springfield: Charles C. Thomas Publisher.

APPENDIX

The TCN Professional Practice Survey

1. Which best describes your current <u>clinical</u> practice? (check one only)

✕ Clinical Neuropsychology   ✕ Clinical Psychology   ✕ Counseling Psychology
✕ Developmental/School Psychology   ✕ Cognitive Psychology   ✕ Behavioral Medicine
✕ Rehabilitation Psychology   ✕ Other:

2. Which best describes your current work status in clinical neuropsychology? (check one only)

✕ Full-time active employment   ✕ Part-time active employment
✕ Training; fellow, intern, student, etc.   ✕ Retired, but work occasionally
✕ Other: please describe:

******** **PRIMARY EMPLOYMENT** ********

In this section please respond to the questions only in terms of your *primary* (i.e. regular, salaried, tenured, institutional, etc.) employment setting. If you are exclusively employed in an independent private practice, skip the following questions and turn to question number 24.

3. Which describes your *primary* employment setting in clinical neuropsychology? (check one only)

✕ University hospital/medical center
✕ Non-university hospital/medical center
✕ Independent or free-standing rehabilitation center/facility
✕ School system
✕ Psychological, psychiatric, neurological, or medical *group* practice
✕ Community mental health center/clinic
✕ Other : Please specify:

4. In this *primary* employment setting are you involved in setting fees for neuropsychological services?

✕ Yes   ✕ No

5. How is billing done for neuropsychological assessment in your *primary* work setting? (select <u>one</u>; if more than one select the one which best describes the way billing is done in your *primary* work setting)

✕ An *hourly* rate → What is your hourly adult rate? $_____   hourly child rate $ _____

         Average hours per adult assessment? _____   per child assessment? _____

✕ A *fixed* rate per patient. → What is your per patient rate for <u>adults</u>? $_____.

         What is your per patient rate for <u>children</u>? $_____.

✕ By the type of protocol or referral question (e.g. diagnostic, screening, forensic, etc.) → Please specify or send a copy of such per protocol charges.

✕ On a per-test basis. → Please specify or send a copy of your per-test charges.

6. Do you provide neuropsychological <u>treatment</u> services to patients in your primary employment position?

✕ Yes   ✕ No → skip to question number 9

7. Of all the neuropsychological <u>treatment</u> services you provide in your *primary* employment setting, what percentage is spent in the following activities? (percentages should sum to 100%)

_____% cognitive remediation/rehabilitation
_____% vocational and employment counseling/guidance
_____% remedial educational services to learning impaired patients
_____% psychotherapy
_____% consultant to a health care organization
_____% other treatment services. → Please specify:

8. What is your hourly rate for treatment services $_____.
   If your billing is other than an hourly rate charge, please specify:

9. What percentage of your clinical time in your *primary* employment setting is spent in the following (percentages should sum to 100%)?

   _____ neuropsychological assessment
   _____ neuropsychological treatment (direct contact and involvement with patients)
   _____ neuropsychological consultation (organizations, attorneys, physicians, etc.)
   _____ other → Please specify:

10. Indicate the percentage of patients you see in your *primary* employment setting which come from the following sources:

   _____% Health Maintenance Organizations (HMO's)
   _____% Preferred Provider Organizations (PPO's)
   _____% Other pre-paid groups
   _____% Criminal Cases
   _____% Personal Injury
   _____% Other Civil
   _____% Other → Please specify:

11. If you see personal injury cases in your *primary* employment setting, what percentage of the time does your referral source represent;

   _____% the plaintiff
   _____% the defendant
   _____% neither
   _____ I do not see personal injury cases

12. In your *primary* employment setting which patient groups (if any) are you not able to provide services to due to the low payment schedule offered?

   ❏ None.

13. In your *primary* employment setting what percentage of your total clinical time is spent working with the following age groups for both assessment and treatment? (percentages should sum to 100%)

   _____% infants _____% children _____% adolescents _____% young adults
   _____% older adults _____% geriatrics

14. In your *primary* employment setting what percentage of your total clinical time is spent working with the following patient groups? (percentages should sum to 100%)

   _____% Head trauma _____% Seizure _____% Stroke/Vascular
   _____% Pain _____% Psychiatric _____% Learning Disabled
   _____% Substance Abuse _____% AIDS _____% Demyelinating
   _____% Toxic/Metabolic _____% CNS Tumor _____% Forensic/Legal
   _____% Dementia _____% Other

15. The monetary compensation I receive for neuropsychological assessment in my *primary* employment setting is satisfactory. (check only one)

   ❏ Strongly Agree ❏ Agree ❏ Uncertain ❏ Disagree ❏ Strongly Disagree ❏ Does not apply to me

16. The monetary compensation I receive for neuropsychological treatment services in my *primary* employment setting is satisfactory. (check only one)

   ❏ Strongly Agree ❏ Agree ❏ Uncertain ❏ Disagree ❏ Strongly Disagree ❏ Does not apply to me

17. In your *primary* employment setting, are technicians, psychometrists, or psychological assistants employed to administer neuropsychological tests?

    ❑ Yes → How many?_____   ❑ No → (skip to question 19)
    How many neuropsychologists do they serve?

18. Are they paid by:

    ❑ An hourly rate. → Rate $_____

    ❑ A per patient fee. → Adult Fee $_____   Child Fee $_____

    ❑ Students/interns in exchange for supervision.

    ❑ Other → Please specify:

19. In my *primary* employment setting I have direct contact with the patient either through a face to face interview or by administering certain tests:

    ❑ Always   ❑ Usually   ❑ Half the time   ❑ Seldom   ❑ Never   ❑ Does not apply to me

20. In my *primary* employment setting I meet with the patient, a significant other, or parent of the child for a follow-up session to discuss the test results:

    ❑ Always   ❑ Usually   ❑ Half the time   ❑ Seldom   ❑ Never   ❑ Does not apply to me

21. In your *primary* employment setting how many neuropsychological assessments do you do per month?

    _____ Total per month   _____ Adults?   _____ Children?

22. In your *primary* employment setting how many patients do you see for neuropsychological treatment per month?

    _____ Total per month   _____ Adults?   _____ Children?

23. Please describe the neuropsychological assessment method/approach/battery which you most typically employ in your *primary* employment setting:

    What state are you employed in?   _____

    What professional groups in <u>neuropsychology</u> do you hold membership in?

Which best describes your response to the TCN Salary Survey (Vol. 3, No. 2)?

    ❑ It was helpful in salary negotiations.

    ❑ I found it interesting and informative.

    ❑ I have not read it.

    ❑ I read it but did not find it useful.

    ❑ Other: please explain:

All comments are welcomed and appreciated.

210

210

******** INDEPENDENT PRIVATE PRACTICE OFFICE ********

In this section please respond to the questions only in terms of your independent private practice office employment, whether or not this is a full time involvement or in addition to another position. If you are **not** in private practice and have completed the previous section please return the questionnaire in the self-addressed stamped envelope.

24. In your independent private practice office how is billing done for neuropsychological <u>assessment</u>? (select <u>one</u>; if more than one, select the one which best describes the way billing is done in your private practice office)

 ❑ An *hourly* rate → What is the hourly adult rate? $_____ hourly child rate $_____.

     →Average hours per adult assessment? _____ per child assessment _____

 ❑ A *fixed* rate per patient → What is your per patient <u>adult</u> rate? $_____.

     → What is your per patient <u>child</u> rate? $_____.

 ❑ By the type of test protocol or referral question (e.g. diagnostic, screening, forensic, etc.) → Please specify or send a copy of such per protocol charges.

 ❑ On a per-test basis. → Please specify or send a copy of your per-test charges.

25. Do you provide neuropsychological <u>treatment</u> services to patients in your independent private practice?

    ❑ Yes   ❑ No → Skip to question number <u>28</u>

26. Of all the neuropsychological <u>treatment</u> services you provide in your independent private practice what percentage is spent in the following activities (percentages should sum to 100%)?

 _____% cognitive remediation/rehabilitation
 _____% vocational and employment counseling/guidance
 _____% remedial educational services to learning impaired patients
 _____% psychotherapy
 _____% consultant to health care organization
 _____% other treatment services. → Please specify:

27. What is your hourly rate for <u>treatment</u> services $_____.
 If your billing is other than an hourly rate charge, please specify:

28. What is <u>your</u> standard hourly fee for the following professional activities?

 ❑ I am not involved in such activities.

 $_____ forensic consulting, depositions, testimony, etc.
 $_____ consulting to an organization (e.g. rehabilitation center, nursing home, etc.)
 $_____ other. → Please specify:

29. What percentage of your clinical time in your independent private practice is spent in the following (percentages should sum to 100%)?

 _____% neuropsychological assessment
 _____% neuropsychological treatment (direct contact and involvement with patients)
 _____% neuropsychological consultation (organizations, attorneys, physicians, etc.)
 _____% other → Please specify:

30. Indicate the percentage of your total patients in your independent private practice which come from the following sources:

 _____% Health Maintenance Organizations (HMO's)
 _____% Preferred Provider Organizations (PPO's)
 _____% Other pre-paid groups
 _____% Criminal cases
 _____% Personal Injury
 _____% Other Civil
 _____% Other → Please specify:

31. If you see personal injury cases in your independent private practice, what percentage of the time does your referral source represent;

_____% the plaintiff
_____% the defendant
_____% neither
_____ I do not see personal injury cases

32. Which patient groups are you not able to provide services to (if any) in your independent private practice due to the low payment schedule offered?

❒ None

33. In your independent private practice what percentage of your total <u>clinical</u> time is spent working with the following age groups for both assessment and treatment? (percentages should sum to 100%)

_____ % infants _____ % children _____ % adolescents _____ % young adults
_____ % older adults _____ % geriatrics

34. In your independent private practice what percentage of your total <u>clinical</u> time is spent working with the following patient groups? (percentages should sum to 100%)

_____ % Head trauma _____ % Seizure _____ % Stroke/Vascular
_____ % Dementia _____ % Psychiatric _____ % Learning Disabled
_____ % Substance Abuse _____ % AIDS _____ % Demyelinating
_____ % Toxic/Metabolic _____ % CNS Tumor _____ % Forensic/Legal
_____ % Pain _____ % Other

35. The monetary compensation I receive for neuropsychological <u>assessment</u> in independent private practice is satisfactory. (check only one)

❒ Strongly Agree ❒ Agree ❒ Uncertain ❒ Disagree ❒ Strongly Disagree ❒ Does not apply to me

36. The monetary compensation I receive for neuropsychological <u>treatment</u> in independent private practice is satisfactory. (check only one)

❒ Strongly Agree ❒ Agree ❒ Uncertain ❒ Disagree ❒ Strongly Disagree ❒ Does not apply to me

37. In your independent private practice do you employ technicians, psychometrists, or psychological assistants to administer neuropsychological tests?

❒Yes → How many? _____ ❒ No → (skip to question 39)
*. How many neuropsychologists do they serve? _____

38. Are they paid by:

❒ An hourly rate. → Rate $_____

❒ A per patient fee. → Adult Fee $_____ Child Fee $_____

❒ Students/interns in exchange for supervision.

❒ Other. → Please specify:

39. In my independent private practice I have direct contact with the patient either through a face to face interview or by administering certain tests:

❒ Always ❒ Usually ❒ Half the time ❒ Seldom ❒ Never ❒ Does not apply to me

40. In my independent private practice I meet with the patient, a significant other, or parent of the child for a follow-up session to discuss the test results:

❒ Always ❒ Usually ❒ Half the time ❒ Seldom ❒ Never ❒ Does not apply to me

41. In your independent private practice, how many neuropsychological assessments do you do per month?

_____ Total per month   _____ Adult?   _____ Children?

42. In your independent private practice how many patients do you see for neuropsychological treatment per month?

_____ Total per month   _____ Adult?   _____ Children?

43. Please describe the neuropsychological assessment method/approach/battery which you typically employ in your independent private practice?

44. What state do you currently practice in? _____

45. What best describes the area your independent private office is located in?

❏ Major City   ❏ Suburban to a Major City   ❏ Rural   ❏ Other: please describe:

All comments are welcomed and appreciated.

The Clinical Neuropsychologist
1991, Vol. 5, No. 2, pp. 103-124

213

The *TCN* Professional Practice Survey: Part II: An Analysis of the Fees of Neuropsychologists by Practice Demographics

Steven H. Putnam
University of Michigan

John W. DeLuca
Lafayette Clinic

ABSTRACT

Fee and clinical practice data for 872 members of the American Psychological Association's Division of Clinical Neuropsychology (Division 40) were further analyzed by the following parameters: area of clinical practice, employment setting, assessment methodology, and United States geographic region. The primary institutional – private practice distinction produced the most prominent differences in fees, with the latter charging lower hourly rates, higher fixed rates per patient, performing longer neuropsychological examinations, and paying higher hourly wages to technicians. Those designating themselves as neuropsychologists charged higher rates than clinical psychologists for neuropsychological services and averaged more examinations per month. The West, New England, and South Atlantic regions of the U.S. reported the highest fees for services, while the East South Central region was found to have the lowest fees. Respondents in university-based hospitals reported higher rates for assessment than in other employment settings. Those endorsing a fixed or standard battery approach to neuropsychological assessment tended to report lower hourly rates for examinations but few other differences were noted on the basis of reported assessment methodology. Fees for neuropsychological services provided to adults *vis-a-vis* children were very comparable across the majority of parameters examined.

This paper presents a further analysis of the data obtained from 872 clinically active members of the Division of Clinical Neuropsychology (Division 40) of the American Psychological Association. A detailed discussion of the study methodology, respondent characteristics, and principal findings are contained in Part I

The authors would like to express their gratitude to Ms. Annunciata Porterfield and Linas A. Bieliauskas, Ph.D. for their contributions to the development of this manuscript.

Accepted for publication September 30, 1990.

(Putnam & DeLuca, 1990). The emphasis in Part II is on greater specification and elucidation of fee and practice characteristics by the following respondent parameters: primary employment setting, geographic region, area of clinical practice, and methodological approach to neuropsychological assessment.

The data presented here are intended as a reference source for the practitioner of neuropsychology in evaluating fee schedules for clinical services. The analyses presented are necessarily "fine-grained," reducing the number of cases for most of the variables examined. These descriptive data appear to be representative of the practices and fees of neuropsychological practitioners in the United States. Confirmation of the generalizability of these data must of course await follow-up study.

FEE STRUCTURE

Hourly Assessment Charges
As evident in Table 1, the hourly rates charged for neuropsychological assessment of adult patients tended to be higher in university hospitals than other employment settings. The rates charged for the assessment of children did not appear to significantly differ from the adult rate charges.

Table 1. Hourly Rates Charged for Neuropsychological Assessment by Employment Setting.

	University Hospital	Non-University Hospital	Rehabilitation Center	Private Practice	Primary Employment of Entire Sample
Adults					
N	72	42	27	386	275
Mean	$118	$102	$100	$100	$105
SD	($32)	($28)	($27)	($25)	($32)
Mode	$100	$90	$80	$100	$100
75%	$150	$110	$122	$110	$125
Mdn	$110	$100	$100	$95	$100
25%	$95	$90	$80	$80	$85
Children					
N	49	24	18	261	176
Mean	$113	$101	$97	$100	$103
SD	($30)	($24)	($17)	($25)	($29)
Mode	$100	$85	$100	$100	$100
75%	$132	$107	$115	$115	$120
Mdn	$105	$100	$98	$95	$100
25%	$94	$85	$82	$80	$85

Respondents were asked to indicate their area of current clinical practice. The overwhelming majority indicated clinical neuropsychology or clinical psychology; 57% and 30% respectively of the 872 respondents. Throughout this paper these two groups will be identified as clinical neuropsychologists and clinical psychologists. However, this is a self-designation; no attempt was made in this study to evaluate formally the credentials or competence of either group of respondents.

Table 2 presents data for these two groups in both primary institutional employment and private practice settings. On the average, neuropsychologists charge from $10 to as much as $17 more per hour than clinical psychologists for neuropsychological assessment. This was true across primary employment and private practice settings, as well as the assessment of adults and children. This was the only instance where professional designation appeared to be more distinctly associated with a difference in fees than the primary employment-private practice distinction. That is, neuropsychologists in private practice settings reported higher hourly fees than clinical psychologists in primary institutional employment settings.

In an effort to capture the diversity of assessment methodologies represented by the Division 40 membership, an open-ended question format was employed which addressed this issue. Indeed, there are few respondents who are "pure" in

Table 2. Hourly Rates Charged for Neuropsychological Assessment by Area of Clinical Practice in Primary and Private Practice Employment Settings.

	Clinical Neuropsychology		Clinical Psychology		Entire Sample	
	Primary	Private	Primary	Private	Primary	Private
Adults						
N	164	175	61	133	275	386
Mean	$110	$103	$93	$94	$105	$100
SD	($30)	($24)	($32)	($24)	($32)	($25)
Mode	$100	$100	$85	$90	$100	$100
75%	$131	$120	$108	$100	$125	$110
Mdn	$100	$100	$90	$90	$100	$95
25%	$90	$90	$75	$80	$85	$80
Children						
N	101	114	41	91	176	261
Mean	$105	$104	$96	$92	$103	$100
SD	($28)	($24)	($30)	($22)	($29)	($25)
Mode	$100	$100	$85	$90	$100	$100
75%	$126	$120	$116	$100	$120	$115
Mdn	$100	$100	$90	$90	$100	$95
25%	$87	$88	$80	$80	$85	$80

216

their endorsement or practice of a given methodology. As Adams (1987) has noted, "the general inventiveness of the neuropsychological community..." has resulted in numerous modifications, variations, and permutations in assessment approaches and methods. As such, an attempt to ascertain respondents' assessment methodology via a mailed questionnaire is subject to many delimiting factors. Finally, the intention here was not evaluative, nor to foster parochialism, but rather to investigate possible differences in fees and practice characteristics associated with the various assessment approaches utilized by practitioners of neuropsychology.

Table 3 presents hourly charges for neuropsychological assessment by methodological approach. A respondent's approach was categorized as "flexible" if it was described as nonuniform across patients and "fixed" if was described as standard or uniform across patients. However, if the approach was identified with a particular established or popular approach (e.g., Boston Process) it was categorized accordingly.

A review of Table 3 suggests that those respondents utilizing a "fixed" or "standard" battery approach (Halstead-Reitan Neuropsychological Test Battery, Luria-Nebraska Neuropsychological Test Battery, Fixed Battery) charge lower hourly rates than those utilizing a "flexible" battery approach (Boston Process, Flexible Battery). The median rates for adult and child assessments are comparable across different methodological approaches.

For several variables data are presented by the geographic region of the respondents. The nine divisions employed were taken from the U.S. Bureau of the Census (1967) and are as follows: the *Pacific* region includes Washington, Oregon, California, Nevada, and Hawaii; the *Mountain* region includes Montana, Idaho, Wyoming, Utah, Colorado, Arizona, and New Mexico; the *West North Central* region includes North Dakota, South Dakota, Minnesota, Nebraska, Iowa, Kansas, and Missouri; the *West South Central* region includes Oklahoma, Texas, Arkansas, and Louisiana; the *East North Central* region includes Wisconsin, Illinois, Michigan, Indiana, and Ohio; the *East South Central* region includes Kentucky, Tennessee, Mississippi, and Alabama; the *New England* region includes Maine, New Hampshire, Vermont, Massachusetts, Connecticut, and Rhode Island; the *Middle Atlantic* region includes New York, Pennsylvania, and New Jersey; the *South Atlantic* region includes West Virginia, Virginia, Maryland, District of Columbia, Delaware, North Carolina, South Carolina, Georgia, and Florida. Questionnaires were returned from all states except for Wyoming and Alaska. The total number returned from each state was presented in Part I (Putnam & DeLuca, 1990).

Tables 4 and 5 present the hourly rates charged for neuropsychological assessment by U.S. geographic region. The *Pacific* region, represented largely by California, tends to show higher hourly charges than other regions. The *difference* in mean fees between primary institutional and private practice settings was most extreme in the *New England* region (i.e., $25 adults, $29 children). The variability in charges was consistently greater in primary employment than private prac-

Table 3. Hourly Rates Charged for Neuropsychological Assessment by Methodological Approach in Primary and Private Practice Employment Settings

	HRNB		LNNB		Boston Process		Flexible Battery		Fixed Battery		Entire Sample	
	Primary	Private	Primary	Private	Primary	Private	Primary	Private	Primary	Private	Primary	Private
Adults												
N	90	154	9	20	55	57	61	79	25	45	275	386
Mean	$97	$96	$96	$99	$113	$104	$109	$102	$105	$99	$105	$100
SD	($26)	($22)	($20)	($38)	($30)	($25)	($35)	($22)	($36)	($32)	($32)	($25)
Mode	$100	$100	$90	$100	$90	$100	$100	$100	$100	$90	$100	$100
75%	$110	$100	$120	$120	$135	$120	$130	$115	$130	$125	$125	$110
Mdn	$95	$90	$90	$95	$110	$100	$100	$100	$100	$90	$100	$95
25%	$80	$80	$80	$70	$90	$87	$90	$90	$80	$80	$85	$80
Children												
N	63	11	6	14	30	39	42	47	12	29	176	261
Mean	$98	$96	$107	$84	$115	$104	$100	$102	$88	$99	$103	$100
SD	($26)	($21)	($28)	($29)	($28)	($28)	($32)	($23)	($17)	($32)	($29)	($25)
Mode	$100	$100	$120	$70	$90	$90	$100	$100	$70	$80	$100	$100
75%	$110	$100	$128	$105	$140	$125	$125	$115	$100	$125	$120	$115
Mdn	$100	$90	$105	$80	$110	$95	$100	$100	$90	$90	$100	$95
25%	$80	$80	$85	$70	$90	$85	$85	$90	$75	$80	$85	$80

Table 4. Hourly Rates Charged for Adult Neuropsychological Assessment by Nine U.S. Geographic Regions in Primary and Private Practice Employment Settings

	Pacific		Mountain		W.N. Central		W.S. Central		N.E. Central	
	Primary	Private	Primary	Private	Primary	Private	Primary	Private	Primary	Private
N	42	111	12	31	26	22	20	21	59	50
Mean	$118	$107	$95	$95	$97	$91	$110	$104	$100	$93
SD	($36)	($26)	($34)	($17)	($31)	($30)	($22)	($17)	($28)	($22)
Mode	$120	$100	$90	$100	$85	$75	$100	$100	$100	$80
75%	$150	$125	$120	$100	$111	$113	$130	$108	$125	$100
Mdn	$120	$100	$90	$90	$95	$88	$105	$100	$100	$88
25%	$100	$90	$76	$85	$85	$75	$90	$95	$80	$80

	E.S. Central		New England		Middle Atlantic		S. Atlantic		Entire Sample	
	Primary	Private	Primary	Private	Primary	Private	Primary	Private	Primary	Private
N	13	15	21	29	38	41	43	63	275	386
Mean	$92	$89	$113	$88	$102	$100	$106	$102	$105	$100
SD	($18)	($16)	($36)	($20)	($33)	($25)	($33)	($29)	($32)	($25)
Mode	$90	$90	$90	$80	$100	$90	$100	$100	$100	$100
75%	$100	$100	$145	$95	$115	$125	$130	$120	$125	$110
Mdn	$90	$90	$100	$85	$100	$90	$100	$100	$100	$95
25%	$80	$75	$90	$80	$84	$85	$90	$80	$85	$80

Table 5. Hourly Rates Charged for Child Neuropsychological Assessment by Nine U.S. Geographic Regions in Primary and Private Practice Employment Settings

	Pacific		Mountain		W.N. Central		W.S. Central		N.E. Central	
	Primary	Private	Primary	Private	Primary	Private	Primary	Private	Primary	Private
N	24	71	9	21	18	13	10	11	47	34
Mean	$115	$106	$79	$94	$101	$96	$108	$106	$103	$95
SD	($29)	($26)	($24)	($15)	($30)	($31)	($23)	($21)	($27)	($25)
Mode	$120	$100	$85	$100	$85	$100	$100	$100	$100	$75
75%	$130	$125	$95	$100	$110	$125	$130	$125	$125	$100
Mdn	$110	$100	$85	$90	$95	$100	$100	$100	$100	$90
25%	$100	$90	$75	$80	$85	$80	$90	$90	$85	$80

	E.S. Central		New England		Middle Atlantic		S. Atlantic		Entire Sample	
	Primary	Private	Primary	Private	Primary	Private	Primary	Private	Primary	Private
N	12	11	8	18	19	27	29	52	176	261
Mean	$88	$90	$115	$86	$107	$100	$102	$99	$103	$100
SD	($16)	($19)	($33)	($12)	($25)	($23)	($35)	($28)	($29)	($25)
Mode	$100	$100	$85	$80	$100	$90	$100	$90	$100	$100
75%	$90	$100	$140	$95	$115	$110	$130	$118	$120	$115
Mdn	$88	$90	$105	$80	$100	$90	$100	$95	$100	$95
25%	$76	$75	$90	$80	$90	$80	$80	$80	$85	$80

tice settings. On the whole, there does not appear to be an appreciable difference in the rates charged for child and adult neuropsychological assessments in these data.

Fixed Rate Per Patient Charges

Table 6 presents the fixed rate per patient charges for neuropsychological assessment in different employment settings. In certain instances the number of cases is small and the values should be cautiously weighed against the values based on the entire sample. However, the overall variability in a number of categories is modest and reflects a strong central tendency.

As was the case with hourly assessment charges, neuropsychologists report higher average fixed rate charges than clinical psychologists. However, with both groups the private practitioners showed higher average charges and greater overall variability in charges than those in institutional settings (Table 7). The fixed rates for the clinical psychologists in primary employment settings were well below the rates reported by others and would rank near the 25th centile relative to the scale for the entire sample. This may be associated with the finding that clinical psychologists tend to report shorter average times for neuropsychological assessment (Tables 13, below).

Table 6. Fixed Rate Per Patient for Neuropsychological Assessment by Employment Setting.

	University Hospital	Non-University Hospital	Rehabil-itation Center	Private Practice	Primary Employment of Entire Sample
Adults					
N	30	10	6	126	88
Mean	$700	$745	$955	$805	$680
SD	($212)	($130)	($197)	($330)	($215)
Mode	$500	$650	$750	$800	$500
75%	$865	$820	$1128	$950	$800
Mdn	$730	$735	$960	$755	$700
25%	$540	$645	$750	$600	$535
Children					
N	26	10	3	91	73
Mean	$725	$660	$975	$815	$685
SD	($271)	($203)	($289)	($330)	($245)
Mode	$1000	$480	$650	$600	$500
75%	$900	$805	$1200	$1000	$825
Mdn	$725	$700	$1080	$750	$700
25%	$490	$480	$650	$600	$490

Table 7. Fixed Rate Per Patient for Neuropsychological Assessment by Area of Clinical Practice in Primary and Private Practice Employment Settings

	Clinical Neuropsychology Primary	Private	Clinical Psychology Primary	Private	Entire Sample Primary	Private
Adults						
N	60	71	17	30	88	126
Mean	$727	$814	$540	$798	$680	$805
SD	($211)	($309)	($182)	($386)	($215)	($330)
Mode	$500	$600	$550	$600	$500	$800
75%	$869	$1000	$685	$931	$800	$950
Mdn	$733	$800	$550	$710	$700	$755
25%	$600	$600	$375	$550	$535	$600
Children						
N	47	55	14	20	73	91
Mean	$760	$855	$484	$764	$685	$815
SD	($238)	($308)	($169)	($364)	($245)	($330)
Mode	$1000	$1200	$350	$600	$500	$600
75%	$900	$1000	$620	$925	$825	$1000
Mdn	$750	$840	$490	$625	$700	$750
25%	$610	$650	$349	$563	$490	$600

When fixed rate charges were analyzed by U. S. geographic region, the number of cases in most groupings was <15. However, in eight of the nine regions the average fixed rate charge reported in private practice settings exceeded the charge in primary employment settings by $55 to $125. This held true for rates pertaining to both adults and children.

Table 8 presents fixed rate charges by the respondents' methodological approach to neuropsychological assessment. It can be seen that private practitioners charged higher fixed rates than those in primary practice settings across all methodological approaches with the exception of those using the Luria-Nebraska Neuropsychological Test Battery with adults. However, the number of cases in this grouping was particularly small. While the average fixed rate charges for the entire sample were slightly higher for children than adults, those utilizing a flexible battery approach tended to report much higher mean charges for child assessments.

Charges for Neuropsychological Treatment

An inspection of Table 9 indicates that no salient differences were found in the hourly rates charged for neuropsychological treatment services across primary employment settings. However, the hourly charges reported by private practitioners

Table 8. Fixed Rate Per Patient for Neuropsychological Assessment by Methodological Approach in Primary and Private Practice Employment Settings

	HRNB		LNNB		Boston Process		Flexible Battery		Fixed Battery		Entire Sample	
	Primary	Private	Primary	Private	Primary	Private	Primary	Private	Primary	Private	Primary	Private
Adults												
N	40	56	7	5	6	18	19	22	8	14	88	126
Mean	$650	$810	$789	$658	$775	$795	$675	$806	$605	$780	$680	$805
SD	($188)	($336)	($255)	($152)	($204)	($260)	($244)	($340)	($210)	($380)	($215)	($330)
Mode	$500	$800	$450	$500	$1000	$850	$700	$600	$225	$650	$500	$800
Mdn	$650	$750	$810	$600	$775	$850	$700	$750	$615	$705	$700	$755
Children												
N	30	38	7	4	7	16	15	14	4	9	73	91
Mean	$595	$790	$774	$925	$765	$765	$795	$925	$565	$768	$685	$815
SD	($202)	($335)	($282)	($570)	($216)	($255)	($290)	($315)	($301)	($322)	($245)	($330)
Mode	$500	$650	$350	$500	$1000	$400	$700	$700	$225	$650	$500	$600
Mdn	$590	$725	$810	$720	$800	$825	$700	$825	$540	$650	$700	$750

Table 9. Hourly Rates Charged for Neuropsychological Treatment by Employment Setting.

	University Hospital	Non-University Hospital	Rehabilitation Center	Private Practice	Primary Employment of Entire Sample
N	51	44	30	306	234
Mean	$98	$100	$102	$92	$97
SD	($25)	($23)	($23)	($18)	($24)
Mode	$100	$100	$100	$90	$100
75%	$106	$110	$120	$100	$110
Mdn	$95	$100	$100	$90	$95
25%	$80	$85	$80	$80	$80

tended to be approximately $10 less per hour. See Part I (Putnam & DeLuca, 1990) for presentation of the different treatment activities and their clinical time distribution.

Respondents identifying themselves as neuropsychologists reported average rates $5 to $10 per hour more for treatment services than clinical psychologists. This pattern was maintained across primary and private practice employment settings.

As seen in Table 10, hourly treatment rates were uniformly higher in primary employment settings regardless of geographic region, a pattern noted earlier for hourly assessment rates (Tables 4 and 5). Rates tended to be higher in the western regions but at the same time they were also more variable. No noteworthy differences in treatment rates were observed on the basis of methodological approach to assessment.

Hourly Rates Paid to Neuropsychology Technicians

Hourly earnings paid to technicians were very similar across primary employment settings (Table 11). However, the average hourly wages paid to technicians employed by clinical psychologists were slightly higher than those working for neuropsychologists. As displayed in Table 12, technicians appear to receive higher hourly wages in the *Pacific* region than other regions. While this may be associated with the increased cost of living and higher earnings for Division 40 members in this region (Putnam, 1989), technicians in the state of California are required to hold a master's degree and a limited license in order to be permitted to administer psychological tests (Department of Consumer Affairs, 1987). Thus, their responsibilities may extend beyond test administration and they may demand higher wages as a result. No obvious difference was noted on the basis of assessment methodology. The most consistent finding was that technicians in private practice settings typically received $6 to $7 more per hour regardless of the other characteristics examined.

Table 10. Hourly Rates Charged for Neuropsychological Treatment by Nine U.S. Geographic Regions in Primary and Private Practice Employment Settings

	Pacific		Mountain		W.N. Central		W.S. Central		N.E. Central	
	Primary	Private	Primary	Private	Primary	Private	Primary	Private	Primary	Private
N	31	68	11	26	15	10	16	25	55	45
Mean	$105	$99	$100	$88	$98	$96	$102	$98	$93	$83
SD	($28)	($18)	($30)	($19)	($24)	($21)	($25)	($14)	($19)	($11)
Mode	$100	$90	$90	$100	$135	$85	$85	$100	$75	$80
75%	$118	$110	$128	$100	$112	$120	$110	$100	$105	$90
Mdn	$100	$95	$90	$85	$100	$85	$95	$100	$90	$80
25%	$90	$85	$80	$80	$80	$80	$85	$90	$75	$75

	E.S. Central		New England		Middle Atlantic		S. Atlantic		Entire Sample	
	Primary	Private	Primary	Private	Primary	Private	Primary	Private	Primary	Private
N	13	12	15	28	37	47	41	43	234	306
Mean	$89	$86	$91	$88	$98	$93	$95	$95	$97	$92
SD	($22)	($17)	($23)	($13)	($28)	($18)	($23)	($22)	($24)	($18)
Mode	$100	$75	$75	$80	$100	$90	$100	$90	$100	$90
75%	$100	$98	$110	$92	$108	$100	$108	$100	$110	$100
Mdn	$90	$85	$90	$85	$95	$90	$95	$90	$95	$90
25%	$73	$75	$75	$80	$75	$80	$80	$80	$80	$80

Table 11. Hourly Rates Paid to Technicians by Employment Setting

	University Hospital	Non-University Hospital	Rehabil-itation Center	Private Practice	Primary Employment of Entire Sample
N	32	18	10	125	132
Mean	$12	$13	$15	$21	$13
SD	($5)	($5)	($6)	($11)	($6)
Mode	$9	$9	$12	$15	$9
75%	$15	$15	$21	$25	$15
Mdn	$11	$12	$13	$18	$12
25%	$9	$9	$10	$13	$10

ASSESSMENT CHARACTERISTICS

Average Hours Per Assessment

Private practitioners tend to perform longer neuropsychological assessments irrespective of employment setting, geographic region, assessment methodology, and clinical practice. Data for the latter are presented in Table 13. When all parameters are examined, the highest average adult assessment time found was 7.9 hours reported by private practitioners in the *Pacific* and *Mountain* regions (Table 14). This value exceeds the average for the entire sample by approximately one hour. Conversely, the lowest average assessment time for adults was 4.7 hours found in primary employment settings in the *East South Central* region (Table 14). This average was more than an hour below the average for the entire sample. A similar pattern was found for child assessment practices. More specifically, private practitioners in the *Pacific* region reported the longest average assessment times (i.e., 7.3 hours), while respondents in primary employment settings in the *East South* region reported the lowest average time for children (i.e., 3.6 hours) (Table 15). This latter value is more than two hours below the mean for the entire sample for those in primary employment settings. On the whole, the average time for the assessment of children was slightly less than that obtained for adult assessments. Respondents employed in independent or free-standing rehabilitation centers averaged approximately 1 to $1^{1/2}$ hours more for neuropsychological assessments than those in hospital settings (6.3 to 7.0 hours in rehabilitation centers, 4.9 to 5.6 hours in hospital settings).

Average Number of Neuropsychological Assessments Per Month

Clinical neuropsychologists employed in institutional settings examine an average of 12-14 patients per month, while clinical psychologists in similar settings average 6-8 examinations on a monthly basis (Table 16). Respondents working in university hospitals appear to average more examinations per month than those in other employment settings (Table 17). The average number of assessments

Table 12. Hourly Rates Paid to Technicians by Nine U.S. Geographic Regions in Primary and Private Practice Employment Settings

	Pacific		Mountain		W.N. Central		W.S. Central		N.E. Central	
	Primary	Private	Primary	Private	Primary	Private	Primary	Private	Primary	Private
N	11	29	1	13	14	6	8	15	25	18
Mean	$18	$25	$15	$17	$12	$17	$13	$18	$12	$19
SD	($13)	($13)		($6)	($4)	($10)	($5)	($11)	($4)	($12)
Mode	$10	$25		$15	$9	$12	$12	$10	$8	$10
75%	$25	$29		$20	$14	$24	$15	$25	$14	$25
Mdn	$11	$22		$15	$12	$14	$12	$15	$11	$15
25%	$10	$15		$14	$9	$11	$9	$10	$9	$11

	E.S. Central		New England		Middle Atlantic		S. Atlantic		Entire Sample	
	Primary	Private	Primary	Private	Primary	Private	Primary	Private	Primary	Private
N	2	3	8	8	16	3	24	20	132	125
Mean	$11	$17	$17	$16	$12	$21	$14	$23	$13	$21
SD	($0.7)	($3)	($7)	($4)	($5)	($14)	($4)	($12)	($6)	($11)
Mode		$14	$25	$15	$9	$8	$13	$20	$9	$15
75%	$11	$20	$24	$20	$12	$35	$15	$29	$15	$25
Mdn	$11	$18	$17	$15	$10	$20	$13	$20	$12	$18
25%	$10	$14	$10	$14	$9	$8	$10	$14	$10	$13

Table 13. Average Number of Hours Per Neuropsychological Assessment by Area of Clinical Practice in Primary and Private Practice Employment Settings

	Clinical Neuropsychology		Clinical Psychology		Entire Sample	
	Primary	Private	Primary	Private	Primary	Private
Adults						
N	138	149	49	114	232	324
Mean	5.8	7.3	5.9	6.7	6.0	7.0
SD	(2.1)	(2.4)	(1.9)	(2.2)	(2.1)	(2.4)
Mode	4	6	4	6	4	6
75%	7	9	8	8	7	8
Mdn	6	7	6	6	6	7
25%	4	6	4	5	4	5
Children						
N	88	96	32	79	155	219
Mean	5.8	6.9	5.3	6.4	5.8	6.6
SD	(2.0)	(2.4)	(1.7)	(2.5)	(2.0)	(2.4)
Mode	6	5	4	6	6	6
75%	7	8	6	8	7	8
Mdn	6	7	5	6	6	6
25%	4	5	4	5	4	5

appears to be lower in rehabilitation centers than hospital settings. However, as noted earlier, the average amount of time per assessment is higher in rehabilitation centers. There may be some regional differences in regards to this variable; in primary employment settings respondents in the *West North Central* region perform an average of 16 assessments per month while respondents in the *Middle Atlantic* region report an average of 9 per month. In the *East Central* region private practitioners perform an average of 11 assessments per month, in contrast to only 4 per month reported in the *Middle Atlantic* region. Across all parameters, those in primary employment settings averaged more assessments per month than those in private practice. The single exception to this pattern was found among private practitioners utilizing the Halstead-Reitan Neuropsychological Test Battery (Table 18).

SYNOPSIS OF COMMENTS

In general, many respondents commented on the challenging and very time-consuming task of attempting to keep pace with developments in the laws and policies that are shaping the practice of clinical neuropsychology. In short, state agencies and regulatory bodies maintain assorted standards and laws impacting

Table 14. Average Number of Hours Per Adult Neuropsychological Assessment by Nine U.S. Geographic Regions in Primary and Private Practice Employment Settings

	Pacific		Mountain		W.N. Central		W.S. Central		N.E. Central	
	Primary	Private	Primary	Private	Primary	Private	Primary	Private	Primary	Private
N	40	94	11	27	21	17	18	19	48	45
Mean	6.3	7.9	6.4	7.9	5.5	6.3	5.7	6.4	6.0	6.0
SD	(2.2)	(2.6)	(2.3)	(2.4)	(1.9)	(1.7)	(1.3)	(1.6)	(2.3)	(2.0)
Mode	6	8	7	8	4	6	5	5	4	6
75%	8	10	7	10	8	7.5	7	7	8	7
Mdn	6	8	6	8	5	6	5.5	6	6	6
25%	4.2	6	5	6	4	5.5	5	5	4	4.5

	E.S. Central		New England		Middle Atlantic		S. Atlantic		Entire Sample	
	Primary	Private	Primary	Private	Primary	Private	Primary	Private	Primary	Private
N	9	12	18	23	28	33	38	50	232	324
Mean	4.7	5.3	5.1	6.3	6.8	6.8	5.7	7.1	6.0	7.0
SD	(1.3)	(2.1)	(1.9)	(2.2)	(2.1)	(1.8)	(2.0)	(2.2)	(2.1)	(2.4)
Mode	3	3	4	5	8	7	4	6	4	6
75%	6	7.5	6	8	8	8	7	8.2	7	8
Mdn	5	5	5	6	7	7	5	7	6	7
25%	3.5	3.2	4	5	5	6	4	5	4	5

Table 15. Average Number of Hours Per Child Neuropsychological Assessment by Nine U.S. Geographic Regions in Primary and Private Practice Employment Settings

	Pacific		Mountain		W.N. Central		W.S. Central		N.E. Central	
	Primary	Private	Primary	Private	Primary	Private	Primary	Private	Primary	Private
N	25	66	8	19	16	10	9	9	38	29
Mean	6.3	7.3	5.8	7.0	5.3	5.9	5.3	6.2	5.4	5.4
SD	(2.1)	(2.8)	(2.6)	(2.0)	(2.1)	(1.6)	(1.0)	(1.7)	(2.1)	(2.0)
Mode	4	6	5	8	4		5	6	4	4
75%	8	10	7.5	8	7	7.2	6	7	7	6
Mdn	6	7.5	5.5	8	5.5	6	5	6	5	5
25%	4	5	4.2	6	4	4.7	4.5	5	4	4

	E.S. Central		New England		Middle Atlantic		S. Atlantic		Entire Sample	
	Primary	Private	Primary	Private	Primary	Private	Primary	Private	Primary	Private
N	8	8	8	15	18	21	25	39	155	219
Mean	3.6	5.5	5.8	6.6	6.5	6.3	6.4	6.9	5.8	6.6
SD	(0.9)	(3.1)	(1.1)	(2.4)	(1.9)	(2.2)	(2.1)	(2.3)	(2.0)	(2.4)
Mode	4	2	5	6	5	5	5	6	6	6
75%	4	8.7	6	8	8	7.5	8	8	7	8
Mdn	4	4.5	6	6	6.5	6	6	7	6	6
25%	3	2.5	5.2	5	5	5	5	5	4	5

Table 16. Average Number of Patients Seen Monthly for Neuropsychological Assessment by Area of Clinical Practice in Primary and Private Practice Employment Settings.

	Clinical Neuropsychology		Clinical Psychology		Entire Sample	
	Primary	Private	Primary	Private	Primary	Private
N	319	257	120	168	528	521
Mean	14	9	6	5	11	7
SD	(10)	(9)	(7)	(4)	(10)	(7)
Mode	10	2	4	2	4	2
75%	20	12	8	6	15	10
Mdn	12	6	8	6	8	5
25%	7	3	2	2	4	2

Table 17. Average Number of Patients Seen Monthly for Neuropsychological Assessment by Employment Setting

	University Hospital	Non-University Hospital	Rehabilitation Center	Private Practice	Primary Employment of Entire Sample
N	118	66	38	521	528
Mean	15	12	9	7	11
SD	(10)	(11)	(7)	(7)	(10)
Mode	4	4	2	2	4
75%	20	15	12	10	15
Mdn	12	10	6	5	8
25%	8	4	4	2	4

on the practice of clinical neuropsychology across the country. Similarly, there is considerable variability amongst insurers with respect to policy coverage and financial reimbursement.

More specifically, the overwhelming majority of respondent comments were concentrated on three principal issues: (1) conflict with insurers regarding reimbursement for services, (2) punitive restrictions on the use of neuropsychology technicians in some states, and (3) the impact of poorly trained practitioners on the field.

The issue commented upon by the largest number of respondents concerned insurance and other third party reimbursement, a finding also noted in the *TCN Salary Survey* (Putnam, 1989). Indeed, an inescapable tension exists between 3rd party payors and those delivering clinical services. This tension is in part related

Table 18. Average Number of Patients Seen Monthly for Neuropsychological Assessment by Methodological Approach in Primary Employment and Private Practice Settings

	HRNB		LNNB		Boston Process		Flexible Battery		Fixed Battery		Entire Sample	
	Primary	Private	Primary	Private	Primary	Private	Primary	Private	Primary	Private	Primary	Private
N	171	126	23	31	101	83	117	104	54	59	528	521
Mean	11	12	8.3	5.8	10	7	12	6.4	13	8	11	7
SD	(11)	(16)	(7)	(4.2)	(7.6)	(6.7)	(10.3)	(5.9)	(10.2)	(9.1)	(10)	(7)
Mode	4	2	1	2	12	2	4	2	10	2	4	2
75%	15	14	12	8	14	9	16	8	20	10	15	10
Mdn	8	5	7	6	8	5	10	5	10	5	8	5
25%	4	2	2	2	4	2	4	2	5	2	4	2

to the fact that the patient is rarely responsible for payment of the services he or she receives, a model seemingly unique to the health care delivery system. It also appears to be further exacerbated by the relatively recent emergence of clinical neuropsychology onto the health care scene and the dissimilarity of neuropsychological methods with the more familiar psychological assessment and neurological examination procedures. Insurers and other 3rd party payors have applied guidelines and criteria established for traditional psychological assessment procedures to the neuropsychological examination. Neuropsychological assessment is of course far more comprehensive and cost, time, and labor intensive. One respondent described how Blue Cross/Blue Shield (BC/BS) in a *South Atlantic* region state recently imposed a $300 per day cap on psychological testing, purporting that this figure ranked at the 90th centile for psychological assessment reimbursement. The absence of uniform current procedural terminology (CPT) codes for neuropsychological services is *the* fundamental problem in the view of a large number of respondents.

In certain states, BC/BS and other major insurers have reportedly refused to cover neuropsychological services rendered by a neuropsychological technician or psychological assistant. In fact, a recent BC/BS newsletter in Michigan proposed screening guidelines stating that "psychological tests . . . may be administered by a licensed psychologist or limited-licensed psychologist" (Blue Cross and Blue Shield of Michigan, 1989); any mention of trained technical personnel was conspicuously omitted. Independent of the philosophical debate associated with the issue of technician use, the hardship that such policies impose on a practitioner attempting to remain competitive in the rapidly changing health care marketplace whose service delivery is built around the technician model can indeed be formidable. Restrictions regarding the deployment of technical personnel in some states seem archaic and regressive and antithetical to the emphasis on cost-effective health care delivery which the technical model can provide (Task Force on Marketing and Promotion of Psychological Services, 1986; DeLuca, 1989). Moreover, the utilization of adequately trained technical personnel is earnestly supported by the American Psychological Association (APA, 1981a; APA, 1981b; APA, 1987a; APA, 1987b).

There are, of course, no simple solutions on the horizon to the issue of poorly qualified practitioners attempting to practice clinical neuropsychology, although guidelines have been established regarding appropriate training (Reports of the INS/Division 40 Task Force on Education, Accreditation, and Credentialing, 1987). Clinical neuropsychology is a most appealing discipline which can yield substantial financial rewards. The lure of supplemental income along with the availability of continuing education workshop training may be contributing to the influx of inadequately trained practitioners into the neuropsychological marketplace. This is in spite of the guidelines established by the Division 40 Task Force on Education, Accreditation, and Credentialing, asserting, "Individuals who lack formal and extensive background in clinical neuropsychology should not approach CE workshops individually or in combination (e.g., basic and advanced workshops) as an acceptable method of obtaining basic competence in clinical neuropsychology . . . Those psychologists who propose to respecialize or expand their areas of specialty must do so within the context of an institutional program that incorporates the APA guidelines on respecialization" (p. 28) (Bornstein, 1988).

While this issue will not soon be resolved, some interesting ideas were expressed by several respondents. It was suggested that a central source or state by state data bank of neuropsychological practitioners be developed listing those who have met the INS/Division 40 training guidelines. Such a reference source could be utilized by 3rd party payors and other consumers (e.g., physicians, attorneys, etc.) when making decisions concerning the referral of patients or clients. Such a listing of practitioners whose education and training have been reviewed by individuals knowledgeable about established standards could sophisticate the referral process for users. One result would be to make referrers less dependent upon "word of mouth" or other informal means of finding practitioners of neuropsychological services. While such a system would necessarily increase competition among practitioners, this would presumably have the same effect on the field as it does in other businesses, namely, to increase the overall quality of the product and service. Those whose *only* background training in neuropsychology was workshop attendance would not meet the criteria for entry into such a register until they fulfilled the necessary training requirements established by the INS/ Division 40 Task Force. While the organizers or administrators of such a data bank would have no regulatory authority, they could serve to help educate consumers of neuropsychological services about the self-monitoring guidelines and standards of training which have been established by the field.

REFERENCES

Adams, K.M. (1987). Reitan's neuropsychology: Take it or leave it. *Journal of Clinical and Experimental Neuropsychology, 9*, 235-242.

American Psychological Association (1981a). Specialty guidelines for the delivery of services by clinical psychologists. *American Psychologist, 36*, 640-651.

American Psychological Association (1981b). Ethical guidelines for psychologists. *American Psychologist, 36*, 633-638.

American Psychological Association (1987a). General guidelines for providers of psychological services. *American Psychologist, 42*, 712-723.

American Psychological Association (1987b). Model act for state licensure of psychologists. *American Psychologist, 42*, 696-703.

Blue Cross and Blue Shield of Michigan (1989). Hospital News.

Bornstein, R.A. (1988). Guidelines for continuing education in clinical neuropsychology. *The Clinical Neuropsychologist, 2*, 25-29.

DeLuca, J.W. (1989). Neuropsychology technicians in clinical practice: Precedents, rationale, and current deployment.*The Clinical Neuropsychologist, 3*, 3-21.

Department of Consumer Affairs (1987). Laws and regulations relating to the practice of psychology. State of California Board of Medical Quality Assurance, Psychology Examining Committee. Sacramento, California.

234

Putnam, S.H. (1989). The *TCN* salary survey: A salary survey of neuropsychologists. *The Clinical Neuropsychologist, 3*, 97-115.

Putnam, S. H. & DeLuca, J. W. (1990). The *TCN* professional practice survey: Part I: General practices of neuropsychologists in primary employment and private practice settings. *The Clinical Neuropsychologist, 4*, 199-244.

Reports of the INS/Division 40 Task Force on Education, Accreditation, and Credentialing (1987). Guidelines for doctoral training programs in clinical neuropsychology. *The Clinical Neuropsychologist*, 1, 29-34.

Task Force on Marketing and Promotion of Psychological Services of the APA Board of Professional Affairs. (1986). *Marketing psychological services: A practitioners guide*. Washington, D.C.: American Psychological Association.

U.S. Bureau of Census. (1967). *Statistical abstracts of the United States (88th ed.)*. Washington, D. C.: Government Printing Office.